FROM
SNAKE CHARMERS
TO
MOUSE CHARMERS

MODERN INDIA UNDER
NARENDRA DAMODARDAS MODI

Surendra Nathan Madhurakkandy

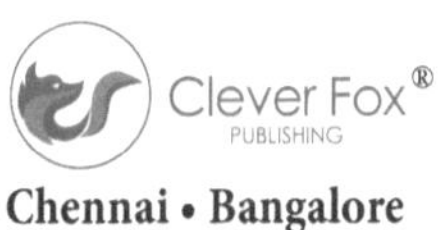

Clever Fox®
PUBLISHING

Chennai • Bangalore

CLEVER FOX PUBLISHING
Chennai, India

Published by CLEVER FOX PUBLISHING 2023
Copyright © Surendra Nathan Madhurakkandy 2023

All Rights Reserved.
ISBN: 978-93-56485-85-3

No page or part of this book may be reproduced in any form or transmitted by any means – electronic, mechanical, postal or otherwise – including photocopy, xerox copy, recording or any information storage and retrieval system without prior permission in writing from the author, except for brief passages quoted in the book as reference.

The images in this book are used in the belief that they are not "copy-right protected" material and by my fair use of the same I have absolutely no intention of whatsoever nature in infringing any copy rights if at all claimed by anybody on these images.

In the event any issues or disputes are raised either on the images or of the contents of certain essays of this book by any alleged vested interested party or parties, such ill-advised disputes and/or issues shall be dealt with and defended by the author himself alone in his individual capacity which shall be at the entire risks as to costs and consequences to such dispute raiser(s) or litigant(s) before any court or authority of competent jurisdiction. The publisher of this book, either jointly or severally, shall in no way be responsible or liable for the contents or images of this book.

FROM SNAKE CHARMERS TO MOUSE CHARMERS
[MODERN INDIA UNDER NARENDRA DAMODARDAS MODI]

[A collection of selected Essays penned by the Author at different points of time, some of which were already published in periodicals in India and abroad, pertaining to the period commencing from NDA Government under Prime Minister Narendra Modi assuming power in 2014)

PUBLISHED BY

Jawaharlal Nehru, the first Prime Minister of free India, is said to have given wide publicity across the world regarding the snake charmers of India. Here in this photo snap Nehru and his sister, Vijaya Lakshmi Pandit, are shown marketing snake-charmer image of India to US First Lady Jackie Kennedy, Circa 1950.

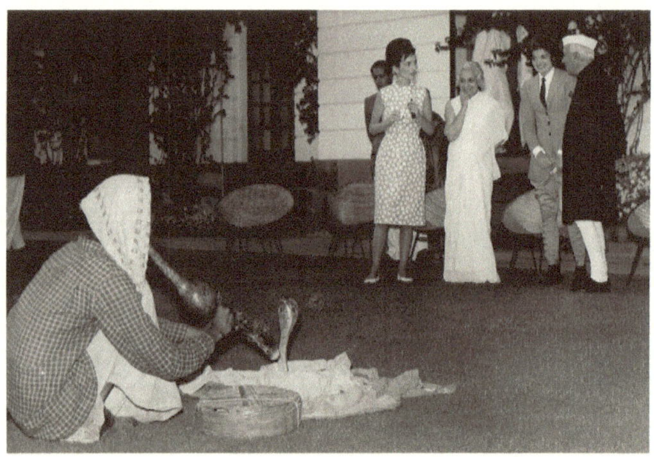

Image Courtesy: www.oldindianphotos.in

DEDICATION

With great love and gratitude stemming from the bottom of my heart, I dedicate this book to all those patriotic Indian citizens who woke up from their "slave mode" and took part in the "second freedom struggle through the Ballot Box" in 2014 and brought freedom for them particularly for the Hindus of this ancient land and saved the country from disintegration and catastrophic doom from the successive Nehru Dynastic governments, ending with the decade-long regime of the unconstitutional United Progressive Alliance (UPA) headed by an uneducated Italian woman [the widow of the third generation Dynasty Prime Minister, Rajiv Gandhi], who was remotely controlled by the Vatican and who harbor utter contempt towards Hinduism or Sanathan Dharma.

[M. Surendra Nathan]

ACKNOWLEDGMENTS

*W*hen I think of the acknowledgment part of this book, the names and images of a few personalities, who were part of my journey through life, particularly in my journalistic forays, come to the surface of my mind.

The first and foremost is Late Shri Daivamuthu Nadar of Mumbai. Shri Nadar had been an RSS *Pracharak* for most part of his life. He had been an ardent admirer of Prime Minister Modiji. How he happened to be an Editor and Publisher of a magazine has this interesting anecdote:

In 2002, during the period when Modiji was the Chief Minister of the State of Gujarat, the Islamic fundamentalists of Gujarat, without any provocation whatsoever, burned down a passenger-train bogey after shutting down all the escape doors from outside in which hundreds of Hindu pilgrims, mainly women and children, were returning home after performing pilgrimage, thereby inhumanly killing all of them in cold blood. As usual, there was no adequate reaction or response from the then Congress Government at the Centre to this inhuman perpetration of burning down a complete bogey and killing innocent people inside it.

Acting on a sudden impulse in the same year, viz. 2002, Shri Nadar ventured into the highly competitive field of print journalism by starting a news-magazine, called "Hindu Voice" (HV) on a shoe string budget, mainly to air out the injustices perpetrated upon the majority citizens of the country by the successive Nehru Dynasty governments and also to report about the positive news regarding Hinduism which was deliberately neglected and missed out by the mainstream sold media in India which were mostly controlled by foreigners.

Thus, from 2002 the growth of Hindu Voice (print edition) has been a phenomenal success and it has since then carved a niche for itself. All the contributors to HV were intellectuals from all over the world belonging to all the major religions such as Dr. David Frawley (Pandit Vamadeva Shastri - world-renowned Western authority on Yoga, Ayurveda and Vedanta of USA), Ms. Maria Wirth (a great lover of India living in West Germany, arguing for making India as a "Hindu *Rashtra*" for maintaining peace and harmony across the world,) Francois Gautier (renowned contemporary Indologist from France), Ms. Taslima Nasreen (well-known writer from Bangladesh), Late Tarek Fatah (a Canadian citizen of Pakistani origin and a Motivating Orator, Author, T.V. Personality and above all a lover of Hinduism), Dr. Subramanyan Swamy (formerly Professor at Harvard University), Late Arun Jaitely (former Finance Minister of India), Late Ram Jethmalani (renowned legal luminary of India) etc.

I am immensely indebted to Late Shri Daivamutu for single-handedly starting Hindu Voice and HV E-Bulletin and for publishing many of my essays in them; a few of which are included in this compilation. Unfortunately, however, due to the sad and sudden demise of the Founder Editor & Publisher of HV, Shri Nadar, its publication was abruptly discontinued, leaving enough scope for some good Samaritans coming forward and restarting the defunct magazine.

I would most respectfully thank Shri Prafulla Ketkar, the highly erudite and charismatic Editor of "Organiser" New Delhi, one of the oldest and respected magazines of India, for publishing my essays in it from time to time out of which a couple of essays are taken and included in this book (after carrying out appropriate editions/revisions in them, keeping in mind the efflux of time).

I would be failing in my duty if I do not express my sincere thanks and gratitude to the Editorial Team of "NRI Internet.com" & "NRIpress.com" of USA, which are the most-trusted name in the NRI Media Worldwide, for publishing my article: "The Role of NRI American Intellectuals Forum in making Narendra Modi as Prime Minister of India" in 2014. I particularly express my sincere gratitude to Mr. A. Gary S. Grewal, one of the founders of these popular internet-based periodicals, who is a prominent US citizen of Indian origin. Indeed this essay had evinced great interest amongst the people of Indian origin settled in America and elsewhere in the world, particularly Late Shri Narain Kataria, former President of Indian American Intellectual Forum which had established a deep and abiding friendship between him and me. Sadly, Shri Kataria passed away in 2016, after witnessing the successful culmination of his efforts in making Modi as the PM of India. He was an ardent fan of Modi right from the days Modi became the Chief Minister of Gujarat for three consecutive tenures. Shri Kataria relentlessly worked for the success of the then Prime Ministerial candidate, Modi, from the USA when he had left no stone unturned in ensuring Modiji's thumping victory at the democratic polls of 2014 as the Prime Minister of India. I have described about these efforts of Indian Diasporas settled in the USA under the leadership of Shri Kataria in my essay included in this book.

Shri Kataria was a great inspiration for me in my foray into freelance journalism. He used to call me from New York almost every week-end over the phone and had regularly kept in touch with me by E-mails until his last breath. In fact, it was his last suggestion to me to compile all my essays and publish them as a book, adding; "essays of good intellectual values published in periodicals have only a short shelf life, whereas the same essay published in a book will have an enduring or permanent shelf-life".

On one occasion Shri Kataria had flown down to Mumbai specifically for meeting with me with regard to his proposal for compiling my essays and publishing them as a book. Unfortunately, however, I could not meet him on that occasion as I had to rush to New Delhi upon short notice in connection with a litigation before the Hon'le Supreme Court of India. I have therefore a sentimental reason to see the compilation of these essays published as a book soon in the pious memory of my fruitful association with a great son of Bharat Mata, Late Shri Narain Kataria. Although his "Karma Bhoomi" was USA, he had tirelessly worked for the progress and prosperity of his "Janma Bhoomi", that is Bharat.

I would also most sincerely thank my colleagues at the Bombay High Court, particularly Adv. Shuchi S. Halwasia, a prominent Mumbai-based Lawyer and Convener of Mumbai BJP Legal Cell, as well as Adv. Shankar Pai, a prominent Testamentary Lawyer, for appreciating my views expressed in my essays which were already published in periodicals as mentioned above and encouraging me to take up the "project" of compiling them and publishing them as a book.

I owe special regards and gratitude to Professor Nicola Stewart, Wenatchee WA, Central Washington University of USA, for patiently going through the manuscripts of my book amidst her busy schedules and suggesting appropriate corrections and also for helping me dot the i's and cross the t's which have greatly enhanced the accuracy and pleasantness in going through the book.

Last but not the least, I regard it as my ardent duty to express my sincere thanks to the Management and Staff at the J.N. Petit Institute, a prominent Parsi benevolent Institution of Mumbai, running one of the largest and oldest Libraries and Reading Rooms [for the general public of Mumbai and for the student communities for facilitating them to prepare for competitive examinations] for making available to me numerous old issues of newspapers, books, periodicals and other reference material which have considerably helped me in preparing and editing these essays amidst my busy legal professional life in the bustling city of Mumbai. I would particularly offer my sincere thanks in this regard to Shri Sachin G. Zalte, a Library Assistant at the Institute/Library.

ABOUT THE AUTHOR

*M*adhurakkandy Surendra Nathan [M.S. Nathan] is a Mumbai-based Lawyer, Law-Lecturer, Freelance Journalist and public orator. He has been practicing Law since the last quarter century. He is holding multiple Post-Graduate Degrees such as M.A. (Philosophy), PGDHR, BJMC, LL.M., etc. from Central and State Universities in India. He has also served as Visiting Faculty Member in several colleges affiliated to University of Bombay.

Prior to his enrolment as Lawyer about a quarter century ago, he had been leading a successful career life in the Administration and Legal fields with Central Government and Private Sector organizations in India such as Bhabha Atomic Research Centre, NITIE, The Tata Iron & Steel Co. Ltd. [TISCO, now "Tata Steel"] etc. as well as in the Middle Eastern countries such as the Kingdom of Bahrain, Sultanate of Oman, Kingdom of Saudi Arabia, etc. During his life in the Middle Eastern countries, he contributed essays in the newspapers published in those countries on current affairs and on political issues and he had also travelled through many parts of the world.

Adv. Nathan has Rashtriya Swayamsevak Sangh (RSS) background and he has benefitted himself – bodily and mentally – by participating in its Camps. Presently he is an active member of BJP Legal Cell in Mumbai.

Adv. Nathan has been leading a spiritually-oriented life and he has exposed himself to various spiritual traditions and disciplines from across India, right from the Himalayas to the Rameshwaram (the Southern tip of India), such as Swami Sivananda Ashram (The Divine Life Society) at the foothills of the Himalayas, Sai Baba of Shirdi, Sri Sathya Sai Baba of Puttaparthy, AC Bhaktivedanta Swami Prabhupada (the founder of ISKCON), Sri Sri Ananda Murthy (founder of Ananda Marga), Ramana Maharshi's Ashram at Thiruvannamalai (Tamil Nadu), Paramahansa Yogananda, (the Founder of Self-Realization Fellowship of USA & Yogoda Satsang Society of India), etc.

After undergoing an in-depth training imparted by Yogoda Satsang Society of India, Ranchi (Bihar), Adv. Nathan was awarded the title "Kriyaben" by Late Sri Sri Daya Mata, a direct disciple of Paramahansa Yogananda and Former President of Self-Realization Fellowship of USA/Yogoda Satsang Society of India.

During his journey through life, Adv. Nathan had golden opportunities to come in contact with many illustrious people of India and abroad. One such personality was Late Dr. A.P.J. Abdul Kalam (whom he was fortunate enough to meet and exchange pleasantries at the Ashram of Sri Sathya Sai Baba of Puttaparthy on an occasion when Dr. Kalam delivered a Convocation address at the Sri Sathya Sai University). Adv. Nathan has written an obituary on Dr. Kalam which was originally published in "Hindu

Voice" and after appropriate rewriting it has now been included in this book.

One of the living role models of Adv. Nathan is Mr. Alfred Ford (aka Ambarish Das), the Great Grandson of Henry Ford of USA. Alfred Ford has gifted his entire wealth for the construction of world's largest and magnificent ISKCON Temple at Mayapuri in West Bengal. He and his family have dedicated their lives in pursuit of the spirituality of India and they regard Bhagavad Gita as the "Manual of their Lives".

When a Reporter asked Mr. Alfred at the beginning of his temple project as to why he was willing to spend huge sum of money on a temple and why couldn't he build hospitals instead, his apt reply was: *"The best thing you can give someone is spiritual knowledge. Hospitals and food are temporary. But spiritual knowledge transforms your life – then maybe you will have less and less need for hospitals! Your life changes for the better. That is what the temple is all about. You will discard all your unhealthy habits and with a positive lifestyle, there is healing of mind, body and soul; there will be peace and harmony. Less greed and more selfless services would lead mankind to a blessed life for which a Temple dedicated to Lord Krishna is essential"* (as reported in The Times of India, Mumbai, issue dated 08/12/2003).

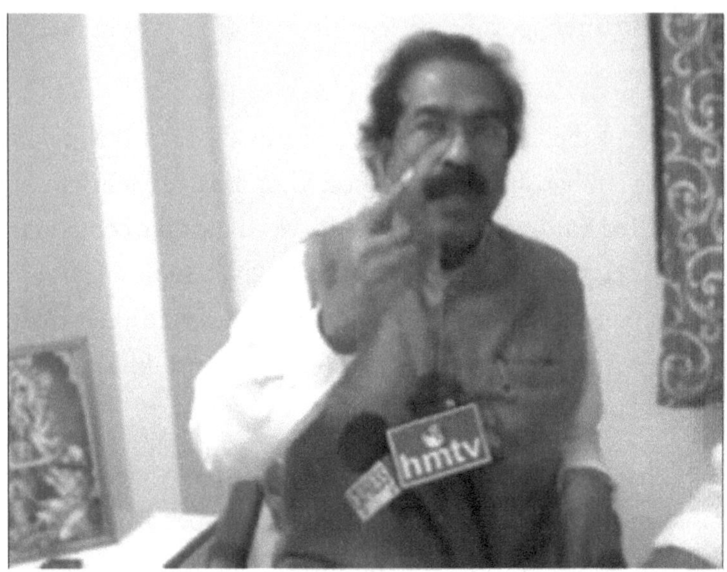

A screen-grab of an interview given by the Author on demand from few news-channels with regard to the controversy created by his article titled "Kerala: God's Own Country or Godless country" published in "Organiser" Weekly, New Delhi in 2015 (included in this compilation after appropriate edition). The YouTube video can be watched by the words link: "Adv. Surendra Nathan". [For accessing from foreign countries, add the words: "…Kerala Gods own country or Godless country"].

PREFACE

*I*t is with immense pleasure that I would like to state here that this book has been blessed with a Foreword by none other than Dr. S.L. Bhyrappa, a living legend of Bharat's literary landscape.

Dr. Bhyrappa needs hardly any introduction to the reading public. In any case out of my gratitude towards him I am duty-bound to write the following few words about him:

Dr. Bhyrappa's career in literature is spanning over five decades. Although all of his twenty-five-odd novels were originally published in his mother-tongue, Kannada, English has been his language of love as well as his medium of communication with the rest of the world, and he is equally conversant with the English, particularly because many of his Kannada-novels have been translated into English. He is an avid reader of non-mainstream journals and periodicals of India which are as he put it: "carrying news and views deliberately left out by the sold mainstream media".

Dr. Bhyrappa was bestowed with the prestigious Padma Bhushan Award by Government of India for his life-long contributions to the field of literature and education. (He was already conferred upon the Padma Shree award in 2016).

Dr. Bhyrappa is the Recipient of *Sahitya Akademi* Award as well as *Saraswati Samman*. In addition, he is also the Fellow of Sahitya Akademi. He has been conferred upon Doctor of Literature by six prominent universities in the country. Presently he has been designated as the National Professor of Literature. Most of his novels were translated into all the Indian languages, including Sanskrit. He is the highest-sold-author since the last four decades in Kannada and Marathi.

His book "Aavarana: The Veil" in English was published by a renowned publisher, which has created a sort of publishing record in India by publishing ten editions of the book in three years on account of demand from the reading public.

Over the years, Dr. Bhyrappa have been offering the highest quality of literature to the erudite reading public in India and abroad during his illustrious journey through life.

I have read almost all the books authored by Dr. Bhyrappa which were translated into English, and I derive a great amount of inspiration from them in my forays into freelance journalism. I am also sentimental to the fact that Dr. Bhyrappa has read the entire manuscripts of this book and he has fully appreciated them, which enabled him to write the Foreword for this book.

The process of writing the essays included in this book by me are by way of snatching away time from my otherwise busy professional life as a Lawyer & Law Lecturer and converting it into "literary time", as I feel Law & Literature often go together. The views and opinions presented in this book are my own, and there are bound to be mismatch with my views vis-a-vis that of the reading public. Hence, anybody can dissent from my views which will only re-vitalize the concept of freedom of expression and enrich the literary-lives in a democratic society.

Dr. Bhyrappa has regularly read all my essays published in Hindu Voice which was a prominent print magazine published from Mumbai carrying thought provoking essays from intellectuals and Indologists from all over the world and has commented upon many of my essays published in periodicals in India and abroad.

I regard my readers as the greatest source of inspiration and I present this book to them with the same devotion as any devote Hindu would offer flowers at the Lotus feet of Goddess Saraswati, who is the embodiment of knowledge and wisdom.

M. Surendra Nathan
Advocate,
Mumbai.

FOREWORD

Shri Madhurakkandy Surendra Nathan (M.S. Nathan), who is a Mumbai-based Lawyer, Law Lecturer and freelance journalist, has been known to me since the last several years through his writings published in various magazines and periodicals, particularly in the "Hindu Voice", a print magazine published from Mumbai. He has requested me to write a Foreword for his book: "From Snake Charmers to Mouse Charmers – Modern India under Narendra Modi", which is a compilation of his essays some of which were published in different magazines and periodicals in India and abroad since the time Narendra Modi assumed his office as PM of India in 2014.

Somebody has commented that "essays are the freest form of literature". I feel it is the essays published in magazines and periodicals which, at first, generate literary interest and veer round public opinion in the minds of the reading public on various issues concerning the nation. However, since the "shelf-life" of the magazines and periodicals are regarded to be of short period, it has always been a practice in the literary world to compile the essays of enduring values in a book so as to increase their utility, popularity and durability. I, therefore, feel that these types of books serve as a kind of tribute to those periodicals and magazines in which some of the essays included in this book have first appeared.

Being a Lawyer, Adv. Nathan's essays have acquired the characteristics of sharpness and analytical skills of the legal profession coupled with the suaveness and niceties of literature. The essays included in this book are analysis and commentary upon various events and subjects such as political ideas and movements, the Leftist Activism and the greatest harms being caused to the nation, personal profiles of eminent personalities like Late Dr. APJ Abdul Kalam, the roles played by Indian Diaspora in strengthening the democracy in India, the current political climates in the country, etc. In short, these essays shall give the reader variegated views of the events, political atmosphere, etc. of India, which is regarded as the largest democratic country in the world, characterized by its vastness, vibrancy, diversity, plurality, etc.

In this regard it is pertinent to state here that amongst the comity of nations, India is fast emerging as the epicenter of positive, fruitful and peaceful changes with the government's motto of "sab ka saat sab ka vikas aur sab ka viswas". All the rating agencies around the world have unanimously rated India's growth rate as the fastest and the nation would soon emerge as one of the superpowers, overtaking countries like China. Adv. Nathan's book attempts to capture a bit of these preliminary periods of rapid progress that are being witnessed in India and its image abroad within a short time frame.

In addition to the all-round progress witnessed within the country ever since the change of government at the Centre in 2014, there has never been such a great interest amongst the Indian Diasporas around the world who are keenly watching the growth oriented developments in the country of their birth or family connection. Literature plays a major role in these upward marches of the development of the country. Judging from the steady growth of publishing industry in India, particularly in the English language, it can be seen that readers of books pertaining to India's politics, corruption-free government, growth and welfare oriented policies of the government, growing medical tourism, its ancient spiritual wisdom, traditions and cultures like Kumbh Mela, Yoga, etc., one can reach to an unmistakable conclusion regarding the great interest amongst the youths of India and amongst the Indian Diasporas around the world towards India.

I am sure Adv. Nathan's book will be read by all the like-minded persons in India and the "India watchers" around the world with great interest.

I wish his book all success in scaling to greater heights in the literary landscape of India in the years to come.

[PADMA BHUSHAN Dr. S.L. BHYRAPPA]
KANNADA & ENGLISH LITERATI
[RECIPIENT OF SAHITYA AKADEMI AWARD &
SARASWATI SAMMAN]

1007, Udayaravi Road,
Kuvempunagar,
MYSURU – 570 023.

CONTENTS

INTRODUCTION

$\mathcal{T}$he essays selected and compiled in this book were all penned by me at different points of time, some of which were published in the past in periodicals such as USA-based NRI Press, Hindu Voice, Hindu Voice E-Bulletin, Organiser, etc., which are revised and edited for including them in this book. All these essays are pertaining to the period commencing from the time Narendra Modi emerged as the undisputed national leader of India in the general elections conducted in the year 2014. This compilation contains a kaleidoscopic view of the political atmosphere since then involving both friends and foes of Modi living in India as well as amongst the People of India Origin (PIO) living abroad.

The first Chapter of the book is an essay containing a brief survey of the Nehru Dynasty government from the time the country attained independence in 1947 until Modi assumed power in 2014 at the Center.

Keeping the background of the Nehru Dynasty period, the change of government with its wide-ranging political views and developments, I have made a feeble attempt to capture at least a fraction of these momentous turn of events in the history of modern India from the time PM Modi assumed power in 2014.

The remarkable growth and progress made by India under his dynamic leadership such as successfully navigating the country through the world-wide Covid-19 Pandemic while simultaneously helping all the countries of the world by supply of vaccine made in India thereby saving millions of people from the scourge of the Pandemic; leading the country to become 5th largest economy in the world, making the country a Space Super Power with the landing of Chandrayan-3 on the hither-to unexplored surface of the moon, etc. are only just a few milestones achieved by the country out of many other accomplishments.

There is an interesting background with regard to the title of the book, viz. "From Snake Charmers to Mouse Charmers – Modern India Under Narendra Modi". The name is pertaining to an anecdote related by Modi at an election campaign speech in 2013. To put it briefly, during the time when Modi was the Chief Minister of the State of Gujarat, he happened to make an official business trip to South Korea. While in Korea, Modi has had chances to interact with the common people of that country and many of them asked him regarding the snake catchers and charmers of India. Modi replied to them that there were no longer snake catchers or charmers in India "But we are now only a nation of mouse-charmers", referring to the growing "Indian tribes" of software professionals thriving in India as well as flourishing in the advanced Western and European countries.

It is indeed a pleasant coincidence that South Korea is presently engaged in setting up "World's Largest Cell-phone Manufacturing Factory" in India under the Make in India initiative introduced by Modi. In fact South Korea is the first country to invest in the industrial sector in India immediately after the Initiative was proposed by Modi Government on assuming power in 2014. The giant South Korean automobile manufacturer Kia Motors invested US$ 2 Billion by setting up its plant at a place called Penukonda in Anantapur District of Andhra Pradesh. The backward District of Anantapur with perennial dry season and potable water shortage is fast transforming itself into a major industrial hub, providing livelihoods to over 10,000 unemployed youths, famished farm workers and villagers directly and indirectly. It is again sentimental to me that I happened to meet few corporate executives and entrepreneurs from South Korea during the "Make In India Week" in 2016 at Mumbai. I had covered the Event for "Hindu Voice" as a freelance reporter, which was published in HV and is included in this book.

Anantapur, where the Kia Motor Factory is located is near to Sri Sathya Sai Baba's Ashram at Puttaparthy, which is my second home-town and I have had a chance to visit the thriving Kia Factory Complex in 2017.

As I had lived and travelled through many parts of the world prior to my entry into the legal profession quarter century ago, I had experienced and observed while living abroad that Indians were looked down upon as a sort of primitive tribe, often equating with Negros of the African Continents. The anecdote related by Modi has, therefore, deeply touched the inner most recess of my mind and hence the title of the Book.

The sleeping ancient giant, called Bharat, which had been invaded and plundered through the millennia by the marauding foreign forces, has now woke up and with her teeming millions of citizens, estimated to be equivalent to one fifth of human race inhabiting the earth, is marching to become a prosperous super power in the near future under the dynamic leadership of Modi, who has been rightly described by many contemporary patriots of India as "God's Gift to India".

It has been said that "the collective public memory is short". In a democratic country like India, every citizens should keep alive the public memory by some means or methods with a view to avert recrudescence of unfavorable events harmful to the country. The one method of keeping alive the public memory is to write about the events and personalities of the bygone period and get them published so that it would guide the electorates when exercising their franchise during democratic elections. It was Professor George Santayana, the Spanish-American Philosopher, who said: "Those who do not learn from history are doomed to repeat it".

Thus, in India the bygone periods particularly of the erstwhile regime of the United Progressive Alliance (UPA) was full of audacity and bluntness with which the gigantic corrupt machinery was operated. Each and every Minister of the UPA was the epitome of corruption such as 2G Spectrum scam, (When A. Raja, one of the former UPA Ministers, was reported to have paid Rs.3000 crores as bribes), CWG Scam (CBI filing charge sheets against Congress stalwarts like Suresh Kalmadi), Chopper scam (involving Augusta Westland and huge payments as kickbacks to politicians in Italy and India), Tatra Truck Scam, cash for vote scam, Congress Minister, Sukh Ram's bags and six suitcases stacked with currency notes worth Rs.2 crores meant for payment of bribes, Harshad Mehta's Stock Market Scam, etc.

etc. were forgotten by the public as their collective memory was short.

Ever since Modi came to power as the Prime Minister of India, apart from the all-round phenomenal social and economic growth of the country, as rated by all the world-wide rating agencies and International organizations, there are unprecedented enhancements of respect and recognition of the caliber of Indians all over the world which were all made possible only because of various progressive measures initiated by Modi, including his historic addresses at foreign shores - be it at the Madison Square of USA or the Islamic country of UAE where a mind-boggling Indian diasporas numbering over 50,000 - heard Modi's address in animated attention.

Each of his State visits to the Buddhist, Christian, Islamic, Western and European countries in his capacity as the PM of India, have paid rich dividends by way of getting in return strategic partnership and mutual benefits between India and those countries. These are all regarded as giant steps redounding to the successful onward march of Bharat and the enhancements of the world-wide images of its citizens as a whole.

Apart from the overseas images of Indians getting overturned from "Snake Charmers" to "Mouse Charmers" on account of the modern "Human Dinosaur", called "Modi" traversing the earth, the Hindus of India who were regarded by the Islamic countries as "infidels" are now being given the status on par with the Muslim citizens of the Islamic countries, judging from the heroic red-carpeted welcome accorded to Modi in all the Islamic countries he visited within the short span of his assuming power.

It was indeed a remarkable event in the entire history of Islam that an "infidel" Hindu man, whose name was used as fuel for the purpose of running the false propaganda machinery in his own country by the anti-national elements, leftist ideologues, foot-soldiers working and flourishing in the country at the instance of anti-India international Islamic fundamentalist networks and Christian Missionaries involved in conversion business, etc. as well as the mainstream sold media as "hard-core Hindu fundamentalist", "saffron terrorist", "Architect of Genocide of Gujarati Muslims", "Hitler of India", etc. etc. was conferred upon the highest civilian honor the "King Abdullaziz Sash" by Kingdom of Saudi Arabia, which is regarded as the citadel of Islamic fundamentalism in the world! The matter does not end there. The Saudi authorities readily signed a Memorandum of Understanding (MOU)/Treaty with regard to the contract of supplying laborers from India thereby ensuring better favorable treatments to the Indian workers by the Saudi employers. In addition, many of the Arab and Muslim countries have made huge direct investments in India which was only because of the abiding faith, trust and confidence reposed by them upon an "infidel", called "Modi".

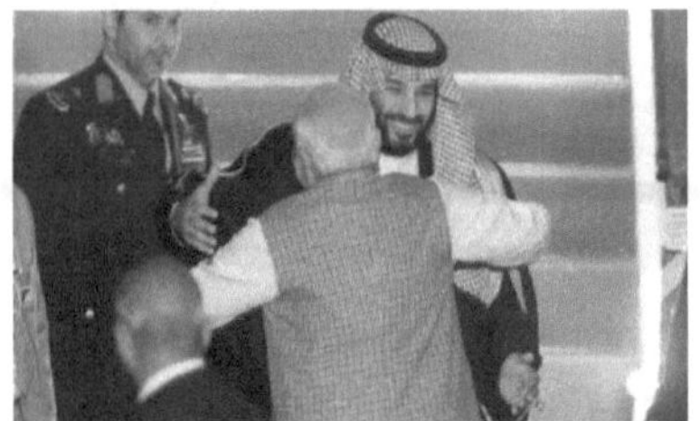 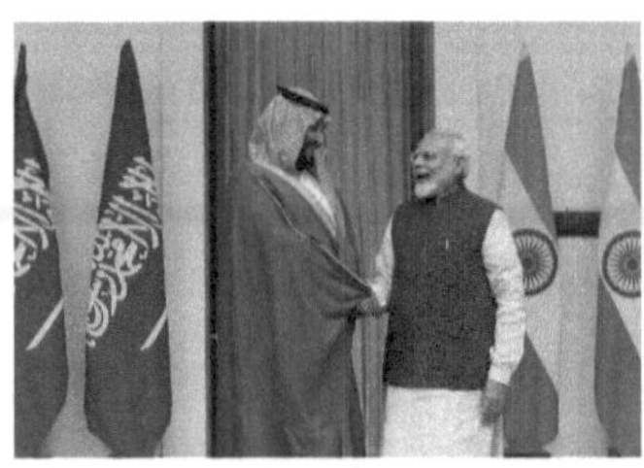

Picture courtesy: Arab News

It is all the more hilarious in the entire history of Islam that the decade-long false propaganda machinery ran by the anti-Modi and anti-India brigades of the country irreparably broke down when Modi, who since his childhood has been a "Pracharak" of RSS, which was equated by a U.P. Muslim Minister on par with ISIS, was conferred upon numerous Civilian Order and Awards by all the other major Muslim countries such as "State Order of Ghazi Amir Amanullah Khan" by Afghanistan, "Grand Collar of the State of Palestine" by Palestine, "Order of Zayed" by the United Arab Emirates, "Order of the Distinguished Rule of Izzuddin" by Maldives, "King Hamad Order of the Renaissance" by the Kingdom of Bahrain, "Order of the Nile" by Egypt… and the list goes on and on.

Yet another historic event is his visit to the Islamic country of UAE. It was for the first time that all the male members of the ruling family (by discarding their usual protocol) received Modi at the airport and during his sojourn of couple of days in that Group of Islamic Countries the authorities announced gifting of a huge track of land in UAE for the construction of a magnificent Hindu Temple – again first time in the history of Islam. In addition, the rulers had also donated adequate money for the said construction. The sight of all the senior Arab Ministers of UAE taking part in the Vedic rituals conducted at the ground-breaking ceremonies as preliminary to the construction of the temple is indeed a remarkable milestone in the evolution of human history. The visuals of the event are available on the YouTube which is a "must-watch" video for every peace-loving, secular citizens of the world.

As already mentioned above, the essays included in this book were penned by me at different points of time between the period 2014 and 2022. Hence, as these essays are pertaining to the bygone years, they are datelined so that the reader will be able to recall or reconnect the issues involved, the political atmosphere then prevailing, the turn-of-events transpired over the years, etc. as it is often said: "Coming Events Cast their Shadows" and these "shadows", I believe, are the images of the period commencing from the Modi Era.

Going through these essays one could get a kaleidoscopic view of the political scenario which prevailed in India ever since Modi came to power. I earnestly hope that my views as expressed in my essays would be appreciated by all the right-thinking people living in India and abroad irrespective of their religious affiliations or nationality identities in the spirit of "Vasudhaiva Kutumbakam" (the world is one family), the ancient philosophy enshrined in the only surviving civilization of mankind called, "Hinduism", which is not a religion but a way of life called "Sanathan Dharma".

[M. Surendra Nathan]

A BRIEF SURVEY OF THE DYNASTIC POLITICAL PERIOD OF INDIA FROM 1947 UNTIL THE BJP-LED NDA GOVERNMENT UNDER NARENDRA MODI CAME TO POWER IN 2014:

*J*awaharlal Nehru became the first Prime Minister of free India only by unfair means and not by any democratic credentials or any personal merit. The archival records of the period would reveal that just prior to the country attaining independence in 1947 there were already feverish activities and deliberations by and between the then prominent Indian National Congress (INC) party members on the question of electing the first Prime Minister.

With a view to elect a leader of the INC party and the Prime Minister, these Congress leaders conducted an election amongst the top notch leaders, who were regarded as the ad hoc decision making body, to elect the leader of the Party, and it was decided that whoever scores the highest number of votes would be appointed as the leader of the INC party and then he/she would be appointed as the Prime Minister.

In the ensuing election Jawaharlal Nehru did not get even a single vote while Sardar Vallabhbhai Patel, who was then a prominent Barrister and was well-known all over the country as the "Iron Man of India" who had tirelessly worked for unifying all the varying Princely Kingdoms, numbering over five hundred, and integrated them with the Indian Union, scored 12 votes out of a total of 15 votes (3 members abstained from casting votes).

Thus, as per the election results, Patel was to become the leader of the INC Party by virtue of which he was qualified to be the first Prime Minister of India as of his right. However, as Jawaharlal Nehru did not want to take up any secondary position, he pressurized Mahatma Gandhi to intervene and make him the Prime Minister. Accordingly, Gandhi prevailed upon Patel to withdraw his candidature/nomination with a view to appoint Nehru as the Prime Minister.

On becoming the Prime Minister, without winning any democratic election, Jawaharlal Nehru bestowed upon himself the title "Bharat Ratna", India's highest Civilian Order. A video recording of a conversation between a journalist/reporter and Dr. Subramanian Swamy, which is available on YouTube, shows that when Dr. Swamy was the Union Minister of Law, he happened to peruse an office file containing recommendations for the award of Bharat Ratna. In that file Dr. Swamy found a recommendation made by Nehru himself in his own handwriting to the effect: "*I,*

Jawaharlal Nehru, hereby award the Bharat Ratna to myself…" and signed by himself. Nehru did not have even an iota of goodwill or generosity towards those nation-founding heroes of the period as well as the stalwarts of freedom struggle like Mahatma Gandhi, Vallabhbhai Patel, Subhash Chandra Bose, etc., who were in the forefront of the country attaining independence, to recommend awarding such a Civilian Order. Many of the prominent freedom fighters of the period had proposed to Nehru to bestow Bharat Ratna on Dr. B.R. Ambedkar, one of the greatest intellectuals of India, who had dedicated his life for the causes of downtrodden masses and Dalits of India and he is regarded as the "Father of Indian Constitution". However, Nehru out rightly rejected their proposal. [In fact, the Bharat Ratna was subsequently bestowed on Dr. Ambedkar in 1996 when for a brief period the INC government was voted out of power and a non-INC government came to power under Atal Bihari Bajpai].

Since the time India attained independence from England in 1947, successive governments at the Centre under INC Party relentlessly assaulted everything that was dear to Hinduism and Sanathan Dharma. Jawaharlal Nehru, the first INC Prime Minister of free India, established a Dynastic Political set up and while in Office he groomed his daughter, Indira Priyadarshini Nehru, to step into his shoes upon his demise.

After the partition of the country into India and Pakistan, Nehru kept himself totally aloof from any public discourses pertaining to the mainstream Hindu citizens, although the Muslims of this ancient land had seceded themselves from India as they were unable to peacefully coexist with the majority Hindus, whom they call "infidels".

Nehru, though born into a Hindu family, practiced a crude mixture of antipathetic policies towards the Hindus and showed excessive partiality and appeasements towards the Muslim minorities of the country who could not opt for the "Rule by the Quran", viz. the theological State of Pakistan, largely on account of their bodily infirmities, old age, poverty, etc. which had restrained their physical movements, accentuated by lack of proper transportation towards the seceded region during that early period. The navigation from India to the newly created theological region of Pakistan had become even more difficult for those Muslim men with numerous prodigies out of four wives. In addition, there were hard-core Islamic fundamentalists who had kept pursuing their long-cherished dream of converting the entire country into a Gaz-ba-E Hind, which is one of the fundamental tenets of Islam by way of striving to populate the country with Muslim progenies and also by way of converting Hindus into Islam [as in the case of Lebanon. Watch a video on YouTube by the link words: "Shocking testimony of Brigitee Gabriel on the Islamization of Lebanon". Also watch video on YouTube by the link words: "How Lebanon was converted into Islamic country within few years? – Pankaj Saxena"].

Nehru projected his policies and practices as "secularism" although since the birth of the nation and during its onward journey through life, these were found to have done greatest damages and prejudices to the majority citizens professing Hinduism as the concept of "secularism" professed by the Nehru Dynasty members turned out to be total neglects of the human-values oriented Hinduism or Sanathan Dharma. He projected the foreign-originated Islamic ideologies as paramount in governing the country.

The whole personality of Nehru was far away from the collective consciousness of the majority citizens professing Hinduism, then comprising about 85% of the Indian population. His whole upbringing was through anglicized education.

B.R. Nanda in his book: "Jawaharlal Nehru: Rebel & Statesman", wrote about Nehru as follows:

QUOTE:

Jawaharlal Nehru was very vocal about his views on religion. In his presidential address to the Lahore Congress in 1929, Nehru admitted that although he was born a Hindu, he does not know how far he is justified in calling himself one or speaking on behalf of the Hindus.

UNQUOTE

A contemporary of Nehru was Late Dr. Narayan Bhaskar Khare, an erudite scholar and politician, who was the founder of Marathi newspaper, "Tarun Bharat", succinctly summarized the personality traits of Nehru in the following words: "Nehru is English by education, Muslim by culture and Hindu by an accident of birth".

Nehru's antagonistic relationship with Hinduism, his affinity towards the Muslim citizens of India, his inborn contempt towards Sanathan Dharma, etc. have clearly vindicated the words on Jawaharlal Nehru quoted above.

Judging from the life and time of Nehru and the numerous legislations and policies made by his government any impartial political analysts could emphatically say that he was hostile to the very idea of survival of Hinduism and its ancient wisdom, human values oriented Hindu scriptures, etc., collectively named "Sanathan Dharma".

Nehru assigned top priorities in promoting Islamic cultures and ideologies. It is this reason that 90% of his policies and programs were seriously prejudicial to the majority Hindu citizens, yet helpful to the Muslim citizens who remained in India after partition of the country at their instance in pursuing their long-cherished dream of working for and converting India which they regarded as dar-ul-harb (land of infidels) into dar-ul-Islam (Land of Muslim). Towards this end, Nehru Dynasty Government under the INC Party enacted various Muslim-beneficial legislations, such as The Waqf Act, 1995, The Places of Worship Act, the Minority Commission Act, etc., which were all seriously prejudicial to the majority Hindus who were per force made second-class citizens of India.

As mentioned above, Nehru had harbored an inborn contempt and animosity towards Hinduism and its ancient wisdom. He particularly disliked the Hindu Saints. It was during the early period of independence that Nehru instructed one Dr. Harry Verrier Holman Elwin to prepare an agreement for facilitating easy conversion of Tribes of North Eastern States of India into Christianity. Thus, an agreement was prepared by Elwin at the instance of Nehru which was signed by him on behalf of the Government of India. Under the terms of this agreement Hindu saints were prohibited from entering into Nagaland as also from constructing any Hindu monasteries and temples in that North Eastern State.

Dr. Verrier Elwin was sent to India by the Vatican for converting all Hindus and Tribes into Christianity just prior to the country attaining independence. For this purpose he had established the first Church in Nagaland and appointed himself as its Head. Thus, since the day of his arrival in India Dr. Elwin had relentlessly pursued his assigned tasks for converting all the Tribes into Christianity – an outstanding success - which could not have been possible had there been no active support and cooperation from the then Congress government at the centre under Prime Minister Jawaharlal Nehru.

Nehru deliberately neglected the ancient wisdom of Hinduism, the study of Sanskrit language, the Gurukula systems of education, the health inducing ancient science of Yoga and meditation, the human-values-oriented scriptures, etc. He did not allow these benign characteristics of Hinduism to ever enter into the educational sectors of India and let them pass into oblivion as he believed that patronizing these age-old essential features of Hinduism might come in the way of "secularism" followed by his government.

With a view to strictly adhere to these Muslim-beneficial policies and practices, Nehru ensured that for the higher cabinet-rank Ministerial positions of the Union Education Ministry, only Muslims should be appointed. Accordingly, for the next three decades of the Dynasty period from 1947 until the year 1977 the Union Education Ministers were Maulana Abbdul Kalam Azad (born in Mecca, Kingdom of Saudi Arabia), Saiyad Nurul Hasan,

Humayun Kabir, Fakhruddin Ali Ahmed and Mohammadali Carim Chagla. During this thirty-year period Madrasas and mosques mushroomed into the length and breadth of the country and conversely Hindu Gurukulas, Sanskrit and Veda Padhasaalas, Yoga Institutions, etc. were vanished into thin air. It was during the successive tenures of these Muslim Central Ministers that India became the only non-Muslim country in the world with the largest concentration of mosques and Madrassas compared with the world-wide Islamic countries.

The medieval period of India had suffered greatest tragedies in its civilizational evolution as the foreign Muslim invaders adhering to a single "Holy Book" and assuming different nomenclatures such as Arabs, Persians, Mughuls, Taliban, etc. had turn by turn invaded India for nearly 800 years and they plundered the magnificent Hindu temples and monuments built by incredible technological and architectural marvels unknown to the rest of the world. These Muslim invaders of India demolished all the advanced centers of learning like the world-renowned ancient universities and large libraries, etc. by adhering to the fundamental tenets of the Arabian-desert-originated religion – to destroy everything established by the infidels - which was an inalienable part of the Islamic traditions since its inception. There are incontrovertible historical evidences and relics of the past to show that the ancient Library of Alexandria in Egypt was burned down on the orders of Caliph Omar bin Al-Khattab on his belief that the Quran is the direct words of Allah and it contained all the knowledge and wisdom that humanity could possess, and he reasoned that the man-made books contained in the library were an insult to Quran.

Caliph Omar had been quoted as saying of the books contained in the Library: "They will either contradict the Koran, in which case they are heresy or they will agree with it, so they are superfluous". Accordingly, Caliph Omar ordered his army to burn down the library. In fact, this ancient Library was so vast and grandeur that it took nearly six months to burn all the books, manuscripts and records preserved at the Library and reduced them to ash.

It is because of this spirit of Islam since its inception that in the recent past the Taliban invaded Afghanistan and sporadically destroyed the ancient libraries of that country, proving that it is the inalienable hall mark of Islamic regime to set on fire the Universities and libraries, if they were found to have established by the non-Muslims (infidels).

A short list of ancient universities and libraries destroyed by the Muslim invaders is at Appendix-1.

In fact, it was these Islamic invaders who plundered India and delivered a death blow to the country's ancient education systems by destroying its renowned centers for higher learning, magnificent Universities and sprawling libraries that they inflicted untold miseries and tragedies to the soul of the country. It is these reasons that every patriotic Indian citizens feel that Nehru, instead of appeasing the Muslim minority citizens and tampering with Hinduism, should have made it a top priority to regain the lost glory of the past by appointing responsible secular minded Hindus with impeccable track records of setting right any man-made calamities as Central Education Ministers who would have taken appropriate steps in regaining these lost glories of the past.

It was indeed due to the negative approach and white washing efforts by these successive Muslim Central Education Ministers that they twisted the true history and grandeur of India and fabricated stories so as to suit the Islamic ideologies which they introduced in the text books produced and distributed to the schools and educational institutions run by the government. These text books glorified the Mughal invaders of India like Babur, Aurangzeb, Khilji, Tippu Sultan, etc. while at the same time they neglected the immense contributions made by the Hindu intellectuals, scientists and Rishis of yore who had dedicated their lives in the fields of Mathematics, Astronomy, Medicine, Yogas, Vedic sciences, etc. Had there been direct corrective approach on the part of the then central government in regaining the lost glories, particularly by way of reviving the Vedic sciences, Mathematics, Astronomy, etc. taught by these destroyed ancient Universities, India would have become, inter alia, a Space Super power much before the historic event of Chandryan-3 landing on the moon.

It is not out of place to mention here that these Central Education Ministers had deliberately commissioned Hindu-academicians professing leftist ideologies and Jihadi-minded Muslim scholars for the job of preparing text books for government-run schools and educational institutions across the country who filled these books with spurious and fabricated contents. The entire textbooks produced for schools and colleges prepared under the guidance of these Muslim Central Education Ministers were a crude attempts to white wash the barbaric conducts of the Muslim invaders, as for example the entire textbooks kept reiterating as to who killed Mahatma Ghandi.

However, it is amazing, to say the least, that there is not even a whisper regarding the heinous crimes, barbaric tortures and killings of the Great Sikh Gurus by these Muslim invaders. For instance, the four Gurus of Sikhism were executed one after the other by the Mughal rulers in most heinous and barbaric ways: These Gurus were: (1) Guru Tegh Bahadur, the ninth Guru of Sikkism, was executed by decapitation on the streets of Delhi on the orders of Aurangzeb (2) Guru Gobind Sing was also decapitated in one blow by the Muslim Executioner on the orders of Aurangazeb, (3) Guru Arjun Dev was executed on the orders of Mughal Emperor Jehangir, (4) Banda Bahadur was executed on the orders of Aurangzeb, etc. Likewise, the much revered Chatrapati Shivaji Maharaj's kid Sambhaji was executed on the orders of Mughal Emperor Aurangzeb.

The barbaric and most cruel conducts of these Muslim invaders are such that prior to the public execution of these Gurus and kid Sambhaji the Mughal invaders had inflicted greatest tortures and cruelties which included plucking out their eyes and tongue, pulling out their nails and removing their skin for about a fortnight. The only reasons for these merciless killings were that they refused to convert themselves into Islam.

The entire history of the Mughul invaders was full of brutalities and blood curdling atrocities against the infidels and inflicting horrendous wounds into the soul of India.

Thus, Babur, the first invader and founder of Moghul Dynasty was a drunkard and homosexual. He demolished numerous ancient Hindu temples upon invasion; Akbar was a sex-starved maniac. He raped his own daughter in law, in addition to having a harem of 5000 women; Jahangir blinded his own son with his own hands; Aurangzeb beheaded his own brother and imprisoned his father and while his father was incarcerating in jail, Jahangir sent him the severed head of his brother. In short, almost all the Mughal invaders were involved in brutally killing their relatives such as sons, siblings, parents, etc. in addition to destroying everything dear to Hinduism. [Further authentic details in this regard can be had from a popular research-based book, titled: "The Naked Mughals: Forbidden Tales of Harem and Butchery" By Vashi Sharma & Sanjeev Newar].

In spite of the availability of truckloads of evidences of the horrendous cruelties and human right violations carried out by the Moghul invaders of the past, all the Central Muslim Ministers, who were appointed by the successive Nehru Dynasty regimes, deliberately concealed these realities concerning the Muslim invaders. There is ample evidence to show that these Central Education Ministers had sympathy with the invaders and they sided with them in solidarity with their common religious threads and adhering to common Holy Book which prompted them to glorify these barbarians.

[It may be recalled that the NCERT history textbooks had contained false narratives regarding the Mughal Rulers, as for example in one of the history text books it was stated that "Shah Jahan and Aurangazeb issued grants to repair temples which were demolished during the war". However, when a social activist filed an RTI Application, seeking proof of such an affirmation, a reply was received by him stating that no proof existed. Thereupon he filed a petition before a Court of Law in Rajasthan which issued a notice to the Union Ministry of Education directing them to expunge the baseless glorifications of Mughal Rulers from all the text books published by NCERT].

With these personality traits ingrained in Nehru, particularly with regard to his policy decisions of appointing only Muslims as Central Education Ministers he pursued pseudo secular policies and programs for governing the country, under which the academic study of any Hindu scriptures, particularly Bhagavad Geeta, Upanishads, etc. were banned in the school and college curriculums across India. Even the study of the world-renowned ancient epics of India like Ramayana and Mahabharata were prohibited in the public discourses of the government. For instance, when the Ramayana T.V. Serials were sought to be telecast by the Government-owned Doordarshan (TV) in the 1980s, when the broadcasting business in India was the monopoly of the Government, it was tooth and nail opposed by the then INC stalwarts on the illogical reason that "It is against the concept of secularism followed by the government".

It is indeed heartening to note that on account of the sustained efforts and policies pursued by the present day government under Prime Minister Modi in adhering to the essence of the Hindu scriptures and Yogas in his day to day life schedule, the study of which were all neglected by the Nehru Dynasty members for over 70 years since the country attained independence, the hard-core Islamic counties like the Kingdom of Saudi Arabia has now included the study of these epics of India like the Ramayana, Mahabharata, etc. in their educational systems.

It is therefore quite unfortunate that those who were born and brought up after independence were totally deprived of any understandings of India's rich heritage, healthy cultural traditions, including the study and practice of the ancient health inducing science of Yoga, etc.

It was in line with the policies and program beneficial to only the Muslim citizens of India as pursued by Nehru since independence that his government enacted a central legislation called, The Waqf Act, 1995 (43 of 1995). This legislation was communal in its entirety as the provisions of the Act were solely for serving the interests of the Muslim citizens of the country which ran counter to the very concept of democracy, secularism, etc. By this legislation the hard core Muslim citizens came under the umbrella called: "Waqf Board", who started usurping land belonging to government entities and non-Muslim private citizens of India through various modus operandi.

Since the time the Waqf Act came into force in 1995, there were thousands of instances of the Waqf Board encroaching upon the prime land belonging to both government and private non-Muslim citizens across the country. Over the years the Waqf Board has turned out to be the only statutory communal body in India with the largest number of litigations filed against it. As per media report as on 2023 there are over 58,000 land encroachment complaints filed against the Board by private non-Muslim citizens across the country. [Refer The Times of India, issue dated 01/08/2023].

While it would be a herculean tasks in compiling all the cases of lands usurped by the Waqf Board, it would be suffice at this juncture to mention below only three instances of land grabbing by the Board in the recent past:

(1) Thiruchenthurai is a village on the banks of Cauvery river in Tiruchirapalli District of Tamil Nadu. The village also boasts an ancient 1,500 year old Hindu Temple, known as "Sundareswarar Temple". The Tamil Nadu Waqf Board claimed the ownership of this entire village along with the ancient temple. The villagers could not believe the claim of the Board and they became panic. They beseeched the District Administrations' Headquarters along with the documentary evidences and other documents of title to prove their respective ownerships upon the land in question when the concerned officer told them that all of the lands in Thiruchendurai village belong to the Waqf Board and anyone wishing to sell them must obtain NOC from the Board at the far-off Chennai which is the capital of the State of Tamil Nadu. [Report in Hindustan Times, issue dated 15/09/2022].

(2) It could be for the first time in the history of judiciary in India that the land upon which the Allahabad High Court was constructed was declared to be owned by the Uttar Pradesh Sunni Central Waqf Board, claiming that a mosque was already constructed inside the High Court premises. The High Court knocked the doors of the Supreme Court to reclaim its own land. The case is still pending to be resolved. [Report by "Op India", issue dated 13/03/2023].

(3) In New Delhi a large piece or parcel of land surrounding the Parliament House is known as "Central Vista", which is the administrative heart of the Central Government. Over 75% of this area has been encroached upon and claimed by the Delhi Waqf Board. At present the Central Government is fighting against the Board in an attempt to regain the prime government assets encroached upon by the Board. The case

has not yet been resolved [Report in The Times of India, issue dated 22/09/2021].

It is pertinent to state here that unlike the rest of the regular courts and tribunals across the country, the Waqf Tribunal is manned exclusively by the hard-core Islamic clergies, bent upon promoting their foreign-originated ideologies in India by grabbing the land belonging to the infidels.

It was with a view to safeguard the land captured by the Board, a provision was engrafted in the Waqf Act by which a bar of jurisdiction was placed for the unrestrained function of the Board. Unlike in the ordinary cases of land encroachment in India, it is extremely cumbersome, time consuming and heart-burning for any private non-Muslim citizens of India in reclaiming the land usurped by the Waqf Board. Section 85 engrafted in the Act provides as follows:

QUOTE:

No suit or other legal proceedings shall lie in any civil court in respect of any dispute, question or other matters relating to any Waqf, Waqf property or other matters which is required by or under this Act to be determined by a Tribunal.

UNQUOTE:

Based on the Census of Land Holdings, the Waqf Board enjoys the 3rd largest ownership of land after Railways and Defense. As per Sachar Committee Report (2006) they have 5 lakh properties comprising 6 lakh acres of land whose value is Rs.1.2 lakh crores. It is unfortunate that in spite of such a large land holdings across the country, Muslim citizens occupy public places like roads, railway land, public parks, etc. for performing five times Namaz in addition to illegally constructing mosques and Mazar at the railway station premises, High Court premises, etc. across the country as in the case of the mosque having been constructed deep inside Allahabad High Court premises, mentioned above.

Over the years, the Waqf Act has become a political tool in the hands of unscrupulous, selfish and shameless political party leaders in India for the purposes of appeasing the Muslim minorities and garnering their votes with a view to cling to power by hook or by crook. For example, as per the response received on an RTI application, ever since the AAP party came into power at the Union Territory of Delhi, the Arvind Kejriwal-led government has been making financial grants to the Delhi Waqf Boad and as on 2022 they had made grant to the tune of over Rs.101 crores.

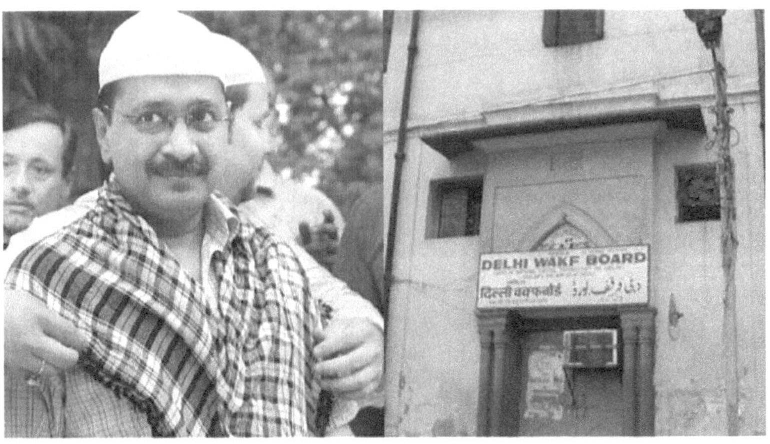

[AAP Chief Minister, Arvind Kejriwal, at the Delhi Wakf Board premises
Photo credit: Op India News portal]

It is indeed a curious case that Kejriwal-led Delhi government has time and again excused themselves for not being able to pay in time the salaries and dues to the government employees, property tax due to the Municipal Corporation of Delhi, etc., citing lack of financial resources while at the same time his government pays out huge sum of money to the Waqf Board year after year without any statutory obligations, without any statutory demands from the Board and without any rhyme or reasons except for appeasing the Muslim communities of Delhi aimed at garnering votes from them so as to cling to power.

Thus, the Waqf Act enacted at the instance of Jawaharlal Nehru has become a piece of draconian legislation slowly and steadily eating away the land owned and possessed by non-Muslim citizens of India leading to the fulfillment of Muslim citizens' dreams of converting India into a dar-ul-Islam. The very enactment of this communal Act is a serious assault upon the democratic and secular credentials of India, which would only promote the interests of foreign-originated Islamic ideologies at the cost of India's sovereignty, integrity, democratic and secular credentials.

Coming back to the subject of Nehru Dynasty government, after the demise of Nehru on 27th May 1964, his daughter Indira Priyadarshini Gandhi became the president of the INC Party. During the next few years she occupied various ministerial posts and in 1971 she was elected as the Prime Minister of India. However, on account of proved charges leveled against her, the Hon'ble High Court of Allahabad struck down her election as unconstitutional on account of corrupt electoral practices and she was barred for contesting any election for the next six years.

Strangely, however, with a view to circumvent the order of the High Court, on her advice to the then President of India, Fakhruddin Ali Ahmed, he proclaimed a state of nation-wide emergency on 25th June1975 which lasted for 21 months. During this period democratic elections were suspended and civil liberties for the common people were curtailed. Wide spread human right violations and atrocities were carried out during this period, including forced mass sterilizations on illiterate citizens which were spearheaded by the late son of Indira Gandhi, Sanjay. Indira Gandhi ruthlessly suppressed the functioning of all democratic institutions and she imprisoned thousands of her opponents and clamped censorship upon the press. This period is known as the darkest period in Indian history.

During this period when the emergency was in force Indira Gandhi surreptitiously carried out an amendment to the Constitution of India by adding the word "Secular" in its preamble without adopting any of the well-established constitutional procedures, parliamentary debates, etc. for such an amendment. This conduct of Indira Gandhi has done great harm and prejudices to the majority citizens professing Hinduism and its human-values oriented Sanathan Dharma for the simple reason that Hinduism or Sanathan Dharma has always been secular for over ten millenniums of its inception in the ancient land of India. Hinduism has no "founder" or Prophet, it is not based on a single holy book but the whole library containing classic spiritual and philosophical doctrines, books and treatises which are the bed rocks on which Hinduism evolved for over ten millenniums. It has no absolute dogmatism. It is these reasons that "fundamentalism" can never be attributed to Hinduism.

Again it is these reasons and backgrounds that the Hon'ble Supreme Court of India has peremptorily ruled that Hinduism is NOT a religion, but a way of life. Its core values are universal brotherhood and welfare as contained in all Hindu scriptures, particularly the philosophy of "Vasudeva Kutumbakan" (the world is but a single family), Samastha Lokha Sukhino Bhavantu (Let all human beings, plants and animals be happy"), etc. In other words, adding the word: "secular" to the preamble of the Constitution of India is something like spraying artificially made chemical perfume upon the naturally grown rose flower!

Indira Gandhi, though born to Hindu parents, had led a luscious marital life. In this regard M.O. Mathai, a long-time Personal Secretary of Nehru, had written a book containing incontrovertible documents and noting made by him in his personal diary, named: "Reminiscences of the Nehru Age", the sale of which was subsequently banned by the then Congress Government.

In his book (at Chapter 17), Mathai writes as follows: (only excerpts are reproduced here)

QUOTE:

"Feroze Gandhi, son of a Parsi liquor and provision merchant of Allahabad, in his early days attached himself to Kamala Nehru as Congress Volunteer. He used to accompany her as a helper wherever she went on Congress work in the Allahabad area. He could not be accused of possessing any eagerness for studies.... In 1941 Indira spoke to her father about her wish to marry Feroze Gandhi. Nehru remembered what his wife had

> *told him at Badenweiler and gave her good advice against the marriage. All the members of the Nehru family were also against the marriage. Neither they nor Nehru could reconcile themselves to the idea of Indira marrying the son of a local liquor and provision merchant. ……… For some inexplicable reason, Nehru allowed the marriage to be performed according to Vedic rites in 1942. An interreligious and inter-caste marriage under Vedic rites at that time was not valid in law. To be legal, it had to be a civil marriage. So, strictly under the law, Indira was only a "concubine" and her children are "bastards".*

UNQUOTE:

[Incidentally, in the Social Media in India different stories regarding the family members of Nehru with regard to the religion professed by them are doing the round. However, I feel the above quoted book portion as authentic as they are straight from the horse's mouth. As the book was banned in India, I purchased it while working abroad on the recommendations of my then colleague who was Mathai's relative, hailing from Kerala].

After lifting the emergency, Indira Gandhi came to power again in 1980 and she picked up the threads of her life by pursuing the pseudo secular policies of her father. Under these policies and practices, the successive Congress Governments devised elaborate Muslim Appeasement Strategies aimed at garnering votes from them en masse. For this purpose various enactments, exclusively meant for the welfare of Muslim citizens of India, were promulgated by the Congress Parliament, prominent amongst them being National Commission for Minorities Act,

1992. The provisions of this Act are directly in conflict with the principles of equal treatments of all citizens as enshrined and guaranteed under the Constitution of India. Muslims in India are comparatively better off compared with the rest of the Muslim countries around the world and yet various schemes were framed exclusively for their welfare so as to keep them in good spirit in the belief that they would vote en masse for Congress in all the democratic elections in which the Muslim citizens have no faith as it is opposed to Quran. This Appeasement of Muslims in India is popularly known as "Vote Bank Politics of the Congress".

Indira Gandhi was assassinated by her own Sikh Bodyguards on the 31st October 1984 on account of the "Operation Blue Star" ordered by her which was the military action to remove Jarnail Singh Bhindranwale, a dreaded terrorist and a Khalistani activist along with his followers from the Sikh Holy Golden temple of Amritsar.

After the assassination of Indira Gandhi, her son Rajiv Gandhi was made Prime Minister of India in 1984.

The first major hurdle the new PM had to face was the reprisals of the 1984 anti-Sikh riots. As a revenge for assassinating Indira Gandhi by her Sikh body guards, the then ruling INC Party members started indiscriminately attacking and killing Sikhs on the streets of Delhi, Punjab and Haryana. While the government sources say that 3,500 Sikhs were killed by the rampaging mobs supported by the Congress stalwarts, the independent sources claim that over 5,000 Sikhs were killed on the streets of Delhi alone.

Rajiv Gandhi was naïve about the nature of politics. Prior to becoming the Prime Minister of India, he was an airline pilot and while he was sojourning and sowing his wild oats in England an Italian waitress then serving at an English Restaurant by name Edvige Antonia Albina Maino succeeded in hooking him as her husband and after marriage with Rajiv Gandhi she came to India and started living with him at his ancestral home at New Delhi.

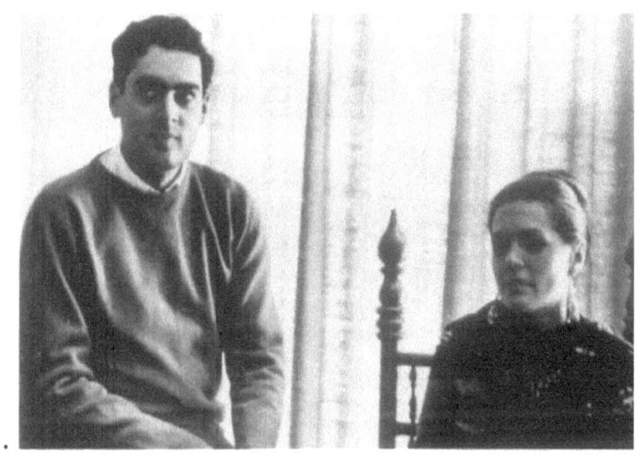

Miss Edvige Maino with young Rajiv Gandhi during her 'hooking period'
Image credit: www.oldindianphotos.in

According to Dr. Subramanian Swamy, Sonia Gandhi's father was Hitler's soldier and her mother was a dedicated follower of Italian dictator, Mussolini.

Sonia played an active role in the personal affairs of Prime Minister Rajiv Gandhi. She had already managed to evict her sister-in-law, Maneka Gandhi, from his sprawling ancestral home at New Delhi.

Sonia is a fun-loving party-going Italian-bred woman, often yearning for enjoying luxurious life style. It was on account of her coercing her hen-pecked husband that in 1987 Rajiv Gandhi took his family, Italian in-laws, foreigners, etc. for a ten-day family holiday at an obscure part of Lakshadweep, Bangaram. For this purpose he used as a personal Taxi the Naval Warship, INS Viraat, which was the only aircraft carrier at that time, in total disregard of national safety and security. A summary of the fabulous holidays as reported from Lakshadweep and published in The Indian Express issue dated 24th January 2088 is reproduced below:

QUOTE:

At least eight foreigners joined the Prime Minister and his family during their New Year holidays here. In all, the group consisted of 24 men, women and children. Looking after their needs were 70 persons from various departments, cooks and servants, and naval personnel. Nearly 1,200 policemen, drawn from Lakshadweep police and Madhya Pradesh, armed special police, etc. were on patrol on the periphery of Bangaram. During the whole period of the holidays, entry of common Indian citizens and international tourists were strictly barred about 100 KMs away from the boundaries of Lakshadweep.

Innumerable boats of the local administration, including 40 HP high-speed boats, and the navy's yachting boats were pressed into service. The navy also provided windsurfers for the use of the holiday-revelers. To ensure security and hospitality, the Lakshadweep Administration reserved as standby nearly 80 private boats and helicopters meant for medical emergencies. In addition services of scores of navy's Sea-King and Chetak helicopters were provided which daily flew thousands of miles to mainland to transport men and material to Bangaram. Bangaram, which was a desert piece of land, was given a new looks. Two new tiled cottages and dining halls were constructed. Two new 30 KV generators were provided.

The VVIP kitchen and the general kitchen were well-stocked, both in food and in drinks. Foreign liquors which included Rajiv's favourite Remy Martin, and Sonia's favourite, Soviet Champagnes, were made available in abundance. Thin Norwegian bread was made available for the foreign guests and to sooth their stomachs digestive substance made in Germany was also made available.

UNQUOTE:

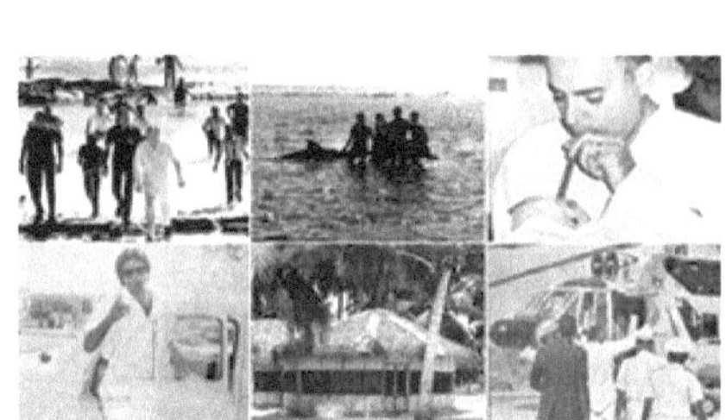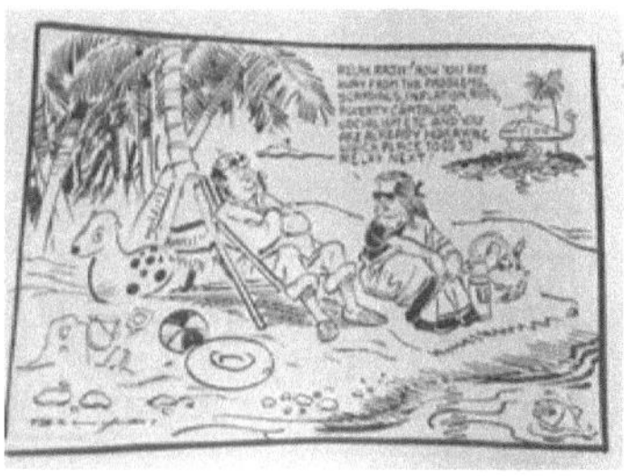

Image Courtesy of the Rajiv Gandhi family holiday: India Today.
Cartoon Credit: R.K. Laxman, The Times of India

Rajiv Gandhi followed the footprints of his mother and grandfather and pursued policies and programs beneficial only to the Muslim citizens of India and during his regime numerous legislations were enacted giving exclusive benefits to the minority Muslims.

One of the most controversial legislations Rajiv Gandhi made was with regard to the marriage obligations of Muslim husbands under the Indian law, which was enacted specifically for enabling the Muslim citizens of India in circumventing the judgment and order passed by the Indian courts of law pertaining to such obligations. This legislation had stemmed from a law suit filed by a Muslim woman against her husband for maintenance under the Indian law, popularly known as "Shah Bano case".

In a nutshell, in this case [Mohd Ahmad Khan Vs. Shah Bano Begum, 1985] a wealthy landlord and a leading Lawyer summarily divorced his long-standing wife by uttering "Talaq" three times. Thus, overnight she became a destitute without any resources for food and shelter. She filed a law suit for maintenance before the Lower Civil Court and after a protracted period of trial it travelled through the labyrinthine judiciary and reached the Supreme Court of India.

Thus, the Apex Court passed a Judgment and Order directing her ex-husband, the wealthy landlord and leading Lawyer, to make certain sum of money as monthly maintenance to his ex-wife. However, he refused to honor the Judgment and order and appealed to his Muslim brethrens across the country for help. Accordingly, large number of Muslim citizens in India resisted the judgment alleging that Muslim citizens in India are governed by their separate personal laws with regard to their marriage and its incidental issues and that they were unable to abide by any judgment passed under "man-made laws" and that too passed by a court presided over by infidels. They further asserted that they would abide only by the verses of God-given Holy Quran and Sharia Law with regard to the issues arising out of their marriages.

Faced by these circumstances with a view to please the Muslim citizens of India, Rajiv Gandhi enacted the legislation called The Muslim Women (Protection of Rights on Divorce) Act, 1986, so as to enable the Muslim husbands in India to rig out the legal obligations as contained in any judgments that may be passed by the Indian courts of law.

At this juncture it is important to deal with the vote bank politics pursued by the successive Nehru Dynasty government under the Congress party. The vote bank politics as devised and practiced by the Congress were most dangerous and risky for India as a whole, which compromised national safety, security, sovereignty and integrity. For example, Assam is one of the North East States in India bordering Bangladesh - a Muslim fundamentalist country earlier seceded from India. Through the porous borders of Assam, lakhs of illegal Bangladeshi immigrants entered into Assam and they slowly, steadily and stealthily settled in various parts of India. On account of this reason there were constant agitations, violence and bloodsheds from the natives of Assam to evict the illegal Bangladeshi immigrants.

Rajiv Gandhi, the then Congress Prime Minister of India, with a view to buying peace, entered into an Accord with the agitating leaders of Assam in 1985 by which it was decided that all the illegal Bangladeshi immigrants who entered into India after 24th March 1971 would be detected; their names from the electoral roll would be deleted and they would be deported within the next three years. However, the successive Congress governments in the State of Assam refused to implement this Accord and kept it in the cold storage solely for garnering votes from these illegal Bangladeshi immigrants, whose names were deliberately included in the electoral roll of the State by the vote-hungry Congress ministers which was in blatant violations of the provisions of the aforesaid Accord.

During this period, the former Congress Chief Minister of Assam, Tarun Gogoi, not only individually met with all the illegal immigrants and assured them that he would not implement the Accord. He had also started dancing in tune with the demands of these illegal immigrants on the unequivocal understanding between Gogoi and the illegal Muslim infiltrators from Bangladesh that they would vote only for the Congress. Thus, instead of Sunday, which had been observed by the Central Government and all other States in India as a public holiday since independence, Gogoi declared Friday as government holiday in his State, Assam. Moreover, in blatant violations of the Accord reached between former Congress Prime Minister, Rajiv Gandhi, and the agitating Assam leaders in 1985, these Congress Chief Ministers in that State allowed the illegal Bangladeshi immigrants to enjoy the benefits doled out to the natives of the State solely for the purpose of clinging to power by getting votes from these illegal immigrants.

When Arnab Goswami of Republic TV interviewed Tarun Gogoi in this regard Gogoi was fumbling for a cogent reply. [Watch video on YouTube by the link words: "Former Assam

CM Tarun Gogoi Speaks to Arnab Goswami"]. Similarly, in all the Congress-ruled States in India the governments freely allowed Bangaldeshi illegal immigrants to settle in their States with impunity and with active connivance of the Muslim staff and officers of Law & Order Enforcing Authorities. [Watch video on YouTube by the words link: "Illegal immigrants from Bangladesh staying in Bangalore …"].

During the Dynasty Period, the majority citizens of India, the Hindus, were treated by the government as "second class citizens" and were made to live in shame just for having been born as Hindus. In this regard a "Letter to the Editor", published in "The Hindu", Chennai, Issue dated 24/03/1984 by a disgruntled Hindu would throw a bit of light regarding the plight of Hindu citizens in India. [See Appendix-2].

The Nehru Dynasty Members regarded the entire landmass of India as their fiefdom. Accordingly, with a view to perpetuate the names of the Dynasty Members, over five thousand entities under various categories such as airports, buildings, roads, hospitals, institutions, tournaments, awards, etc., etc. were named after the successive dynasty members, viz. Nehru, Indira, Rajiv, etc. In this regard a compilation of the few institutions named after the Dynasty Members were done by Dr. A. Surya Prakash [See Appendix-3]. [Please also refer to Dr. Surya Prakash's book: "Public Money, Private Agenda"].

In addition, with a view to perpetuate the names of the Nehru Dynasty members, large chunk of pieces and parcels of prime land at posh/costly locality of New Delhi were acquired at throw away prices through intimidating tactics from the original land owners for erecting "Memorials" in the names of the Dynasty Members. For example, for erecting Nehru Memorial 55 acres of land; for erecting Indira Memorial 45 acres of land and for erecting Rajiv Memorial 15 acres, etc., totaling to 115 Acres (equivalent to 5,56,600 sq. yards) were acquired which would collectively be costing at a conservative estimate to the present market value prevailing in the capital city of New Delhi is of Rs.50,094 crores.

One of the indelible characteristics of the successive Nehru Dynasty is the massive corruption indulged in by all the Ministers of the Congress Party at the heavy cost of the State/ National Exchequer, which has retarded the growth, progress and prosperity of the country from what it could have genuinely achieved in nearly seven decades after the country attained independence.

It is pertinent to mention here with regard to India's growth since independence under the successive Nehru Dynasty governments belonging to INC party, that the party was established in 1885 while the neighboring Chinese Communist Party (CCP) was formed only in 1920. On a careful analysis it can be realized that comparing the growth made by India under the INC government with that of the CCP, China became 2nd most powerful nation in the world with enviable economic progress and prosperity for its people while India under the leadership of INC could reach only 105th position as per Global Economic Growth Index. The reasons behind this wide chasm are undoubtedly the rampant corruption, nepotism and vote bank politics indulged in by all the congress party leaders.

In connection with the misrule of the Congress Party for nearly seven decades after the country attained independence, it would be appropriate to recall an incident in Parliament involving the debate between a veteran trade union leader of the yesteryears, Late George Fernandes, and the congress Members of Parliament (MP) and their supporters.

George Fernandes was the Defense Minister under the non-congress government of Attal Bihari Bajpai. For the purpose of paying homage to Late Fernandes the debate in question is reproduced below verbatim.

Thus, it was in 1998. BJP was single largest party and NDA was the strongest coalition alliance in Lok Sabha. Vajpayee was elected as the PM, when a Confidence Motion was put before the House. Congress and CPM had joined hands to vote against the NDA government in the Motion. Leaders of both the parties were sitting together and attacking BJP & NDA. Whenever Congress leader spoke, the CPM leaders were thumping the desks and vice versa. Likewise, whenever a leader from NDA was attacking Congress, leaders from CPM were aggressively counter-attacking him/her. All so-called "secular forces" were united to topple Vajpayee government.

At this point, veteran Trade Union Leader, George Fernandes, was the Defense Minister of Vajpayee government and he was defending the government. He stood up and spoke: "Speaker Sir, I want to inform you what a strong organization has to say something on Congress Party", whereupon he picked up a book and started reading from it: "Congress party is the fountainhead of corruption…." (big shouting from Congress benches) "….The British left and the Congress party replaced them. Over the past 50 years, Congress has established ever new records in corruption…" (again big shouting from Congress Members).

George Fernandes continued: "Congress party ministers have often been found embroiled in several scams, including Mundra scam, Bofors scam, Sukhram scam (bundles of Indian currency notes stuffed in six large suitcases), Harshad Scam, JMM Bribery scam, Hawala scams, etc. etc., that took place during its regime. Congress has corrupted and misused every institution of the Indian democracy".

At this point, both the Congress and CPM got charged up and said: "Speaker Sir! Please ask the Honorable Member to name the source; we cannot allow him to read from any damn document. Please restrain him".

Fernandes spoke: "Please don't get impatient. I will definitely name the source. But first let me complete what this book says. It says:

"The Congress party's record on secularism too has been chequered. At various times in history Congress goondas took active part in riots and killed innocent people. 3000 Sikhs were butchered by them both on the streets of Delhi and Haryana and Prime Minister Rajiv Gandhi watched them in silence".

Big shouting and noise again rose from the benches of Congress and CPM. After a pause, Fernandes resumed: "Just give me two more minutes…. and then I will reveal the source".

He continued to read from the book: "Speaker Sir, it says: "No country in history has ever progressed with bad governance and excessive corruption as partners. None! The Congress suffers from this twin ailments since decades. Its survival is detrimental to the progress of India as a whole. Therefore, in the interest of this nation, it is important that Congress party is wiped out from this land forever".

Big shouting and noise again rose from benches of Congress and CPM and pandemonium prevailed in the House. They shouted: . "Speaker sir! It cannot go on like this. We will not allow him to speak any further if he doesn't give the source he is quoting from".

"OK,OK", said George, "There is more to read. But since our friends from Congress and CPM are so desperate to know the source, let me tell you what I am reading from…."

"….I am reading from the Manifesto of CPI(M) issued just before these Lok Sabha elections".

Pin drop silence in the House ensued. Leaders from Congress and CPM were starring at each other…

George: "What happened, why you're all silent?. You were shouting we want to know the source, we want to know the source! Once you heard the name of the source, your voices were mute. Shame on your selves! Definitely you should be ashamed…"

"My friends from the Left! Either you don't read your own manifesto or you don't mean a word of it. In either case, you should be ashamed of yourselves. In the name of secularism, you have joined hands with Congress that has broken all records in corruption. I urge you to introspect to determine your future course of action. And if you do not mend your ways, your party will become history, sooner rather than later".

To come back to the Nehru Dynasty rule of India, in 1991 Rajiv Gandhi was also assassinated by the Liberation Tigers Tamil Ealam (LTTE), thus ending the direct lineage of the Dynasty.

When the direct lineage of Dynasty ended with the assassination of Rajiv Gandhi, grandson of Nehru, his Italian widow, assumed the surname of her husband and became "Sonia Gandhi", so as to fool the gullible Hindus of India, although her Christian name as Baptized by her parents in Italy was "Edvige Antonia Albina Maino".

Thus, Sonia Gandhi was voted to power by the slave-minded gullible Hindus and she became the Head of the "United Progressive Alliance" (UPA) which was formed as a fourteen-party coalition arrangement, comprising various regional political factions, splintered national parties, communal parties like Indian Union Muslim League, All India Majilis Ittehadul Muslimeen (AIMIM), etc. In addition, UPA was also supported by Leftist political parties from outside. Thus in a way the UPA government, comprising dedicated communal political parties like Muslim League, was unconstitutional as the Constitution of India unequivocally declares: "India shall always remain secular".

During the decade-long government of UPA, the legacy of the successive congress government of corrupt dealings by all the ministers was consolidated and corruption was at its zenith. Sonia became fourth richest politician in the world (as per the survey conducted by Forbes Magazine). She was also described as "Richer than the Queen Elizabeth and Basser Al Assad put together" in the list published by Huffington Post in 2013, titled: "The Richest World Leaders are Ever Richer than You Thought".

Similarly her daughter's in-laws like husband Robert Vadra and his parents overnight became richest business class people in the country. [For an authentic picture of Sonia Gandhi, the readers are invited to watch a video recording on YouTube by the link words: "Dr. Subramanian Swamy calls for criminal action against Sonia Gandhi Amid RGF Row"].

Sonia Gandhi did not have any educational qualification, experience or understanding of governing such a vast continental-sized country, inhabited by the equivalent of almost one sixth of the human race on earth, called "India". The British mainstream media described Sonia as "Vatican Controlled Waitress". [See news report: "How a Waitress Became a World Leader" by Glen Owen and Nick Meo, The Times, London, May 17, 2004]. Sonia was anxious to become Prime Minister of India. However, apprehending assassination, as was the fate of her husband and mother-in-law, her children advised her against such a choice. Accordingly, Sonia appointed an economist, Dr. Manmohan Singh, as her puppet on the unequivocal understanding that he would have to act only as per her instructions. It is pertinent to state here that Dr. Singh never before won any democratic election and in one election which he contested after elaborate electioneering he was defeated by a huge margin of over 40,000 votes by his rival. Thus, during the whole UPA period the Prime Minister of India, Dr. Singh, was remotely controlled by Sonia, hailing from Italy, from behind the throne, as a result of which there were paralysis of government policies and decisions, which Dr. Singh frequently termed as "Coalition Compulsions".

Thus, Dr. Manmohan Singh became the first non-Hindu de facto Prime Minister of India without winning in any democratic elections. On assuming power and upon the instructions from Sonia, he categorically and openly declared at various public events across India that: "The first priority in the matter of allocation of the national resources shall go to Muslim citizens of India" [See The Times of India, issue dated 9th December 2006], thereby indirectly hinting that the Hindus, comprising about 80% of the population, shall be treated for all intends and purposes as "second-class citizens".

In addition, Sonia ruthlessly ensured that none of the Hindus were appointed in any political or government positions. She specifically chose those who have had track records of Hindu bashing, atheists, Leftist ideologues, hard-core Muslim fundamentalists, etc. etc.

Thus, Sonia appointed Indira Jaising, a hardcore Leftist ideologue who has had track records of spitting venom at the very mentioning of the word "Hinduism", was made the Head of the Legislative Business of the UPA government in the capacity of Additional Solicitor General of India, which is a constitutional position.

Jaising held the aforesaid constitutional position, simultaneously working for numerous International NGOs, such as Open Society Foundation (founded by George Soros), UNIFEM, etc. and she was on their pay-rolls from whom money poured into her personal account. She drafted numerous anti-Hindu legislations for the UPA Parliament with a view to wipe out every trace of human-values oriented social systems from the Hindu societies on the fund remitted to her by the international NGOs and Foundations. The main anti-Hindu legislation out of these numerous legislations exclusively meant against Hindus, was "The Protection of Women from Domestic Violence Act, 2005" for which Jaising was reportedly paid a huge initial sum of Rs.50 crores by UNIFEM. Under this enactment, numerous imaginary concepts were introduced with a view to distract Hindu men from marriage and destroy the very sacrosanct Vedic institution of marriage amongst the Hindus. This enactment has also introduced the concept of Live-in-Relationship in place of marriage for the first time in the spiritual-oriented Hindu society whereby any man and woman can live together without marriage.

The first case of such a live-in-relationship, as reported by a State electronic media, was that of the Communist State of Kerala whose Chief Minister's daughter adopted such a live-in-relationship without marriage for a brief period. Young college-going boys and girls started pursuing this mode of lives without obeying their parents, which invariably resulted into violent crimes, suicides, protracted litigations, etc., leading to serious complications in Hindu societies. In fact this enactment is regarded as the starting point in transforming India's ancient legacy of spiritual-oriented societies into a lust-filled and sex starved promiscuous societies on the lines of the Western societies.

During 2008 in the second term of the UPA government, power seems to have got into the head of this former Italian bar maid as she and her son along with Congress stalwarts surreptitiously made numerous trips to Peking, China, and on one such occasion a Memorandum of Understanding (MOU), containing secret liabilities on passing of internal information pertaining to the defense strategies of India, between the then Indian government under the Italian woman and the Communist

China was got executed. None of the Indian citizens, who voted her to power, ever made to know anything regarding the purpose of their frequent visits to China or the contents of this MOU, which even now is being maintained by the Congress as a closely guarded secret.

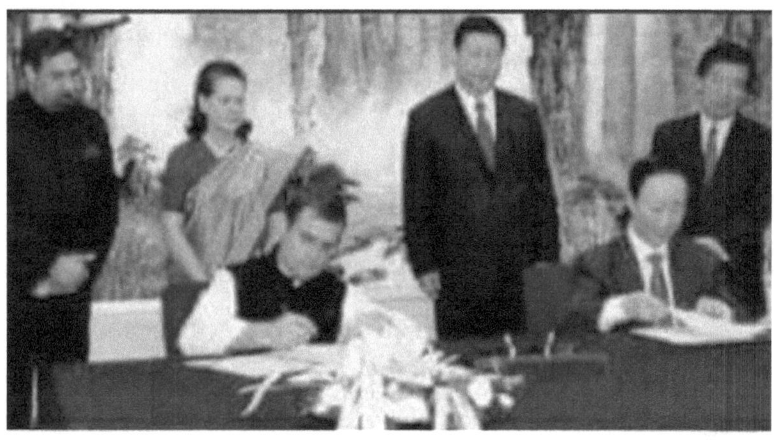

[Rahul Gandhi, son of Sonia Gandhi, executing a secret MOU in the presence of his mother, witnessed by Chinese President and other high-ranking Chinese Defense Ministry Officials at an undisclosed location, near Peking]
Photo Courtesy: Google Images

Like all the leftist ideologues living like parasites and flourishing in India in the absence of any legislations against Leftist ideologies (for annihilating and controlling them, as in the USA and other democratic countries), Jaising throughout her "activism-ridden" life maintained a high degree of double standards on the question of the faiths of Hindus and Muslims. In this regard one of her earliest activism was to repeal all laws pertaining to adultery and she fought tooth and nail for giving freedom and liberty to married Hindu women to utilize their bodies "as per the dictates of their minds rather than living as slaves of their husbands". Conversely when the question of Sharia law comes, which mandates stoning to death of any woman straying away for extra-marital sex outside the wedlock, Jaising whole-heartedly supported the Muslim husbands by saying that the faith was originated abroad and the Muslim citizens of India should be allowed the freedom of practicing their religion. Similarly when the questions of Tripple Talaq, genital mutilation, etc. as practiced amongst the Muslim citizens in India at the behest of their husbands, Jaising fought for their "religious freedom", although throughout her life of "Women's Lib Activism" she projected herself as the "Champion of Women's Equality and Freedom".

The members of the Indian judiciary during the UPA period were also selected by the UPA Parliamentarians who were all totally against the Hindu faith and sentiments. Thus, the Chief Justice of India, who was appointed on the recommendation of Sonia Gandhi was one Justice K.G. Balakrishnan, whose family members have converted themselves into Christianity, professing leftist ideologies, hailing from the communist Kerala. On assuming power, the first major judicial pronouncements in support of the newly introduced concept of Live-in-Relationship which he made was his categorical assertion that: "There is nothing wrong in man and woman living together without marriage because Lord Krishna himself enjoyed sex with numerous women of his choice prior to his marriage". [Refer to internet article titled: "Supreme Court Judges insults Hindus by referring Radha-Krishna as premarital sex partners" – http:arisebharat.com [Accessed by me on 15/8/2020] Large number of slave-minded Hindus with a laid-back attitude, particularly those Hindu comrades of Kerala, remained silent over the aforesaid observations made by none other than the Chief Justice of India. However, certain alert sober-minded people professing Hinduism and Sanadhan Dharma, categorically denied the assertion of Justice Balakrishnan as the entire scriptures and other evidences accumulated over the millenniums clearly show that Lord Krishna never ever had sex with any of his female companions and his relationship was childhood pranks confined only up to the period of His age of eleven. However, there was no voice to represent the sober minded Hindus either in Parliament or in the Ministry.

It was again during the UPA period that the concept of "Single Parenthood" began to take shape in India. Feminists, particularly in the State of West Bengal, started sleeping with different men of their choice and bearing children without marriage and bringing them up singlehandedly. The Madras High Court in a judgment has observed that "Single Parenting was a dangerous concept, which will only criminalize the human societies" [The Times of India, issue dated 11-8-2018].

It is pertinent to place on record here at this juncture while dealing with the question of historic authenticity of Ramayana events, the United Progressive Alliance (UPA), which comprised of a hotchpotch of coalition of Hindu-bashing political parties like that of the atheist communist parties, dedicated communal parties like the Indian Union Muslim League, AIMIE, etc. under the leadership of an Italian fundamentalist Christian woman, the faith of Hindus in Rama had received a serious blow.

Thus, in 2007 the UPA government had sought to demolish the historic relic associated with Ramayana, called "Rama Setu" for which they had floated a global tender to award the contract job of demolition. The said decision of the UPA government was challenged by Dr. Subramaniam Swamy, Member of Parliament, before the Hon'ble Supreme Court.

Upon the direction of Hon'ble Supreme Court, the UPA government had submitted an affidavit in the Hon'ble Court stating therein: "There was no historical and scientific evidence to establish the existence of Rama and the Ramayana". The affidavit was drafted by the then Home Minister, P. Chidambaram, who was also a Supreme Court Lawyer at that time, prior to his going to jail on various corruption charges of great magnitude, involving he and all his family members.

Indeed it was a mile stone in the post independent history of India in the journey towards realizing the aspirations of Bharateeyers that on account of the challenge by Dr. Swamy, the UPA government was restrained from pursuing its decision to demolish Rama Setu, thereby protecting the faith of millions of Hindus of Bharat and around the world and restoring their self-respect.

As mentioned above during the decade-long period of UPA rule, Sonia and her family members looted the country's resources through unfair means and became fourth richest politician in the world according to various surveys conducted by reputed global rating agencies. This "Vatican controlled Waitress" occupied one of the largest estate-like prime lands in the posh locality of the capital city of New Delhi with a sprawling bungalow along with swimming pool, hangar for parking her private jet plane, etc. allotted by the UPA government which she still continues to occupy even after the defeat of UPA government. In no other country can one find an ordinary Member of Parliament occupying a residential complex which is much larger than the elected Prime Minister of the country.

Interestingly, it is not in the Indian public domain that Sonia owned a private jet plane. Initially, she flew this plane to visit her electoral constituency, Rae Bareli in Uttar Pradesh, and to different parts of the country and abroad. However, newspapers published in the Western countries reported that on the instructions of Vatican, Sonia abandoned the usage of her private plane. The Guardian of UK reported: "Sonia Gandhi abandons private plane in an austerity drive. India's ruling party makes symbolic gestures to show it is in touch with the suffering masses". [The Guardian, U.K., issue dated 14th September 2009].

It is worthwhile to mention here that after the assassination of Rajiv Gandhi, Sonia chose Rae Bareli in the largest Indian State, Uttar Pradesh, as her electoral constituency. Rae Bareli is the most backward District in India inhabited by illiterates and poor, carrying on precarious existence, struggling with grinding poverty. The Political Pandits in the know-how of India's poverty often say that if Sonia and her family has had even an iota of sympathy towards the electorates of her constituency, who voted her to power, and if she had donated at least 10% of her wealth for the welfare and progress of the Constituency, the conditions of those miserable people could have been ameliorated. However year after year she only paid lip services by visiting the Constituency in Hindu woman's attire sprouting a large "Tilak" on her forehead, like any other Hindu woman, so as to fool the gullible, illiterate people, although she and her family members are born-again Christians, and harbored utter contempt towards Hindus.

During the whole period of the UPA regime, India was transformed into an Eldorado of both Christian and Islamic missionaries. A report leaked by Wikileaks reveals that Vatican used Sonia for spreading Christianity in India by converting Hindus into Christianity. [Watch YouTube video by the link: "How Vatican used Sonia Gandhi – per Wikileaks"]. Plane-loads of Christian Missionaries were the regular visitors in India for whom Visa regulations were specifically simplified and/or relaxed by the then Government on the instructions of Sonia.

It is pertinent to state here that the Archbishops in India are directly appointed by the Vatican. These Archbishops, Pastors, Bishops, Priests and nuns live in India and act at the behest of their Masters in Rome. On account of exercising this extra-territorial jurisdiction by a foreign power upon India, the Christian citizens of India can do any harm to the integrity and sovereignty of the country. In fact, it was ubiquitous during the decade-long UPA rule that government servants professing Christian religion, including IAS/IFS Officers, serving in various government positions in India and abroad were devoting part of their duty hours in popularizing Bible and clandestinely encouraging non-Christian government employees for converting themselves into Christianity.

During the UPA regime these Archbishops were extremely active and alert in spreading the Gospels of Christ and the conversion rate was the highest which they carried out without the knowledge of the general public for which the UPA government created congenial atmosphere and provided all the necessary logistics. However, when the change of government at the Centre took place in 2014, their large-scale clandestine operation across the country came to the fore. For example, almost all the Archbishops on the payroll of the Vatican have been issuing "Fatwa" to the Churchgoers of the respective Churches under their control. As per the media reports, Thomas Macwan, the Archbishop of Gujarat; Cardinal Oswald Gracias, Archbishop of Mumbai; Anil Couto, Archbishop of Delhi, etc. were in the limelight for issuing Fatwas containing strongly worded warnings to Christians congregating in their churches against voting for BJP in the 2019 general election.

It is worthwhile to mention here that during the UPA period, the rate of conversion of Hindus into Christianity in the communist Kerala was the highest, compared with the other States in the rest of the country. The entire credit for this conversion would go to the then Chief Minister of Kerala, Oommen Chandy, who was a born-again Christian and he had taken numerous pilgrimages to Vatican to pay obeisance to the Pope and taking instructions from him at the cost of the State Exchequer.

It is interesting to state here that the Sonia (Italian) regime at the Centre and the Chandy regime in Kerala had coincided. It was during this period that on the active support and instructions from Sonia at New Delhi, Chandy got the Kerala Legislative Assembly pass legislation for establishing a Financial Corporation named and styled as "Kerala State Development

Corporation for Christian Converts from Scheduled Castes and the Recommended Communities Ltd. [KSDCCCRCL]".
[See news reports: "Loan Waiver Scheme for Christian Converts", The Hindu, June 10, 2010. Also visit official Web Portal of Government of Kerala: https:kerala.gov.in for details regarding this Financial Corporation].

The KSDCCCRCL was specifically established for the purpose of encouraging large scale conversion of Hindus into Christianity. If any Hindu citizen of "Secular" Kerala converts into Christianity, he/she would automatically become eligible for waiver of the loan which he/she had taken while he/she was a Hindu. Nowhere in the democratic world can one find similar instances. Any impartial secular-minded Indian citizen can be sure and certain that if the establishment of the Financial Corporation is put to judicial scrutiny, orders would be passed to out-rightly wound it up. On a closer scrutiny of the structure of the corpus fund for managing this Corporation, one can find that a major chunk of the money for running the Corporation is directed from the revenues received by the Hindu temples across the State which are under the full control of the atheist government (Devosworm Board), who have harbored absolute contempt towards Hinduism. However, the forces of the Hindu leftist ideologies in the State have grown up for over six decades of communist leftist activism in the State that none of the Hindu Comrades in the State has the courage of their conviction to challenge such blatant illegality and injustice. Chandy while expecting large scale migration of Hindus into Christianity under the newly established Financial Corporation, (KSDCCCRCL) which exclusively favored converted Christians, had simultaneously ensured that he left no stone unturned in stopping the Christian citizens of the State from returning back to the Hindu fold, rightly known as "Ghar Vapsi" (returning to one's route). In this regard he had also unsuccessfully filed Writ Petitions before the High Court of Kerala for stopping "Ghar Vapsi", although those Christians desirous of returning to their original faith (Sanathan Dharma or Hinduism) were acting solely on their own accord without any coercion or compulsion from anybody, as alleged by Chandy.

Similar to the Christian conversion-spree during the UPA regime, there were large-scale flows of Wahhabis from Saudi Arabia into India. Hamid Ansari was the Vice President and was also a senior government functionary during the whole period of the UPA regime prior to which he was India's Ambassador to several fundamentalist Islamic countries, notably Iran. During his tenure as Vice President of India he invited large contingents of Wahhabis from Saudi Arabia into India. As per Indian Intelligence Bureau report, during the period 2011-2013 over 25,000 Wahhabis visited India and they were enjoying free access to the students of all Madrassas across India for their radicalization into Wahhabism. [**Visit:** https://www.haaretz.com/middle-east-news/does-saudi-funded-muslim-radicalization-threaten-india-].

It was P. Chidambaram, then a prominent Union Minister of the UPA government, who first coined the phrase: "Saffron Terrorism" and gave it wide publicity across the world. With a view to control the "growing menace of saffron terrorism", Sonia formed a Council, named and titled "National Advisory Council" (NAC). All the members of this apex body directly under Sonia were selected from those who have had proven track records of being hard-core Hindu bashing. These members were also on the pay-roll of various Western/European NGOs. Their main functions were to protect and safeguard international Islamic terrorists attacking India. [See list of people who signed Ajmal Kasab's mercy petition. Appendix-4].

Chidambaram in his capacity as the Finance Minister knew the modus operandi in looting the national resources with the connivance of his former Italian Boss. In short, he turned out to be the fox that guarded the hen house. He and his family members were involved in massive corrupt practices of unprecedented magnitudes and scales. His son, Karthi, who regularly flew down from his Chennai home to Hazratbal Mosque at Sreenagar for offering prayers, turned out to be the biggest beneficiary of the massive empire of corruption built up by his father during the decade long period of the UPA government. [Refer: "Chidambaram Rahasya" by PGurus – Appendix-5].

No summing up of the narration regarding the Nehru Dynasty period since the country attained independence until the NDA government under Narendra Modi came to power can be completed unless and until a reference is made to the 4th Generation Dynasty's (UPA regime) draconian enactment, sought to be used against the slave-minded majority Hindus.

Thus, at the fag-end of the UPA's decade-long regime, it enacted an anti-Hindu Bill named and styled as "The Prevention of Communal and Targeted Violence (Access to Justice and Reparations) Bill 2011". The entire Bill has had frightening provisions to book any citizen of the country found to be professing Hinduism on a purported "communal violence".

Sonia Gandhi, the born-again Italian Christian woman, who harbored pathological contempt and hatred towards Hinduism, piloted the Bill in her capacity as the Chairperson of UPA for which she specifically commissioned all those who have track-records of Hindu bashings as well as those who professed imported leftist ideologies, thereby making a 32-member group for drafting the Bill. It should be recalled at this juncture that during the decade-long UPA period, over 500 international NGOs, mainly from Islamic and Christian fundamentalist countries, were active in India through their foot-soldiers living in the country. In fact, these NGOs made hay while the "Italian sun" shined in India for them. On a closer scrutiny, it can be realized that all the members of the Communal Violence Bill Drafting Group were on the pay-roll of these NGOs who were hard-bent to create anarchy in India and destroy Hinduism. Few of such instances are listed in the highly researched book, "Breaking India: Western Interventions in Dalit and Dravidian Fault lines" by Rajiv Malhotra and Aravindan Neelakandan.

Indeed the whole purpose of this Bill was to make Hindus slaves of Muslim citizens who are part of the world-wide Islamic fundamentalist network of organizations and brotherhood.

The background of few of the members of the Drafting Committee of the Bill is described below in a nutshell:

Harsh Mander: Mandar is a former bureaucrat and a hard-core Hindu basher. He was made Chairman of the Drafting Committee. It has been reported in the media that Mander had received a whopping sum of over Rs.100 crores from various overseas Islamic brotherhood organizations, such as Indian

Muslims Relief & Charities Trust (USA), American Federation of Muslims of Indian Origin, etc. [For further details regarding the activism of Harsh Mander, please read article on UNHCHR included in this book].

Shabnam Hashmi: Hashmi was one of the founders of the Indian NGO, ANHAD, whose parent organization in the USA was a church funded international organization. The FCRA registration of this NGO was cancelled in 2016 by the NDA government on finding subversive and anti-national activities based on incontrovertible documentary evidences and dubious financial remittances into her Account from numerous sources based in Western and European countries.

Ram Puniyani: Puniyani has had excellent track records of harboring hatred against Hindus. He has had scant respect towards the Indian judiciary and had vociferously opposed the hanging of terrorist Afzal Guru even after the Supreme Court Judgment awarding him capital punishment for the dastardly crimes perpetrated upon India. Puniyani's NGO, Centre for Study of Society and Secularism (CSSS) regularly received funds from Christian countries notably the Heinrich Boll Foundation, German Green Party, etc.

Gagan Sethi: Sethi has been a Congress stooge since his college days. He had been a Member of the Planning Commission of India and held various positions of International NGOs, notably Oxfam India, wherein he had been a Board Member.

To come back to the provisions of the Communal Violence Bill, the definition of the Bill categorically defined the "victim group" as only those belonging to a religious minority in a case of communal violence and projected the Hindus as the sole perpetrators of the violence. The entire provisions of the Bill were against the Hindu majority, a few of which are selected at random and given below:

The Bill provided a specific provision which would go beyond the federal structure of the democratic India, as for example in a communal violence, the Bill gave unrestrained power to central government to take over the case from any part of the country and no state government would have any role in investigating the case.

The Bill had a provision for a body named and styled as "National Authority of Communal Harmony" the members of which will not be accountable to anyone for all intents and purposes if the wordings of the Bill were to be read in the right perspective.

It is pertinent to state here that during the erstwhile NDA regime under Atal Bihari Vajpayee Government with a view to prevent the regular terrorist bombings and violence across India, sponsored by International Islamic fundamentalist countries, an enactment, called The Prevention of Terrorists Act (POTA) was made. However, when the slaves of India voted out Vajpayee government and elected the Italian woman as head of UPA government, the first thing she did was to repeal the POTA. Thereafter even a child knows that India was rocked by dastardly terrorist bomb attacks almost every month. Blasts occurring in cities like Mumbai, Varanasi, Delhi, Ayodhya, Jaipur, Bangalore, Assam, Patna, Ahmadabad, etc. were the regular features of the country during the whole UPA regime. In short, terrorist activities had become a regular affair so much so that the people of India had become accustomed to reading and hearing news regarding terrorist violence resulting in loss of innocent lives and destruction of properties across the country with increasing frequency.

To cut short the long turn of events in India since independence, it can be conveniently argued that at time the brain of the slaves of India becomes alert and thus they voted out of power the unconstitutional government of UPA under the Italian woman and brought again the NDA government under Narendra Modi.

The aforesaid regular terrorist strikes in India would become clear taking into account the fact that there has been no terror strike in the mainland of the country beyond Kashmir since the last 8 years of the NDA government. This fact was recognized world over, including USA, UK, Canada, etc. It is indeed heartening that countries like Saudi Arabia, Turkey, etc. had bestowed upon Modi the highest civilian awards of those countries by recognizing his leadership qualities as PM of India and for the genuine secularist policies pursued by his government which are free of appeasement of any groups of citizens for dabbling in vote bank politics.

Since the time Narendra Modi came to power, apart from achieving all-round progress and prosperity within a short span of time, there are world-wide recognitions of his leadership quality. All the impartial world-wide media are unanimous in predicting that India would scale to greater heights under his leadership as for example the media in Singapore has predicted that India would be surpassing all the economic parameters and become a super power under the leadership of Narendra Modi. In this regard a news and image appeared early in November 2016 in a widely circulated English language Newspaper in Singapore is reproduced below:

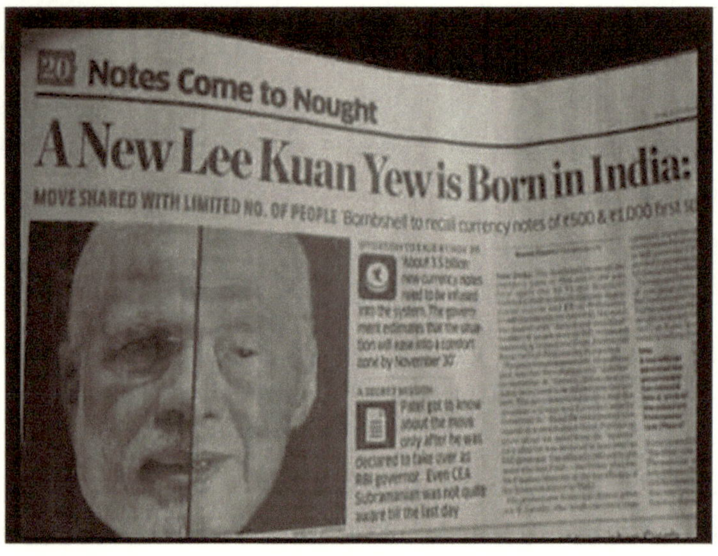

In conclusion, let all patriotic Indians keep their fingers crossed that the success story drafted and enacted by the NDA Government under Narendra Modi for two consecutive terms with absolute majority will continue as the electorates would en masse vote him to power in the ensuing general elections in 2024.

JULY 2022

[An unedited version of this essay was published as a cover story in "Organiser" in its July 17, 2022 issue]

CROSSING THE *LAXMAN REKHA* BY THE JUDGES OF THE HON'BLE SUPREME COURT OF INDIA

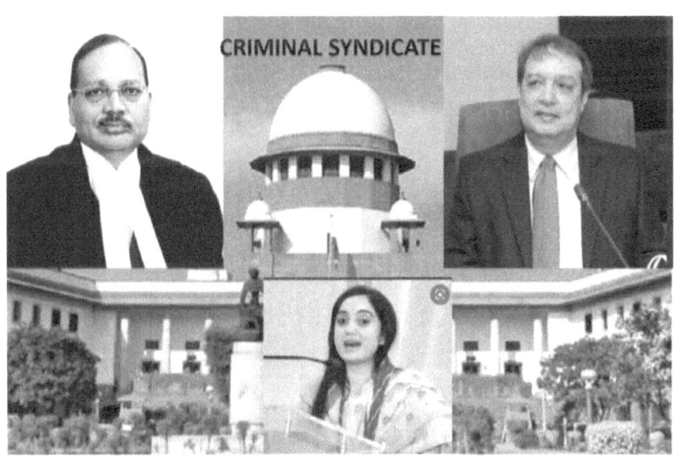

[Image Courtesy: WhatsApp forward, originated from the NRIs of USA]

$\mathcal{A}$t no point of time in the post-independent judicial history of India had there been such a nation-wide mass-scale reaction and outcry when the sitting Judges of the Supreme Court, Mr. Justice Surya Kant and Mr. Justice J.B. Pardiwalla sermonized on the Nupur Sharma episode (while refusing to consider her petition for clubbing together the multiple FIRs lodged against her all over the country).

Amid the unprecedented outbursts of these Judges, they categorically yelled: ***"Nupur Sharma with her loose tongue is single handedly responsible for what is happening in the country, including Udaipur beheading of a tailor this week for allegedly sharing her remarks"***.

These outbursts and unwarranted remarks, uttered without any legal basis or observing any well-established practices and procedures pertaining to adjudication, raises the following frightening questions in the minds of the law-abiding, peace-loving citizens of India, professing Hinduism, which were gleaned at random from these millions of social media postings erupted since the date of the outbursts:

1. Are these judges presiding over a Sharia Court in a Muslim country or a Court constituted under the constitution of democratic India?

2. There is not even an iota of untruth in whatever Nupur Sharma uttered during the democratic debate in question. In fact, the truthfulness of her remarks made during the debate was validated by international authorities on Islam, including the Islamic scholar, Dr. Zakir Naik. Hence did

these Judges throw out the motto of Indian judiciary, viz. "Satyameva Jayathe"?

3. Nupur Sharma made her remarks not in isolation but only when faced by outrageous provocation regarding the religion professed by her as well as the majority citizens of India, the propriety of which was promptly admitted by Islamic scholars from across the border, viz. Pakistan, as per the social media video clips. Hence the question is whether the statutory provisions of the criminal jurisprudence on "provocation" is not available to Nupur Sharma or cannot be appreciated by these Judges?

4. According to the Judges, does opposing participant in the debate in question, who professes a foreign originated religion, enjoy immunity from making any insulting/ disparaging remarks against the religion professed by Nupur Sharma as well as by the majority citizens of India?

5. *On what grounds the Judges burst out against Sharma by alleging that* it was only Nupur Sharma who is **"single-handedly responsible for setting the country on fire"?**

6. The fundamental legal principle on which adjudication is commenced in courts of law in any democratic country is known as "cause of action". The term cause of action as defined under the Civil Procedure Code is **_"... a bundle of facts which allow a person to establish his or her legal rights against another…"_**. When this being the basic tenets of adjudication, the million dollar question is: "What did the Apex Court Judges mean when they repeatedly uttered: **_"Nupur Sharma is single handedly responsible for the …. beheading of an unarmed innocent tailor…" ?._**

7. The fundamental criminal law doctrine of *"**presumption of innocence until proved guilty**"* was thrown into the dustbin by the Apex Court Judges when the fact remains that none of the courts of law in India, where multiple cases were lodged against her, has yet proved Nupur Sharma guilty of any offence.

8. Unlike the Sharia Law, wherein the doctrine of *mens rea* (guilty intention) is totally absent, in Indian law the said doctrine is paramount in considering the gravity of an offence allegedly committed by any citizen. By watching the debate in question Nupur Sharma has had not even an iota of guilty intention (*mens rea*) by uttering the words in question, which were purely out of sudden and aggressive provocation made by the other party to the debate. This is all the more bizarre and strange on the part of the Judges when viewed from the perspective that her words were nothing but unvarnished truth, as certified by all the world-renowned Islamic scholars, including Dr. Zakir Naik, who has dedicated his life for the cause of Islam, and was awarded the highest religious title by Saudi Arabia along with a mountain of monetary reward for his unstinted efforts in spreading Islam in India.

9. Do Their Lordships consider both uttering of words out of provocation is same as that of beheading of an innocent unarmed citizen of India? Does it not amount to taking Sharia law in one's own hands for perpetrating a gruesome crime of beheading of an Indian citizen through treachery and deception by way of creating friendliness of a customer (of the murdered tailor), which is known under Holy Quran as "Al-Taqquiya" (Sura 3 Ayat 28)?

10. The Judges have reportedly posed a query: "Why is she freely moving and not yet arrested"? This query goes to the very root of the human rights as guaranteed to citizens under the Constitution of India. The entire citizens of India and even a child, except the foot-soldiers acting for international Jihadis, know that the multiple FIRs lodged across the country against Sharma are only by the Jihadi/ Sharia elements and not even a single person professing secular values and democratic credentials to which the Jihadi elements have no faith. By filing FIRs by these Jihadi elements through the democratic process of the country, in which they do not have any faith of whatsoever nature as it is opposed to their foreign-originated faith, viz. Sharia, it is only they who force their writ upon the peace-loving law-abiding citizens of the country, whom they regard as infidels. And yet the Judges are anxious to bow down to the Jihadi demands.

11. There is yet another very serious angle to the query posed by the Judges, viz. "Why is she freely moving and not yet arrested"? This query goes not only to the very root of human rights as guaranteed to any Indian citizen under the constitution but also to the root of right to equality, right to freedom to move fearlessly across the country, etc. As the words spoken by Nupur Sharma were triggered ONLY out of disparaging provocation made by her opposing debate member and even a child in India knows that she has not committed any offence of whatsoever nature. Are these Judges extremely cruel by not considering the reality that this young unmarried lady cannot move freely across the country in attending to the hearings of multiple FIRs filed

on false and frivolous grounds without exposing herself into greatest danger and risks to her life? Hence, where is the question of arresting her upon multiple FIRs filed on false and frivolous grounds, as demanded by the Judges?

One of the outbursts made by the Judges is: "……She should have gone to the TV and apologized to the nation…". The million dollar question is: "Is such a demand applicable to only to the Hindu citizens of the country and not to the Muslims"? There are thousands of most heinous crimes perpetrated by the Muslim minorities of the country against the majority citizens. Two instances out of such large number of cases are briefly described below:

(i) In the recent past an incident pertaining to the debate in question occurred. The accused, whose physical appearance resembled to that of the killers of the tailor, made a video showing a mock beheading of Nupur Sharma and uploaded it on social media. The video showed the accused severing the head of a look-alike woman and then he held the severed head in one hand and in the other hand he held the blood-oozing clever/sword. He was arrested by the police and brought before a Magistrate who instantly granted him bail. It took not more than ten minutes for the Advocate of the accused to argue on bail application.

(ii) When Akbaruddin Owaisi, the Hyderabad based Muslim fundamentalist declared at a largely attended public event to the effect that: "if police force are away just for fifteen minutes the Muslims in India could easily eliminate the Hindu infidels". To this nation-wide telecast threat, nobody has filed any FIR against him and when the police suo moto filed case against him, it was heard by a High Court Judge, who let him free by passing a judgment to the effect: "The speech does not amount to hate speech".

Thus, in short, all the Muslim criminals are handled by the Indian judiciary with kid gloves, at the cost of grave threat, dangers and risks to the life and liberty of the Hindu citizens and there is no question of the Judges asking them: "to go to TV and apologize to the nation".

Multiple FIRs were lodged exclusively by the Jihadi/Sharia elements of India with international support from Muslim countries. When Nupur Sharma's application came up before Their Lordships for clubbing together all these multiple FIRs and place them before a single court, her Advocate vehemently argued for over a couple of hours showing exemplarily clear that there is a serious threat to her life if she keeps moving from one State to another for appearing before various courts. However, Their Lordships were not only even slightly satisfied by the arguments but also out-rightly rejected her application, refusing to grant any relief of whatsoever nature. This could be for the first time in the history of Indian judiciary that it has bowed down to the demands of the Jihaadi/Sharia elements and refused to hear the rightful secular and democratic prayers of a young unmarried lady and exposing her into grave dangers and risks from the internationally marauding Islamic forces. Judging from the whole outbursts and remarks of the Judges coupled with their body language, it would be exemplarily clear that the whole "concern" for the Judges was: "Nupur Sharma is a spokesperson of BJP".

The above quoted frightening questions were garnered out of millions of postings flooded in the social media ever since the outbursts of the Judges. Only very few of the same are taken at random and quoted above.

The conducts of the Apex Court Judges shows in clearer light that the Apex Court regards the majority citizens of India only as "second class citizens", not deserving any rights as guaranteed to them under the Constitution of India. Their unwarranted and atrocious outbursts without any rhyme or reasons have serious country-wide repercussions, particularly for the life, liberty and property of the majority citizens of the country, whose lives without the freedom of expression and without the right of self-defense have now become extremely dangerous and risky, a few of which are briefly discussed below:

At the outset, no sooner than the outburst of the Judges came to the public domain than it had become a cause for celebration for all the anti-nationals, anti-Hindus, foot-soldiers working at the behest of their foreign Masters who are rank enemies of infidels of India, international Jihadi elements clandestinely living in India, etc.

Owaisi, the UK qualified Barrister MP in democratic India who has been working round the clock for dividing India once again on religious lines, started addressing his Jihadi followers to take up street activism to free the killers of the Rajasthan tailor from the clutches of the "man-made laws". Similarly the Congress leader, Rahul Gandhi, thanked both the Judges and called up an emergency meeting with all the stake-holders of the erstwhile dynasty rulers, welcoming the utterances of the Apex Court Judges and finding faults with the present Prime Minister of the country and repeating his usual jib: "Chowkidaar Chor Hey".

Nobody professing Hinduism can any more freely move about in the country, leave alone the question of the much abused "freedom of expression", which can only be enjoyed by the minority Jihadi elements of the country against the majority citizens.

The Hindus will now be left with no other alternatives but to take up law into their own hands for saving themselves, their family members as well as their property in India from the world-wide Jihadi attacks.   There are over 57 Islamic countries in the world many of whom have already involved in the Nupur Sharma episode who have now been emboldened in attacking the infidels of India in retribution for a truthful isolated remarks made by an Indian citizen purely out of provocation in a democratic debate.

Needless to mention here that the only citizens in India abiding the law of the land as well as the Judgments, orders and directions delivered by the courts of law are undoubtedly the Hindu citizens. And yet, a pal of gloom, a climate of fear, mutual suspicions amongst the citizens of different religions, etc. have now engulfed India. None of the Hindu citizens of the country would have any confidence upon the judiciary hence forth which would lead to total anarchy across the country.

In the USA the Judges of all courts of law, particularly the Supreme Court are nominated by the President and confirmed by the Senate (which in India is called "Parliament"). Diametrically opposed to this system prevailing in the USA and the other democratic countries in India the appointment of the Judges are done through a mechanism, called 'Collegiums System", which is popularly known as Judges appointing Judges. The successive Nehru Dynasty governments in India since independence took advantages of this system and through corruption and nepotism selected Judges on the choice of the Dynasty Members. On a careful analysis one can discern that almost 80% of the present day Judges at the Apex Court are products of the erstwhile Dynasty Governments. This was the reason that for the first time in the judicial history of India after the first-time-ever nationalistic government assumed power, a gang of four senior Supreme Court Judges walked out of their plush government-allotted bungalows and staged a street "Dharna" to the great chagrin of street dwellers, hawkers, mendicants, etc. which was purely on suspicion upon the newly elected nationalistic government. Similarly, in the recent past a retired Judge of the Supreme Court, Justice Ganguli, a product of the Dynasty Government, who was accused of molestation by several young women, categorically justified the anti-national, anti-Hindu agitation, plannings of waging war against the Government, etc. as was organized by the students of JNU. [Watch a video clip on You Tube by the link words: "Angry Anupam Kher rips apart Rahul Gandhi, Kanhaiya Kumar at the ….."].

The concept of separation of power is part and parcel of democracy. This separation of powers refers to a system of sharing of powers into Branches, each with separate, independent powers and responsibilities in such a way that the powers of one Branch are not in conflict with those of the other Branches.

As far as the democratic countries such as India, USA, UK, etc. are concerned there exists three branches, which are Legislative, Executive and Judiciary. This separation of power can effectively function only when the Judiciary behaves within the powers and responsibilities assigned to them. Since independence the country had been governed by a single family, viz. Nehru Dynasty for about seven decades. During this period, the Dynasty Government had made numerous unethical practices by way of appointing Judges through corruption and nepotism which has now become totally detrimental to the present nationalistic democratic government elected with absolute majority.

Coming back to the aforesaid nation-wide mass-scale reaction and outcries from the social media, it is worthwhile to mention here that several social media postings were agog over the claim that the two Judges involved in the Nupur Sharma episode are the products of the Nehru Dynasty governments. These postings further claimed that Justice J.B. Pardiwala was elevated to the post of SC Judge on the "telephonic instructions" from the former Italian Head of the erstwhile UPA government made to the concerned authorities by virtue of his father, Mr. B.C. Pardiwala, who was a Congress stalwart, having served her as her Friday-Man. Certain postings further claimed that Justice Pardiwala was a Junior Judge of a lesser-known High Court in the country and he was elevated to the SC post by way of superseding many meritorious senior Judges and Chief Justices of several High Courts just because of his father's political connection with the Italian woman.

It is not out of place to state here that ever since the first ever nationalistic government came to power with absolute majority the circumstances were so surcharged for the sitting Judges who were appointed by the successive Nehru Dynasty governments purely on sycophancy that it was something like the stiring up of a hornet's nest. Apprehending unfavorable circumstances for them with the change of government, they started exercising their power far beyond the scope and limit assigned to them without any care of the government. They have not only encroached upon/usurped the jurisdiction of the present government but also started creating stumbling blocks in smoothly governing the country. Law and order problems emanating from the illogical Judgments and outbursts of these Judges are the major concern for the present government.

Unlike the Western democratic countries India cannot afford to treat the divisions as "water-tight compartment" due to various unique social circumstances peculiar to India. There are increasing instances of serious affronts made by the judiciary against the present democratically elected government, enjoying absolute majority, by way of frequent interference in the government function, delivering illogical and impracticable judgments, frequent confrontation with the government authorities, etc. are the present state of affairs with the Indian judiciary.

As mentioned above, the aforesaid conduct of the Apex Court Judges tantamount to serious assault upon the present government. Hence for maintaining law and order situations across the country, which is in the exclusive domain of the Central government, the foreseeable days are going to be extremely dangerous and risky in tackling those problems involving attack against the Hindus by the Jihaadi elements, emboldened by the unwarranted outbursts. The present government came to power with absolute majority on the mandate of the patriotic citizens. If their confidence in the judiciary is shattered by these types of

Judges, it would lead to serious repercussions for the government to function.

Hence when a government is elected to power with absolute majority, such government should have the prerogative in hiring and firing the Judges. The system of impeachment of the Judges in the USA is very effective which is not practicable in India on account of various negative forces at play. Moreover, in the USA there are time-tested stringent measures and Codes of Ethics to discipline and control the judiciary by the government, which are totally absent in the Indian democracy.

In many of the democratic countries the judges do not have immunity from law suit and other legal proceedings and in constitutional democracies judicial misconduct or bad personal behavior is not protected. It is therefore high time for Indian government to sack the aforesaid Judges without looking into the consequences of the same but for saving the country from conflagration.

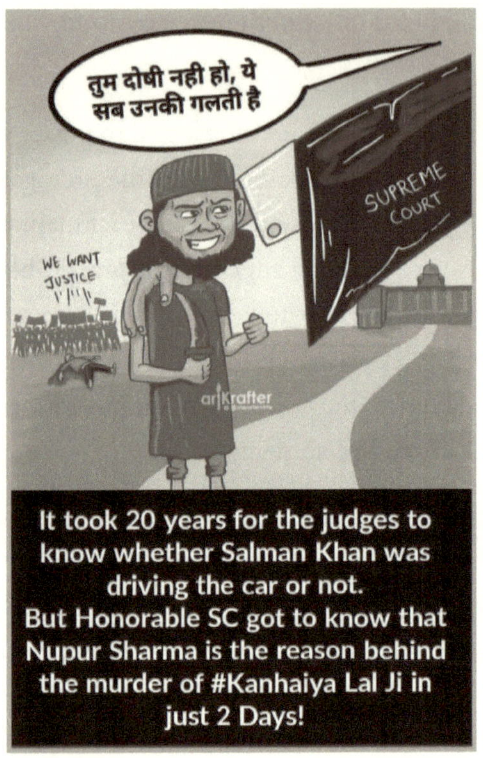

Cartoon courtesy: Social media, WhatsApp forward

Allowing these Judges in occupying their positions in their egoistic belief that they enjoy immunity from removal would be a serious threat to Indian democracy which will put the country into increased instances of Jihadi attacks and violence upon the majority citizens, total loss of confidence in the decisions of the courts, etc., leading to potential civil war.

Hence it is for the lager interest of saving India from disintegration and settling anarchy that these two Judges should be sacked forthwith, which will have full support from the entire right thinking electorates of India.

UNHCHR: THE UNWARRANTED ASSAULT ON INDIA'S SOVEREIGNTY AND INTEGRITY BY THE UN BODY

---

*T*he recent attempts on the part of the United Nations High Commissioner for Human Rights (UNHCHR), Michelle Bachelet, to interfere in a domestic legislation enacted by the Indian Parliament, viz. the Citizens Amendment Act (CAA), should be a serious concern for all peace-loving independent nations around the world, particularly for the democratic member-states of the UNO, as such a brazen interference is fraught with far reaching consequences for the UN Body itself to survive as an impartial, independent umbrella organization.

This unprecedented move on the part of the UNHCHR, as widely reported in the Indian media, for the first time in the legislative history of India, should be condemned by the entire citizens of India.

The UNHCHR has also unabashedly sought to interfere with the independent judiciary of India by seeking to file an intervention application in the Hon'ble Supreme Court over the CAA at the instance of George Soros' Open Society Foundation and his highly-paid foot-soldiers living in India, thereby throwing to the winds the UN charter signed by India which categorically mandates that the UNO and its other Bodies shall not interfere in the internal affairs of member-countries. This conduct being an outlandish incident in the entire history of UNO and India, the Government of India should take out urgent necessary steps to withdraw its membership from the UNO and demand and recover reparation from the concerned officials of UNHCHR in their individual capacities for this high-handed interference, causing embarrassment for India in the eyes of the other member-countries.

A Major investigation by the Indian government along with corrective steps is urgently called for with a view to unravel the anti-India forces living in India like parasites behind such a despicable high-handedness on the part of the UN body in meddling with the internal affairs of the country.

At the outset, it must be unequivocally understood by all the right-thinking people around the world that the CAA is as per the consistent aims and objectives of the founding fathers of India, including Mahatma Gandhi, who is regarded as the father of India, and Dr. B.R. Ambedkar, as the father of Indian Constitution and it is based on the bedrock of human rights. This legislation was strictly in consonance with the age-old tradition of India followed from time immemorial in offering succor to the persecuted human beings around the world.

Thus, in 1893 Swami Vivekananda, one of the greatest philosophers and Saints of Hinduism, when addressing the august gathering of the World Parliament of Religions at Chicago declared:

"I am proud to belong to a nation which has sheltered the persecuted and the refugees of all nations of the earth; I am proud to tell you that we have gathered in our bosom the purest remnant of the Israelites, who came to Southern India and took refuge with us in the very year in which their holy temple was shattered to pieces by Roman tyranny; I am proud to belong to the religion which has sheltered and is still fostering the remnant of the grand Zoroastrian nation….".

Similar to what Vivekananda had echoed more than a century ago to the world at large, in the recent past, the former President of India, Late Dr. A.P.J. Abdul Kalam, spoke at an international event organized by a UN Body regarding India's age-old and consistent philosophy of treating every human being inhabiting the earth as one's own kith and kin, in support of which he quoted India's great Saint-Poet, who lived 3000 years back, viz. Kanniyan Poongundranar, in the following words:

"Where there is righteousness in the heart,

There is beauty in the character;

When there is beauty in the character,

There is harmony in the home;

When there is harmony in the home,

There is order in the nation;

When there is order in the nation,

There is peace in the world".

[The above speech delivered by Late Dr. Kalam at the European Parliament on the occasion of its Golden Jubilee can be watched on YouTube by the link words: "APJ Abdul Kalm inspiring speech on India at European Parliament"].

India's ancient culture and highest moral values have strengthened Indian democracy and secularism which are unparallel in the history of human civilization. It is precisely this reason that when His Holiness the Dalai Lama spoke at the United States Institute for Peace on the 13th June 2016, he called upon the world communities to emulate India in her contributions towards peaceful co-existence which is in consonance with her age-old practice and upholding the highest traditions of Unity in Diversity.

It is, therefore, the legitimate inheritance of these ancient traditions and human values of India that CAA was enacted by the Indian Parliament with a view to fulfill the aspirations of the founding fathers of India and to achieve the objectives of helping the persecuted human being of Indian origin from the neighboring Islamic countries. These countries were parts of India prior to the country attaining independence in 1947, which was divided on the demands of the then Muslim citizens so as to create separate theological country exclusively for governing them under Quran and Sharia laws, so as to maintain their separate Islamic identity from the rest of Indian citizens, whom the Muslims regard as "infidels". These Islamic characteristics are diametrically opposed to the very foundation of India being a democratic and secular country.

The CAA lists the "persecuted persons" as belonging to all religions, except Islam. This is for the elementary logic and common sense that these Islamic countries, which were part of India earlier, are governed by Sharia, originated in the medieval era in the frightening desert land of Arabia, without even an iota of any democratic principles, secularism, etc., which have per force deprived of their non-Muslim citizens of any dignity or equality given to a Muslim Citizens of those countries.

It must be reiterated here in this context that out of all the religions listed in the CAA, Islam is the only religion which is diametrically opposed to the very concept of democracy, secularism and universal brotherhood. It is in this regard what Dr. B.R. Ambedkar said about Islam is noteworthy, the relevant portion of which is taken from his book *"Pakistan or the Partition of India"* and is reproduced below:

QUOTE:

Islam is a close Corporation and the distinction that it makes between Muslims and non-Muslims is a very real, very positive and very alienating distinction. The brotherhood of Islam is not the universal brotherhood of man. It is the brotherhood of Muslims and for the Muslims only. There is a fraternity but its benefit is confined only to those within this Corporation. For those who are outside this Corporation there is nothing but contempt and enmity.

> *The second defect of Islam is that it is a system of social self-government and is incompatible with local self-government because the allegiance of a Muslim does not rest on his domicile in the country, which is his, but truly upon the faith to which he belongs. "Whichever country is well with me that is my country" is unthinkable in a democracy. "Wherever there is rule of Islam there is my own country". In other words, Islam can never allow a true Muslim to adopt India as his own motherland. Likewise a Muslim can never regard Hindu or any non-Muslim citizen as his kith and kin or fellow citizen".*

UNQUOTE:

Hence the question of treating Muslim citizens from these Islamic countries as "persecuted" and including them in the CAA list would be a sheer madness apart from the fact that those dedicated Islamic countries would accuse India at international forums for enticing away their Muslim citizens who are the believers (Momin) into the country inhabited by infidels (Kaffir) with political systems totally opposed to Quran.

It would also be shameful and religiously improper to the believers of those Islamic countries to revert to the earlier positions of their forefathers who had lived with the infidels in India until partition which is being governed by man-made laws, instead of the alleged God-given laws, as prevailing in the Islamic countries.

It must also be born in mind that while there are over fifty Islamic countries in the world, who are Members of the UNO, in the unlikely event any Muslim citizens of these neighboring

Islamic countries are subjected to "persecution", they can easily seek asylum in any such countries which would also help them in getting opportunities to continue to embrace their chosen religion to the fullest extent possible while India is a country inhabited by 80% of, what the Quran describes as "infidels".

In this context, it is noteworthy to mention here that the entire citizens of India, including the patriotic Muslim citizens, welcome this legislation, except those citizens who have been serving as foot-soldiers of overseas Islamic Networks spread across the Western and European countries as well as those Muslims who had illegally crossed over to India through the porous borders in the past with the active help and support of the erstwhile successive Congress Governments. In fact Congress government is well known for indulging in undemocratic practices of "appeasement of minority Muslims" for "vote bank politics" at the cost of the true democratic principle, integrity, safety and security of India as a whole, so as to continue to cling to power.

Keeping in mind these avowed objectives of Congress Party to continue to remain in power for ever, all the consecutive Presidents of the party, who are members of Nehru Dynasty since independence, particularly the modern-day Presidents, like Sonia Gandhi, Rahul Gandhi, etc. keep publicly affirming that the "Congress is an Islamic Political Party".

It is pertinent to state here that just prior to the assumption of power in the year 2014 by the Bharatiya Janata Party-led National Democratic Alliance (NDA) government under Prime Minister Narendra Modi, India was ruled for a decade by a coalition entity, known as "United Progressive Alliance" (UPA) which was a hotchpotch of political affiliations comprised of regional parties, splinter parties who were once part of national parties, etc. many of which were professing Leftist ideologies and Islamic radicalism, as for example All India Majlis-e-Ittehadul Muslimeen (AIMIM), Indian Union Muslim League (IUML), etc., which are dedicated communal political parties, who are opposed to the very ideas of democratic principles, secularism, etc., were coalition partners. Thus, as the UPA government contained dedicated communal political parties, the government was indeed unconstitutional as the Constitution of India categorically provides for the exclusion of all religious political parties in the formation of democratic and secular government.

The AIMIM was promoted by Asaduddin Owaisi, a hard-core Islamic fundamentalist. He harbors contempt towards Indian democratic institutions, judiciary, secularism, Parliamentary systems, its age-old human-values oriented customs and healthy traditions for the simple reasons that the fundamental tenets of Islam are against democracy, secularism, human-made law (instead of "God-given Sharia") and the judiciary formed by infidels. Owaisi often indulges in invoking Indian Constitutional provisions purely for furthering his Islamic expansionist agenda in the country. Every waking moment, Owaisi along with his fundamentalist brother rant against the Hindus and preach hatred, separatism and secession. Most strangely, although these Islamic fundamentalists do not believe in democracy and secularism, the majority Hindu citizens of India, whom these characters call as "intolerant", allow them to stand for democratic elections and win election after elections for furthering their Islamic causes.

Mr. Mohammed Arif Aajakia, a Pakistani-origin human rights activists and YouTuber, presently exiled in London once opined: "Owaisi is behaving like the Mogul Invader of India and not as a citizen of the country". [A video-clip in this regard is available on YouTube].

From time to time Owaisi calls upon all the Muslim citizens of India to unite themselves on the basis of Islamic brotherhood and cast their votes in the democratic elections of India only to a Muslim candidate, thereby attempting to polarize Indian electorates. The Indian Apex Court had time and again warned that "garnering votes on the basis of appeal of religious sentiments is a corrupt practice and such political parties are liable to be derecognized by the Election Commission of India".

However, Owaisi has hardly any respect towards the judgment pronounced upon "man-made laws" by the Indian judiciary comprised of "infidels" and he continues to provoke Muslim citizens to vote only for Muslim candidates with a view to espouse his pet dream of dividing India once again, following the footprints of his predecessor Mohammed Ali Jinnah, who created the theological state of Pakistan.

It should be realized that Owaisis's Islamic political party AIMIM was a coalition partner in the erstwhile UPA government. During the ten-year UPA regime, Islamic terrorism and bombings had grown in leaps and bounds, assuming a diabolical proportion as sporadic Jihadi bombings struck across the length and breadth of the country killing innocent civilians and destroying properties on mass-scale. It should be drilled into the minds of all those who shed crocodile tears on the imaginary concept of *"human-rights violations against Muslims in India*" that none of the UN Bodies has ever raised even an eye brow at these dastardly killings and maiming of innocent Indian citizens or expressed even a word of contempt on the increasing instances of periodic terror strikes across the country.

It must be born in mind that during the decade-long regime of UPA, foreign-funded resident citizens and NGOs were flourishing in India with the unchecked money pouring into their Bank accounts from enemies of Hinduism and anti-India forces living in various nooks and corners of the world to defeat what they perceived as a threat from: "Hindu Right Wing force aiming to capture political power in India". All these individuals and NGOs were given free hand to carry on their nefarious activities harmful to India's internal safety and securities by the erstwhile UPA government by scuttling the provisions of the Foreign Contributions Regulation Act (FCRA).

It is not out of place to state here that upon the first-ever nationalist government assuming power in 2014 after nearly 70 years of rule of India by a single family called "Nehru Dynasty" since attaining independence in 1947, over 5,000 such NGOs working overtly and covertly against India's interest as foot-soldiers of foreign agencies were restrained from receiving foreign funds, who have therefore turned against the present government by way of indulging in world-wide false propaganda and provocation, thereby fomenting troubles for the country in maintaining welfare for all the citizens and ensuring peaceful coexistence amongst the citizens of all religions and creeds through the democratic principles, resulting into eruption of periodic street violence and arson, Jihadi terror strikes, etc. causing irreparable damages to the soul of the country.

There are individuals and organizations living in India and carrying on anti-national and subversive activities, threatening the very existence of India as a sovereign independent democratic nation, who wield enormous clout with the international agencies and the UN Bodies, including the UNHCHR, and as such they have the capacity to get the interference of these foreign Agencies into India's internal affairs. Some of these anti-national forces living in India like parasites are briefly described below:

1. ANTONIA EDVIGE ALBINA MAINO, ALIAS SONIA GANDHI:

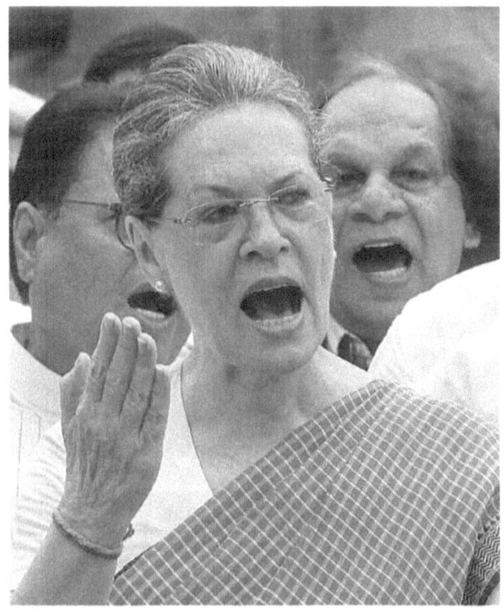

Sonia Gandhi with her most-trusted Political Advisor,
Ahmed Muhammad Patel and other Congress stalwarts.
(Photo credit: PTI)

Sonia Gandhi and her family members are born-again Christians, controlled by Vatican. Although her original name, as christened by the Church in Italy, was Antonia Edvige Albina Maino, she assumed the name as "Sonia Gandhi" with a view to fool the gullible Hindus of India and illiterate masses and garner votes from them in the democratic elections in which she had excelled and had ruled the nation for a decade. She and her family members harbor utter contempt towards the Hindus of India.

Pranab Kumar Mukherjee, the former President of India, in his book "The Coalition Years" states that: "Sonia Gandhi is anti-Hindu and the UPA government under her leadership has done enormous activities harmful to the interest of the majority Hindus of India".

Although, the de-facto head of the erstwhile UPA government, this Italian woman has had no experience or proper education in running such a vast country, housing ancient civilization, called "Sanathan Dharma" with complex social and political characteristics as India. It was E.M. Forster who once rightly observed that "India is an unexplainable muddle". The largest democratic country in the world, called Bharat or India, should have a dynamic person who is capable of tackling such "muddle".

At the fag end of the decade long UPA regime, the majority Indian citizens were already fed up with the anti-Hindu policies and programs discreetly thrust upon them by the UPA government. Then came the general election in 2014, which was billed as the world's largest exercise in democracy. Out of the staggering number of 834 million eligible voters, an adequate number of electorates voted in favor of the national political party, called Bharateeya Janata Party (BJP), thereby constituting it as the majority political party, dedicated to democratic principles, competent to form the government by itself (instead of a stop-gap arrangement of forming a coalition government as in the case of the former UPA government). Thus, its Prime Ministerial candidate, Narendra Damodadas Modi, was elected on a historic mandate from the voters, as the right man who has been endowed with unsurpassed skills of cutting the Gordian knots that is India.

Thus, since losing political power in the 2014 general elections, Sonia and her family members of the Nehru Dynasty are leaving no stone unturned in getting back to the power by hook or by crook. The CAA was a handy tool in their hands for provocations of the Muslim citizens of India in an attempt to create internal unrest or civil war with a view to overturn the Modi government and come back to power.

It might be mentioned here that it was during the Nehru Dynasty period that Citizens Act, 1955 was enacted by the Congress Parliament. Thereafter the same Congress government initiated the exercise called National Registrar of Citizens (NRC). Again it was the same Congress Government who framed rules of what is called: "Citizenships (Registration of Citizens & Issue of National Identity Cards) Rules, 2003". Under the said rules framed by the Congress government, for the first time a new concept was introduced, viz. National Population Register (NPR). To put it simply the CAA, NPR, NRC, etc., which are inextricably intermingled with each other, were introduced by the erstwhile Congress governments, excepting the fact that in the Amendment Act, called CAA, introduced by the present BJP government, Islam was excluded in the "List of Religions" on sound and incontrovertible logical reasoning, as partly mentioned above.

What the present NDA government under Prime Minister Modi did was to continue the same policies as framed by the erstwhile successive Nehru Dynasty Governments. In other words, what the NDA government did was selling the same old wine in new bottle. It was therefore the highest levels of hypocrisy on the parts of the Congress stalwarts that when the CAA was passed by the present Parliament, Sonia and her family members and coteries, kept howling at the top of their voice: "India's Muslims are going to be Stateless people soon" without there being even an iota of truth which had resulted into street violence by a section of the gullible Muslim population, many of whom were illegal immigrants from neighboring Islamic countries, entered into India through the patronage of the successive Congress governments in power.

The notorious 101-days Shaheen Bagh protest against CAA on the streets of capital city of New Delhi which witnessed unprecedented violence, arson and bloodsheds, resulted solely out of provocation by the Indian citizens with vested interest like Sonia, Harsh Mander, etc. without there being any cause or logic, should remain as a reminder in the minds of those who are at the helm of affairs of India's internal security.

During the whole regime of Nehru Dynasty from 1947, which culminated into the coalition government called UPA coming to power in 2004, the biggest problems faced by India as a whole was illegal infiltration of Muslims from Bangladesh and Myanmar. These infiltrators were clandestinely allowed safe passage into India by the Ministers of the erstwhile successive Congress Government and the UPA government and helped them settle down in many parts of the country. [Numerous video-clips of these clandestine *modus operandi* in allowing the illegal immigrants into India by the vote-hungry Congress leaders can be watched on YouTube. The link words for one such video is: "Watch a special show on how illegal migrants cross over to India from Bangladesh"].

As the Congress Party kept affirming from time to time that the "Congress is a Muslim Party", all those Muslims infiltrated into India and settled in many parts of the country, started casting their votes en mass to the Congress. Accordingly, realizing the strength of the vote bank politics involving the infiltrated Muslim, the UPA government shelved the idea of implementing the NRC, NPR, etc. This reality is conspicuous in the State of Assam, bordering Bangladesh. In 2006 Sonia Gandhi addressed the illegal Bangladeshi immigrants and assured them that they will never be deported. The Wiki-leaks has provided numerous documentary and video graphic evidences to show how Sonia and her son Rahul Gandhi took various clandestine steps to protect the illegal immigrants. A video clip is available on YouTube in this regard by the link words: "Did Sonia Gandhi try to prevent deportation of illegal Bangladeshi immigrants?|India First" (India Today TV).

As Sonia, who had been regarded as "Raj Mata" by the slave-minded gullible Hindus, installed Dr. Manmohan Singh on the "throne of the P.M. of India" as her puppet and as she remotely controlled him from behind the curtain it was easy for her to clandestinely work against the interest of India, away from the public glare, by touring through all the fundamentalist Western and European Christian countries and hold secret parleys with the Heads of State of those countries, in her private plane under the pretext of seeking medical treatments for her mysterious ailments. The grapevine Indian media groping in the dark regarding her disappearances from the country tersely reported "Sonia Gandhi left for an undisclosed country for treatments of her undisclosed ailments".

On one such occasion of her "disappearance" from the country the BBC News dated 28/02/2012 briefly reported as follows:

QUOTE:

India's governing Congress party leader Sonia Gandhi has travelled abroad for a "routine check-up". She holds no official post but she considers herself as the de facto Head of the government. Her party has consistently refused to comment on the nature of the illness or where she went. The powerful Nehru-Gandhi Dynasty has ruled India for most of the time since the country gained independence from British Colonial rule in 1947".

UNQUOTE:

Sonia Gandhi also regularly visited China along with her son Rahul since assuming power in 2002 as the *de facto* Head of the Indian Government.

In October 2007 she visited China along with her son Rahul, daughter Priynaka, son-in-law Robert Vadra and their children and Priyanka's in-laws and other relatives of Vadra for witnessing Olympic Games on the patronage of the Chinese government. Since then Sonia has been maintaining a closely guarded liaison with the Chinese leaders.

Keeping with her clandestine anti-India and anti-Hindu operations ever since she was elected to power by the slave-minded Hindus, in 2008 when she was the epicenter of political power in the country, which was accentuated by her position as the fourth richest politician in the world, she along with her son Rahul and party stalwarts secretly travelled to China for months-long sojourn. While in China a secret Memorandum of Understanding (MOU) was signed at the Great Hall of People by Sonia's son Rahul on behalf of the Indian government and the Chinese Vice President Xi Jinping on behalf of the Chinese government for supply of high-level classified information on India and for opportunities to consult each other as and when found necessary.

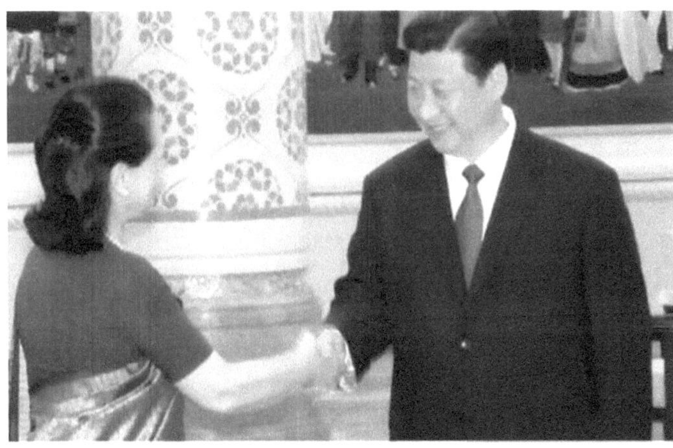

The Italian "Raj Mata" of the slave-minded Hindus and the cunning fox of China at an undisclosed venue near Peking in 2008
[Photo courtesy: Google Images]

The entire secret operations and various other links and documentary evidences conclusively reveal that the Chinese government was slowly and steadily building an elaborate internal spy networks in India exclusively with the Congress party, particularly with the Nehru-Gandhi family which goes beyond the scope of any Indian governments.

It was around this period, as revealed from the FCRA sources, that Rajiv Gandhi Foundation, a private charitable trust founded by Sonia Gandhi received a whopping sum of Rs.1.35 crores from the Chinese Embassy at New Delhi.

In the capacity of the former *de facto* Head of the Indian government and being a staunch adherent of Jesus Christ, controlled by Vatican, it is but natural that Sonia and her family members can easily wield enormous influence and lobby in the entire Christian world and in the Christian-dominated workforce of the UN Bodies. Presently the UNHCHR is headed by a Catholic woman, Michelle Bachelet. It is, therefore, simple logic that Sonia who holds dual citizenships of both Italy and India and is mentally adhered to Vatican, can easily get together and by using their sentimental card of "adherents of Jesus" can directly influence the mind of the UN Body which can easily find India as a "soft target" and pass strictures against the present nationalist government of India, in an attempt to topple the government and help Sonia come back to power.

2. LAWYER'S COLLECTIVE:

The "Lawyers Collective" was established in 1981 as an NGO by a woman, called Indira Jaising, professing hard-line leftist ideologies, who became its Trustee along with one Anand Grover, formerly a UK citizen.

Jaising was born into a Hindu family in the pre-independent Pakistan in 1940 and when India attained independence in 1947 she along with her parents and siblings fled to India on account of persecution by the then Muslim citizens of the newly created Islamic country. She and her family were given shelter by the accommodative Hindu population in the suburb of Mumbai, then known as Bombay. Although Jaising fled from her birth place in an area which had gone to the then newly created Pakistan upon partition, it is most strange, to say the least, that this woman's upbringing was to transform herself into a dreaded Leftist Ideologue. Her entire academic education was through schools and colleges run by Christian Missionaries controlled by the Vatican whose sole aim is converting Hindus into Christianity, by brainwashing the minds of the students and fill them with hatred and contempt towards Hinduism.

Thus, Jaising was a thoroughly brain-washed woman who rose to become a militant feminist Lawyer, professing leftist ideologies. There cannot be any other female amongst Indian citizens as this character, called Indira Jaising, who harbored utter contempt and hatred towards everything dear to Hinduism. Every word of hers published in the media and every public speech delivered by her contained hard-hitting and insulting attacks on the human values oriented healthy traditions and cultures of Hinduism, which she labels as "superstition", "medieval", "abhorrent", "outdated", etc. In short, Jaising spewed venom at the very mention of the word "Hinduism".

Jaising, on account of possessing the proven track records of being a hard-core anti-Hindu during the UPA regime was appointed by the Italian Head of Indian Government, viz. Albino Maino, alias, Sonia Gandhi, as the first ever female Additional Solicitor General of India. Sonia also recommended to the President of India to confer upon Jaising the civilian honor, called "Padma Shree".

It is pertinent to state here that conferring civilian titles has been a practice of the Indian government since independence as a symbolic gesture to recognize the contributions made by Indian citizens or citizens of foreign countries espousing any healthy causes of India towards fostering peace and harmony amongst various multi religious people of India and attaining achievements in various other fields beneficial to India as a whole. However, Jaising's "contribution" was only "Hindu bashings" and "loyal to Nehru-Gandhi Dynasty members" for which she was conferred upon the civilian honor: "Padma Shree" by the erstwhile UPA government.

Thus, in 2008 Indira Jaising became the first female Additional Solicitor General of India at the instance of Sonia Gandhi, the Italian head of the then UPA government. The post of Additional Solicitor General is a constitutional position and is regarded as highly sensitive with regard to the internal security of India, safeguarding its sovereignty, safety and integrity. However, instead of paying attention to her constitutional duties and responsibilities as the Additional Solicitor General of India, she simultaneously and clandestinely focused her whole attention on the duties and responsibilities of various foreign NGOs who are hostile to India.

Accordingly, Jaising through her personal entity "Lawyers Collective", kept receiving huge foreign funds from various foreign NGOs spread all over the Western and European countries such as the notorious George Soros's Open Society Foundation, USA, Foundation Open Society Institute, Switzerland, Lavi Strauus Foundation, USA, etc.

All the above foreign NGOs are concerned with "regime change", aimed at overthrowing the democratically elected government in India by way of surreptitiously exercising extra-territorial jurisdiction upon India with the tacit support and encouragement of the UNO for various subversive activities within the territories of India, which included admitting entry into India millions of Muslims from Bangladesh and Rohingya Muslims from Myanmar as refugees under their pet Utopian ideas of "open society".

During the erstwhile UPA period, a Jaipur based Lawyer, one Mr. Raj Kumar Sharma, filed a Public Interest Litigation (PIL) before the High Court of Delhi seeking investigation into the murky affairs of Lawyers Collective, headed by a person holding the constitutional post of Additional Solicitor General of India, viz. Indira Jaising.

Thus, the investigation conducted as per the directions issued by the Hon'ble High Court of Delhi resulted into the opening up of a whole can of worms. World-wide sources of foreign funds having been pumped into the Bank Account of the Lawyers Collective headed by Jaising by numerous Western and European NGOs hostile to India came to light. On a conservative estimate it was revealed that over Rs.200 crores annual foreign funds were received by the Jaising's NGO by way of flouting various regulations under the FCRA with the connivance of the former Italian Head of the Indian government, for carrying out various subversive activities against India and the majority citizens.

It must be born in mind that by virtue of Indira Jaising simultaneously holding the constitutional post of Additional Solicitor General of India as well as a private entity established by her in her individual capacity, viz. the Lawyers Collective, a false impression was created in the minds of foreign donors and NGOs as well as the UN Bodies who mistakenly believed that the "Lawyers Collective" was also an organization promoted by the Government of India!

Accordingly, on the baseless belief that Lawyers Collective was a government entity, the United Nations Development Fund for Women (UNIFEM) interacted with feminists in India on a regular basis. Thus, a gang of unmarried Western promiscuous women attired in sarees and projecting themselves as the "saviors of exploited women in India" descended on the streets of Delhi and worked along with the militant feminist and leftist ideologue, Jaising, and formulated various schemes to enact legislations in India meant for "saving exploited Hindu women". Thus, to cut a long story short, "The Protection of Women from Domestic Violence Act, 2005" was passed by the UPA Parliament at the instance of UNIFEM. The fund for the same was routed to the Bank Account of Lawyers Collective for which Jaising received over Indian Rs.50 crores. The speed with which the D.V. Act was passed by the UPA Parliament, headed by an uneducated and inexperienced Italian woman by way of scuttling all the procedures and debates to be essentially adopted in a Parliamentary Democracy, was indeed incredible.

The D.V. Act is the first enactment by the Indian Parliament fully sponsored and funded by an outside foreign Body, though the money was routed to India through a private Indian citizen, viz. Indira Jaising.

After the D.V. Act came into force in the year 2005, Jaising sent out to UNIFEM half-yearly Reports under confidential covers, named and styled as "Reports on the implementation of the D.V. Act by the Indian Judiciary" for which she was paid Rs.2 crores per Reports by the UNIFEM. In those reports Jaising picked up Judges who presided over various courts of law across the country and unabashedly accused them of bias and negligence in implementing the provisions of the D.V. Act in letter and spirit for the purpose of consumption by her Western Masters.

Thus, upon the grand success of the Italian-headed-UPA Government enacting numerous anti-Hindu legislations at the instance of Jaising on the foreign fund made available to her by UNIFEM, Jaising was appointed by a UN Body as the Member of the United Nations Committee on the Elimination of Discrimination against Women.

With the money pumped into the Bank Accounts of Jaising from her numerous donors spread across the Western and European countries, she frequently travelled through those parts of the world and kowtowed with the powers at the UN Bodies. Scores of Western women holding various positions at the UNIFEM and other UN Bodies, including the woman called Michelle Bahelet, presently holding the position of Commissioner of UNHCHR, regularly visited India and met with the Italian Catholic Head of UPA, Jaising and other militant feminists and they confabulated on the made up stories of the plight of "Indian Hindu women, exploited by their men".

On account of these international connections and secret rendezvous, Jaising has had ample opportunities to carry on close interactions and establish strong rapport with the officials of UN bodies, particularly the UNHCHR. It is, therefore, anybody's guess that she could easily influence the mind of this woman heading the UNHCHR, Michelle Bachelet, by getting their interference with the Indian legislation and finding fault with every legislation enacted by the nationalistic government.

3. ANAND GROVER:

Anand Grover is a former British citizen. He came to India in the seventies and with a view to get Indian citizenship he had a Marriage of Convenience with Indira Jaising, although in reality Jaising harbored contempt towards the institution of sacramental Hindu Vedic Marriage or any marriage at all.

It is unfortunate that Jaising's foreign originated leftist-ideologies-infused mind can absorb only violence, sense gratification and lustful life. She can never absorb the love, affection, devotion and dedication amongst the Hindu family members as enshrined in the Vedic Hindu Marriage institution from time immemorial on the ten-millennia-old principles of Sanathan Dharma.

In the D.V. Act, it is for the first time that a concept was introduced which is termed as "Live-in-Relationship" carried on by men and women without marriage. Such a practice has done greatest damages to Hindu society delivering a catastrophic blow to the sacramental Vedic institution of Hindu Marriage. Recently, the High Court of Kerala, which has the largest number of such relationships without marriage and the practice is spreading like wild-fire across the State, has observed: *"The younger generation thinks marriage is an evil to be avoided to enjoy sex without any obligations and that the consumer culture of use and throw has influenced the matrimonial relationships which is a dangerous trend".*

Thus, Jaising and Grover demonstrated to the world at large by the enactment of the D.V. Act as to how marriage can be discarded for a live-in-relationship. In other words, Indira Jaising and Anand Grover would go down in modern Indian history as the legally recognized first-ever live-in-relationship couple in India under the provisions of the D.V. Act.

Grover, like his live-in-partner Jaising, has been a rank Hindu-basher and he despised all the healthy traditions and social values of Hinduism. Upon his "marriage" with Jaising he took up various activisms to destroy every tenet of morality as enshrined in Hinduism.

Accordingly, Grover fought tooth and nail for decriminalizing homosexuality by reading down Section 377 of the Indian Penal Code. He was known in India as "Lawyer who fought the 377 law and won". He declared himself as the "Honorary Gay", as though he is ready and willing to impart training to Indian masses on homosexuality. In fact, from time immemorial, Hindu society has been treating homosexuality as a mental disorder which can be cured individually rather than treating such isolated cases of mental aberrations as universal norms of Indian society.

The decriminalization of Section 377 resulted into Indian masses viewing homosexuality for the first time as something like a legally recognized "sports" or approved social behavior and the unscrupulous, sex-starved people started experimenting in it by way of enticing small children (boys and girls) for their sense gratification which in India is now a growing social menace. Prior to the decriminalization of Section 377, there used to be a sense of fear in the minds of the masses and sexual assault upon children had never been a ubiquitous problem in India.

As mentioned above, Indira Jaising had already established an excellent rapport with all the members of the UN body, particularly the UNHCHR. Thus, as Anand Grover was projected to be her "husband", he was appointed on the recommendation of Jaising in a post specifically created for him at the UNO, named and styled as "Special Rapporteur of the High Commissioner for Human Rights on the Right of Everyone to the Enjoyment of the Highest Attainable Standard". This newly created position is more or less concerned about attaining "highest standards" of "bodily enjoyment" [probably including homosexuality as practiced and propagated by Grover, the "Honorary Gay of India"] of the Western promiscuous societies and not at all connected with India's ancient Vedic teachings of mental purity, control of mind, attainment of bliss through Yoga and Meditation, etc. thereby leading blissful life.

In the capacity of UN Special Rapporteur, Grover has had ample opportunities to personally interact and lobby with all the

UNO office bearers and influence their minds against India. It was indeed a joint operation of Indira Jaising and Anand Grover to lobby against India through the office of UNHCHR with regard to the enactment of CAA by the Indian Parliament.

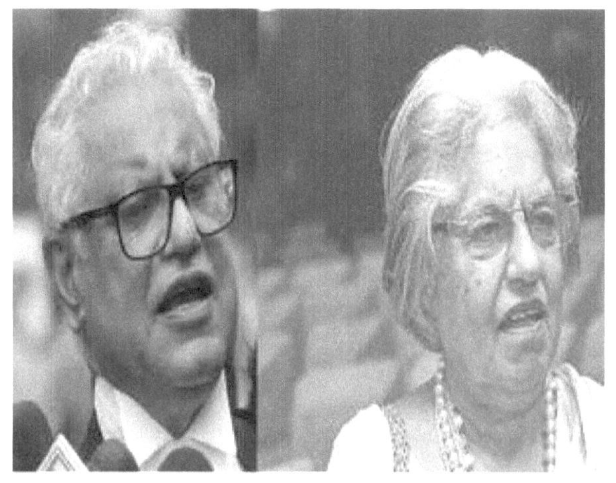

Indira Jaising and her "Chief Live in Partner" Anand Grover
(Photo Courtesy: The Economic Times)

4. HARSH MANDER

Harsh Mander had served as an IAS officer under the successive Nehru Dynasty government in various plum posts. He is a pathological hater of Hindus of the country. He wields enormous influence across the world and has been serving as the foot soldier of numerous foreign NGOs, including world-wide Islamic network.

As the adage goes: "Make hay while the sun shines", during the decade-long Italian-woman-headed UPA government, Mander laid the foundations of a massive world-wide network of

NGOs, outstanding amongst them is what is named and styled as: "Centre for Equity Studies" (CES).

Although CES holds out a secular image, it was a fraudulent façade to hoodwink the Law Enforcing Authorities and the gullible Hindus of the country. CES had been maintaining a clandestine deep-routed nexus between world-wide Western and European Churches who remitted huge funds into the Bank Account of CES for carrying out subversive activities for stopping any so-called "right wing nationalist government ever coming to power in India". It had also its terms of reference to convert Hindus into Christianity en masse by way of disbursements of huge foreign fund at the behest of the world-wide Christian Evangelical Organizations.

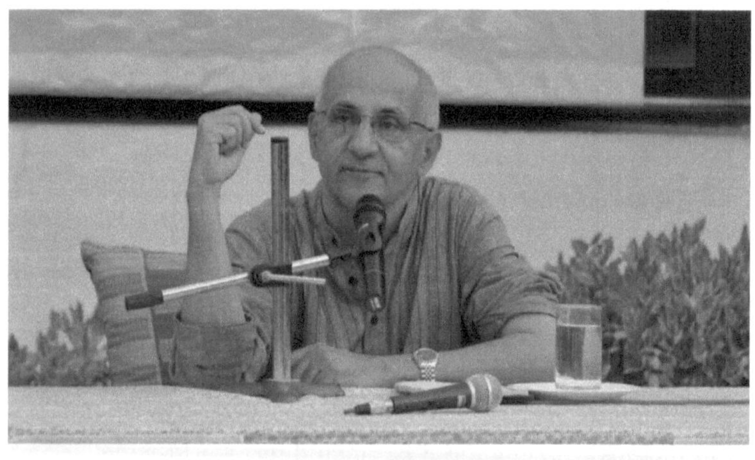

Harsh Mander. Photo Courtesy: OpIndia online portal

Harsh Mander had earned a notorious image during the period when the present Indian Prime Minister Narendra Modi was the Chief Minister of Gujarat. Mander had initiated at the instance of his foreign Masters numerous criminal proceedings against the Modi government as well as filing scores of Public Interest Litigation (PIL) at the instance of his Principals in various parts of the world and accordingly he was nicknamed as "PIL Propagandist".

Mander would often file Writ Petition before the Hon'ble Supreme Court at the drop of a hat on false and fabricated grounds and then flee to any of the Western or European countries for secret rendezvous with his donors, resulting into wastage of valuable time by the Hon'ble Supreme Court. Needless to mention here that as all those Petitions were filed at the instance of his foreign Masters without even an iota of truth or any causes of action based on the ground realities of India which cannot be conceived by any outside agencies, they were all dismissed one after the other by the courts of law in India, finding them as "bogus" and lacking any logic.

In addition to the world-wide Catholic Churches, Christian fundamentalist organizations based in Scandinavian countries, Norway, France, Denmark, etc. had remitted huge funds into the Bank Accounts of various NGOs ran in India by Mander. Two of his major fund remitters are the US based Indian Muslims Relief & Charity Foundation and the UK-based Minority Rights Groups who pumped money from time to time into the Bank Accounts of CES and other NGOs established by Mander.

During the UPA period, Mander was appointed by Sonia as a governing committee member of National Advisory Council (NAC). At this period Mander took upon himself the task of drafting a Bill to be made into an Act of Indian Parliament later on, named and styled as *"The Prevention of Communal and Targeted Violence (Access to Justice and Reparation) Bill 2011"* at the behest of international Islamic network, aided and abetted by Sonia. The Bill contained various frightening provisions against Hindus just for being born as Hindus. Had the Bill been passed by the UPA Parliament, there would have been no peace and harmony between Hindus and Muslim citizens of India. Under the Bill, Hindus were given the status of only second class citizens almost as slaves of the Muslim citizens. Any Tom, Dick and Harry from the Muslim communities could easily get any Hindu trapped by false and fabricated charges of "communal violence" and get him/her arrested and putting him/her behind the bars for protracted period on flimsy and false grounds. While framing the said Bill, Mander had deliberately ensured that no rights of resistance was reserved in it in the event false and fabricated charges are made by a Muslim citizen against any Hindu citizen.

A few of these draconian provisions taken at random from the draft Bill are reproduced below:

QUOTE:

- *A Hindu against whom a Muslim minority makes any complaint shall be presumed in law to be guilty by the police and the court till the accused Hindu proves his innocence.*
- *The accused Hindu shall have to be immediately arrested and all the offences in the proposed Act shall be non-bailable.*
- *This law can be invoked only by the minority Muslim against the Hindus.*

- *The accused Hindu shall not be informed who has made the complaint against him/her.*
- *The minority Muslim is not required to give any evidence to support his complaint against the Hindus.*

UNQUOTE:

Needless to mention here when such a Bill become an Act of Parliament, there would have no other option for a citizen born as a Hindu but to take the law in his or her own hands, resulting into communally surcharged atmosphere creating mutual suspicion, animosity, hatred, fear, ill-will, anger, etc. amongst Hindus and Muslims, leading to potential civil war within India. [There are number of video-clips available on YouTube regarding Mander's round-the-clock activism in getting this Bill enacted by Sonia-led UPA Parliament].

Though Mander has declared himself to be a Hindu during his IAS days with the UPA government, he has dedicated his life to the destructions of Hinduism. All his activisms are at the instance of his foreign masters hostile to Hindus and India for this purpose.

It must be recalled here that during the 26/11 Mumbai Terror Attacks, Mander had played a crucial role by trying in vain for freeing the lone surviving terrorist from the clutches of the Indian Law Enforcing Authorities. The terror strikes, sponsored by Pakistan, had witnessed brutal killings of over 300 innocent citizens and maiming over 500 people, including foreign nationalities, many of whom were made to lead bed-ridden or wheel-chair bound lives until their last breaths. The Attacks had also witnessed large scale destruction of properties and businesses of Mumbai. The competent Mumbai police successfully killed all the terrorists, except a staunch Muslim, called Mohammed Ajmal Kasab. Kasab was arrested and put behind bars. The Hon'ble Supreme court awarded him capital punishment.

At this juncture Mander was in Italy holding secret rendezvous with the Vatican authorities in connection with the job of conversion of Hindus into Christianity entrusted to him on huge Italian funds. When the news of the Supreme Court awarding capital punishment to Kasab reached Mander, he flew down to Mumbai, met Kasab at the High Security Jail and soon he prepared a Mercy Petition to be submitted to the President of India through his Italian Master, Antonia Edvige Albina Maino, alias Sonia, who was reported to have had a motherly affection towards "the young charming Kasab with physique similar to her own darling son".

In the mercy petition prepared by Mander he managed to get over 200 signatories, many of whom were members of the NAC constituted by Sonia. The speed with which Mander arranged to canvass and obtain signatures to the petition was indeed unprecedented in the modern history of India.

[A list of the signatories to the Petition along with the picture of the terrorist, Ajmal Kasab, is at Appendix-5].

It must be born in mind that at the time of partition of India there were 23% of Hindu population in Pakistan. They did not move towards Indian side as they had reposed their full faith and trust upon their Muslim brethrens. However, their number kept on drastically reducing and presently reached to a single digit of 3%. All those "disappeared" Hindus, which included

Sindhis, Sikhs, etc. were subjected to draconian blasphemy laws and eliminated them by cold-blooded murders and by forcible conversion into Islam. [Further details in this regard can be had by watching a video-clip on YouTube by the link words: "India responds to Imran Khan's speech and shames Pak at the UN – Vidisha Maitra, First Secretary, MEA"].

Even the reduced 3% minority Hindus are put to greatest cruelties and persecution for not converting themselves into Islam. These Hindu minorities are given the status of only animals without any dignity, liberty or rights by the Pakistani citizens with the full support of the government. There is no other country as Pakistan where the human rights of these miserable human beings are trampled upon by the government just because they are non-Muslims.

[There are hundreds of video-clips available on YouTube regarding these frightening and draconian states of affairs in Pakistan. However, the readers are urged to watch a video-clip by the link words: "Pakistan is Hell for Hindus: Arif Aajakia, Ex-Mayor, Karachi]".

Conversely, however, at the time of partition there were only 11% of Muslims in India whose percentage has now risen to a staggering unofficial figure of 35%. From these statics one can easily understand the high standard of life of Muslims in India and the miserable plight and grinding poverty of Hindus in Pakistan, thereby the falsehood of Mander would emerge to the surface.

The very aims and objectives of the establishment of UNHCHR are to avert such human right violations in all member-countries of the UNO and take appropriate steps to stop such inhuman treatments meted out to the minorities on the basis of religion. These fundamental duties of UNHCHR were taken by India upon itself and instead of appreciating and rewarding India by this UN Body they are encouraging the perpetuation of such incredible human-right violations and rewarding the perpetrating countries and their foot-soldiers living in India and working for them. This is a very serious issue. It is high time that India withdraw its membership with UNO and in all other UN Bodies with immediate effect before it is too late when the circumstances would become beyond the control of India and the people of India.

It is anybody's knowledge that there are fifty odd Muslim-majority countries in the world which are governed under Quran and Sharia Law. However, in none of these countries can one find any non-Muslims holding any political or non-political posts. On the contrary, in India the percentage of the number of Muslim citizens holding positions with the government, both political and non-political, as well as in the judiciary, Defense, education, police, etc. are disproportionally much higher than the holdings by the majority Hindu citizens. Though the adherents of Islam totally oppose the very idea of democracy and secularism, one can find in India Hindu citizens voting in favor of the Muslim candidates in democratic elections and making them Chief Ministers, Cabinet Ministers, Judges, Chief Justices, President of India, etc.

Similarly, the entire Muslim citizens of India are tempted to go for annual Haj as the Indian government has subsidized their travel expenses by government-owned airline company and had also built ultra-modern Haj Houses in each and every state in India for the comfort of the Muslim citizens intending to go for Haj at huge costs and expenses realized from the taxes paid by the majority citizens and from the income generated from the Hindu Temples which are controlled by the government. On the contrary no such facilities are offered to the Hindus for undertaking any pilgrimage.

During the erstwhile UPA period 75% of the political and non-political positions were held by Muslim citizens. Muslims in India enjoy enormous amount of religious freedoms as for example India has the largest concentration of Mosques and Madrassas compared even with the Muslim countries whereas there cannot be even a single temple or any worshiping place provided to Hindus or to any other non-Muslims in any of the Muslim-majority countries. In Pakistan, even if any Hindu temple is allowed to be constructed, it would be demolished to smithereens by the Muslim citizens of that country with the tacit support and encouragement of the Pakistan law enforcing authorities.

When the Economist, Dr. Manmohan Singh, was installed on the throne of PM of India by Sonia as her Puppet during the UPA regime, he had categorically asserted at all public speeches that "As per our government policies the Muslim citizens of India will get first priority in the allocation of national resources". [The Times of India, issue dated 09/12/2006].

When the present BJP government assumed power under the leadership of Narendra Modi in 2014 the first step he initiated was to enhance the existing allocation of 10% towards the welfare of Muslim Citizens to 18% on his motto of "Sab Ka Sat Sab Ka Vikas" with a view to ensure that the minority Muslim citizens of India should not lag behind when India makes great strides of progress and prosperity under his leadership.

Ever since the assumption of power by the Modi Government in 2014, the welfare measures for Muslims were multiplied as for example providing electricity to Muslim dominated villages, free cooking gas to them, free medical facilities under the world's largest insurance cover, called "Ayushman Bharat", providing subsidized housing and repealing the draconian medieval practice of *tripple talaque*, thereby attaining equal status and dignity to Muslim women. The Modi government has also taken effective steps in facilitating Muslim women to go for Hajj without any accompaniment of men. [A video-clip is available on YouTube of an interview given by the Cabinet Minister of India for Minority Affairs, Mr. Mukhtar Abbas Naqvi to *"Aappki Adalat"* hosted by Mr. Rajat Sharma in this regard].

As mentioned above, the biggest threats faced to the security and integrity of India is illegal infiltrations from the neighboring Islamic countries with the clandestine support and cooperation of Nehru Dynasty members and Congress leaders. [Hundreds of video-clips in this regard are available on YouTube].

As recently as 2010, during the UPA regime, over 25,000 Bangladeshi Muslims were allowed to settle down in make-shift shanties in a marshy land at a place called "Thubarahalli" near Bangalore. All of them were soon issued with ration card and Adhar cards with the help of the Congress leaders with the support of corrupt police and connivance of law enforcing authorities on the unequivocal promises extracted from the settlers that they would vote only for a Congress candidate during democratic elections.

The readers are urged to watch a video-clip on YouTube in this regard by the link words: "Illegal immigrants from Bangladesh staying in Bangalore".

The Al Jazeera Satellite Networks, owned by a Jihadi Muslim Organization from Qatar, through their local Agents at Bangalore, produced a hour-long video showing the lives of the Bangladeshi Muslims at the above-mentioned shanties illegally allowed to settle down by the Congress leaders, for telecasting world over under the title: "The Plight of Indian Muslims under the Right Wing Government".

In tune with the aforesaid telecast by the Al Jazeera Satellite Networks, during the period of Modi government, Harsh Mander wrote an article and published in the year 2018 in The New York Times of the USA, where Mander's major Muslim donors are located and 75% of the media in the USA is largely controlled by George Soros, who is Mander's God Father in the USA, on totally false and fabricated propaganda narratives. A paragraph taken from one of his essays is reproduced below:

QUOTE:

"Muslims are today's castaways, political orphans with no home, for virtually every political party. This despite India being home to a tenth of the world's Muslims, around 180 million people, making it the largest Muslim country after Indonesia and Pakistan. There has never been a harder time to be a Muslim in India, since the stormy months that followed India's Partition as in the present day".

UNQUOTE:

[The "present day" in the above quote was preceded by false narratives of "right-wing government's anti-Muslim policies" in his aforesaid article] Needless to mention here that Mander himself is fully aware that the above allegations are totally false based only on the figment of his imagination for hoodwinking his USA-based Muslim donors, numbering over a hundred NGOs and individual Muslims of Indian origin. Mander often projected himself as the "IAS Officer of the government of India" which carried credence and his every word was rewarded in dollars remitted into his personal accounts in India.

If there is an iota of truth in the above false allegations, the million dollar questions would be:

(1) "Why are the Muslim citizens of Bangladesh and other Islamic neighboring countries straining at the leash to enter into India?" Even a child can answer this question on simple logic that the Muslims find themselves as "in paradise" in India compared with the lives they lead in their own dedicated Islamic countries.

(2) Why does George Soros entrust Harash Mander with an amount of US$1 Billion through his world-wide network of Open Society Foundation to fight against the Indian government for easy immigration of Muslims from Bangladesh and Rohingya Muslims from Myanmar?

[Incidentally the allocation of US$1 Billion was for facilitating millions of Bangladeshi and Rohingya Muslims entering into India as well as for handling legal proceedings to be initiated and defended which are coming before the courts of law and the law enforcing authorities across the country pertaining to the cases of their illegal infiltration into India and deportation from the country].

It might be mentioned here that India is an over populated country inhabited by people almost equal to one fifth of human race of the earth. India's present day population is equivalent to China and is bursting at the seams with regard to living conditions of India's own thriving over population and at that time when Rohingya and Bangladeshi Muslims are facilitated to infiltrate into India upon the lunatic idea of George Soros of "Open Society" with the help of his hugely-paid foot-soldiers in India, it would be as the adage goes: "the last straw that breaks the laden camel's back" with regard to the survival of India as a civilized nation.

And yet Mander, strictly for showing his solidarity and gratitude towards his world-wide Muslim donors, writes such imaginary pulp fictions essays in foreign media. It can, therefore, be easily concluded that the foreign funds regularly received by Mander is so mountainous that the mind of this former IAS Officer got paralyzed, devoid of proper thinking or logical faculties. One would shudder to think what would be the tragedy in store for India had this devilish character continued in the government of India service had the slave-minded Hindus of India voted to power the UPA regime on the third tenure.

It is not out of place to mention here that the American Magazine "Time" in its May 20, 2019 international edition carried a cock and bull story featuring Modi on its cover with the title: "India's Divider in Chief". This story was written by one

Aatish Taseer, who is the love-child of Indian columnist, Tavleen Singh, born out of her rendezvous with the Pakistani politician Late Salmaan Taseer. Although the article carries the name of "Aatish Taseer" as its author, any Indian citizen of ordinary prudence could easily make out, based on several clues, that the article was the brainchild of Mander. By publishing such a pulp fiction, it is only the Time Magazine whose reputation, image, integrity and journalistic ethics were questioned by the reading public. [Readers are invited to watch a video-clip on YouTube in this regard by the link words: "An angry Indian rips into Time Magazine for calling PM Modi Divider-in-Chief"].

The situations presently faced by India as a whole from external threats by way of foreign funds flowing into the hands of the anti-nationals and anti-Hindus are extremely grave on account of the subversive activities overtly and covertly carried out by Indian citizens like Mander.

Being involved in activism in India on behalf of the world-wide Christian Evangelical and Islamic fundamentalist organizations, Mandar has wielded enormous influence across the Muslim and Christian world, which can in turn influence the mind of the UNHCHR in accusing India and get their interference with the legislation enacted by the Indian Parliament.

[A list of the world-wide donors of Harsh Mander is at Appendix-6. The list reflects only 10% of the total amount remitted into his personal account and about 5% of the names of the total world-wide donors. For details regarding the money he received through the decade-long UPA period, the readers are advised to access the website of Ministry of Home Affairs, Government of India].

5. HAMID ANSARI:

Hamid Ansari had served in various plum positions in the Hindu dominated India, particularly during the Nehru Dynasty period, such as Vice Chancellor of Government Universities, India's Ambassador to several countries, etc. which culminated into his appointment as the Vice President of India. Throughout his tenure spanning over a period of four decades, Ansari had remained himself totally aloof from the mainstream public discourses concerning Hinduism. Therefore any Indian citizens of ordinary prudence could easily discern an element of Islamic fundamentalism flowing through his vein. However, it was only on the penultimate day of demitting the office of the Vice President of India which coincided with the initial period of the first-time ever nationalistic government under Narendra Modi assuming power, his Islamic fundamentalism which he had been nurturing within his being over the years "exploded".

Thus, in an interview given by him to the Rajya Sabha TV, he alleged: "There is a feeling of unease and a sense of insecurity amongst Muslims in the country". This false allegation of Ansari, based only on his figment of imagination, is the reason that the very next day the Indian media widely reported that the then UN Commissioner for Human Rights, Mr. Zeid Raad Al Hussein, who is hailing from a Jihadi Islamic country, passing strictures against India and accusing and warning India for the repercussions for the alleged "atrocities against the Muslim citizens of India".

Indeed, it was the case of Islamic solidarity on the part of Ansari demonstrating the bond of world-wide Muslim brotherhoods. One can therefore easily understand the damage deliberately caused to India's image by the false allegations of Hamid Ansari, the former Vice President of India, after enjoying his life in Hindu-majority country to the fullest extent, which can only be called as a treacherous conduct on his part.

It is interesting to note that on the day of Ansari demitting his office, PM Modi gave a farewell speech in the Parliament when Modi, who knew the clandestine operation behind the curtain which was being carried on by Ansari, had "complimented" him by saying: "Sir, you are now free to pursue your own fundamental thought process".

What was this "fundamental thought process" came to the knowledge of Indians as a whole when Ansari joined as one of the office bearers of Popular Front of India (PFI), a South-India based radical Islamic organization, who have had track records of striking terrors across the State, including the chopping off the right hand of Prof. T.J. Joseph on the allegations of his "insult to Prophet Mohammad". [More detailed account of this terror strike is available in Joseph's autobiography in Malayalam, titled: "Attupokatha Ormakal"]. Subsequently, his wife has had to commit suicide due to extreme sufferings and unimaginable hardships she was made to face and the gradual disintegration of his whole family.

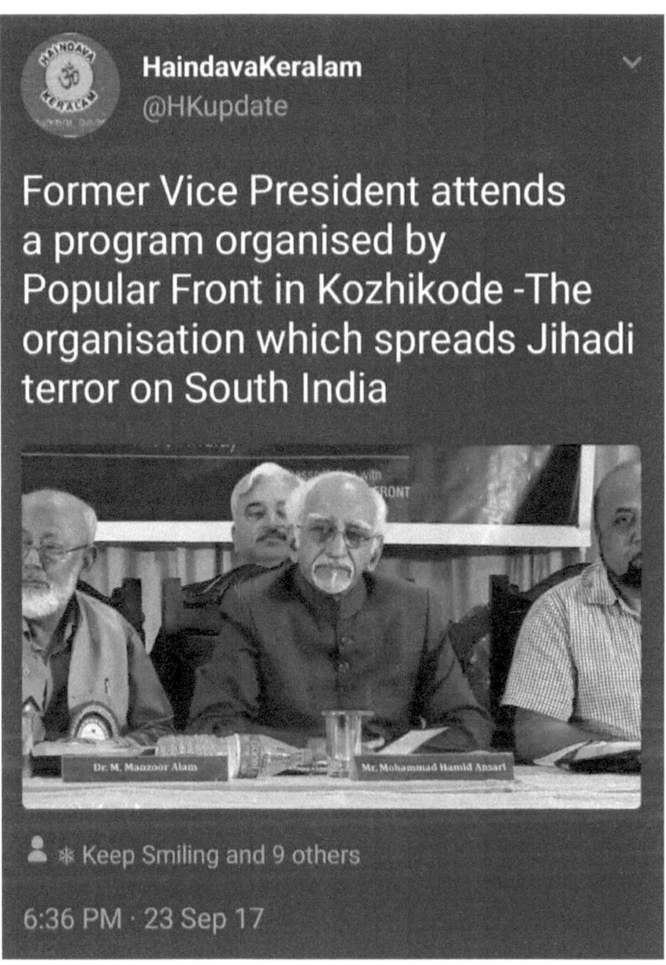

HaindavaKeralam
@HKupdate
Former Vice President attends a program organised by Popular Front in Kozhikode -The organisation which spreads Jihadi terror on South India
Dr. M. Manzoor Alam
Mr. Mohammad Hamid Ansari
Keep Smiling and 9 others
6:36 PM · 23 Sep 17

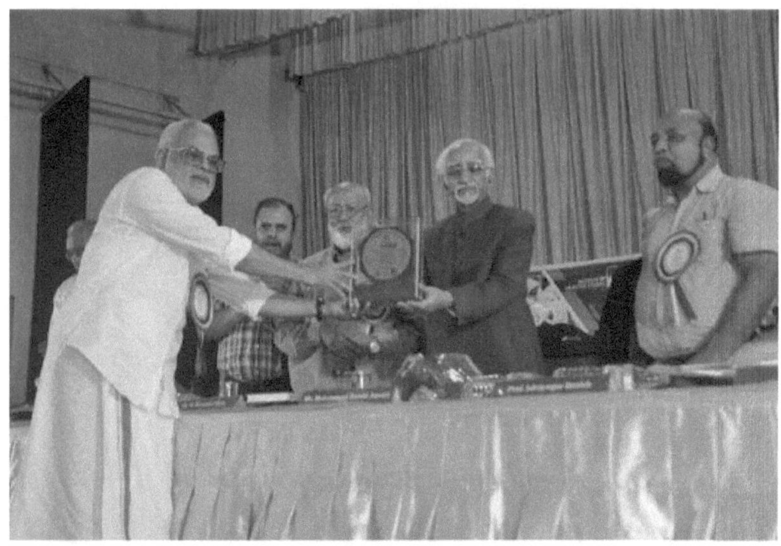

The Chairman of PFI presenting a memento to Hamid Ansari on his joining the organization. Photo Courtesy: The News Minute.

Subsequent to the demitting of the Vice-President's office, Ansari's clandestine operations against India came to light. Thus, when he was appointed as India's Ambassador to Iran in the 1990s, instead of working as a responsible Indian Diplomat, he sided with Iran and carried on various nefarious designs prejudicial to the safety and security of India like a spy so as to espouse the cause of Islamic fundamentalism in India, using his link with the Muslim brotherhood and solidarity.

It is pertinent to state here that a segment of Indian print media had also reported that Ansari's wife has been running one of the largest Madrassas in India, and during his 8-year tenure in Iran as India's Ambassador he took every opportunity to get funding from the authorities in Iran for expanding activities of the said Madrassas and got huge fund from Iran for which Ansari had shown loyalty, solidarity and gratitude towards the Iranian government and harbored hidden contempt and hostility towards the majority citizens of India.

Numerous acts of commission and omission, apart from deliberate misdeeds committed by Ansari in his capacity as India's Ambassador to Iran came to light. In a book titled: "Mission R&WA" by R.K Yadav, who was a former Diplomat, the author had given shocking revelations about Hamid Ansari, which would have endangered the safety and security of India.

It is solely on account of Hamid Ansari's personal rapport with the Islamic Republic of Iran, established by him when he was India's Ambassador to Iran, that Iran's Supreme Leader, Ayatollah Khamenei, and his cabinet Ministers slamming India by using the hashtag #IndianMuslimsInDanger# and tweeting: "The hearts of Muslims all over the world are grieving over the massacre of Muslims in India. The government of India should confront extremist Hindus and their parties and stop the massacre of Muslims in order to prevent India's isolation from the world of Islam". (The Times of India, issue dated 6-3-2020).

Each and every self-respecting Indian citizen must ask himself and herself: "Is there even an iota of truth in what the Ayatollah tweeted?" Ayatollah treats isolated street violence as "massacre" of entire Muslim population of India, concealing the fact that Indian Hindus provided shelter to Muslims in India at the time of partition on religious basis and Muslims in India is the largest minority and is the fastest growing population compared to the rest of the Indian citizens. These Muslim citizens enjoy a status often much higher than the Majority citizens because of various welfare schemes introduced and implemented by the government.

The million dollar question is: "Can the Ayatollah be allowed to defame India in the eyes of the comity of nations on false and unverified accusations and allegations on the basis of false propaganda carried on by Indian citizens professing Islamic fundamentalism like Hamid Ansari?"

It is worthwhile to mention here that Iran has committed extremely cruel human right violations not only against its own citizens but also against the citizens of other Muslim countries, as for example Iraq. Iran had committed aggression upon Iraq and involved in what they regarded as "Holy War" for nearly a decade in the recent past. The war had slaughtered millions of civilian innocent Muslims of that country, destroying their properties, including the oil production facilities, which is the lifeline of Iraq. Where was the UNHCHR at that time?

It is, therefore, shameful on the part of the Supreme Leader of Iran and their Ministers to accuse India when isolated street violence takes place and that too on the provocation of foreign agencies and anti-nationals living in India who are espousing the cause of Islamic fundamentalism.

Iran exercises extraterritorial jurisdiction over the rest of the world as for example when Indian writer, Salman Rushdie, wrote the novel "Satanic Versus", the then Khomeni called upon the Muslims around the world to behead Salman wherever he was found as a result of which Salman had to live underground for over two decades. Can the UNHCHR remain as a silent spectator to these incredible human right violations?

In the same sense of exercising extraterritorial jurisdiction by Iran, it would be ideal for the present Khameni to call upon the Muslim citizens of democratic India to shun Jihadi violence and live in harmony with accommodative spirit with the majority citizens of India. Such a move on the part of Iran would go a long way in ensuring peaceful coexistence with the majority citizens of India rather than precipitating the internal issues of India by attempting to pour "Iranian oil" into the Indian street fire caused by the elements of anti nationals and foreign agencies.

Thus, one can easily get the dots connected with regard to Hamid Ansari's role in fomenting trouble in India and in getting the UN Body's accusation against India by the present UNHCHR, Ms. Michelle Bachelet, who is the immediate successor of Zeid Raad Al Hussein, hailing from a Jihadi Islamic country, who had promptly responded to the false allegations of Hamid Ansari in the past as mentioned above, espoucing the cause of universal Islam.

One thing the world communities must understand is that of all the countries of the world, India is the only country which is housing the oldest civilization which has a track record of over ten millenniums in advocating and maintaining peaceful co-existence and harmony amongst the multi-religious citizens under its time-tested philosophy of "Samasta Lokah Sukhino Bhavantu" [Let every living being be happy].

India's former President was a Muslim, viz. Dr. APJ Abdul Kalam, who is regarded by the entire citizens of India as "People's President", lived his entire life with full of secular credentials of the highest standard and therefore presently after his death his statue erected at his village in the southern tip of India is being worshipped by the Indian masses belonging to all religions. The question, therefore, often hangs in the minds of the majority Hindu citizens is:

"Why don't the rest of the Muslim citizens in India emulate the staunch patriotic and secular life led by Late Dr. Kalam"?

It is noteworthy in this regard that one of the doctrines of Islam is to capture political power in any country they infiltrate by sword and by unleashing violence, which can be easily understood by studying the history of Islam since its advent 1400 years ago. Under this doctrine, the Muslims invariably seek to illegally infiltrate or seek asylum in a country inhabited by infidels and then convert the country of their occupation by gradually increasing their population by procreating through four wives, by way of converting non-Muslims into Islam by instilling fear in their minds of beheading or violence against them and by illegal infiltration through the porous borders.

A classic example in this regard is the history of Lebanon. In the 1950s Lebanon was a thriving Christian majority country. Lebanon believed exactly as India's Hindus – welfare of the humanity as a whole irrespective of the religion in which a person accidentally was born. Lebanon promoted multi-cultural societies, secularism, democracy, etc. At one time it was a country known as a role model for any modern welfare State.

In the 1950s, the Time Magazine described Lebanon as the Garden of Eden. The country had boasted world-class educational system, medical services, gender equality, libraries, sports complexes, etc. They had also allowed asylum to few Muslims.

Slowly and steadily Mosques and Madrassas mushroomed in the length and breadth of the country. In those Madrassas Islamic Terrorism on the detailed guidance as described in the book "Sahih al-Bukhari", are taught to the students, which is regarded by the Muslims as the most important religious book after Holy Quran. Simultaneously, the Muslim men reproduced children through several women (keeping in mind the religious injunction of maintaining a fleet of only four wives at any given time). Thus, over the years each and every village and town was gradually and steadily populated by Muslims and ultimately the Christian Majority country that was Lebanon became topsy-turvy. It became Muslim majority country whereupon the Muslims slaughtered the Christian natives of the country who had to run for their lives. The rest of them were asked to convert into Islam or face the sword. Many of them obeyed and the rest of them were slaughtered. [A brief history of this sordid history of Lebanon can be understood by watching a video-clip on You Tube by the link words: "Story of Christian majority Lebanon, Brigitte Gabriel and the deed…."].

Similar to Lebanon, one can find numerous other countries. Malaysia was once Hindus and Buddhist majority country. Presently, on account of the fast growth of the Muslim populations in that country, which stands at 53% at present, it had adopted Islamic government, declaring Sharia as the State Law. Indian Islamic Terrorist, Dr. Zakir Naik, while fleeing India after committing serious crimes, was invited by Malaysian Government to permanently settle down in that country. Dr. Naik is given all amenities for leading a luxurious life and ultra-modern computerized logistics for preaching world-wide his theories of Islamic superiority. The Malaysian Government has conferred upon Dr. Naik an Arabic Title and when translated into English it is known as "Allah's Guest" who is now living in lavish life styles with abundant resources and forces at his command.

Dr. Naik has now advised the Malaysian government to give an ultimatum to the natives and non-Muslims of that country to embrace Islam or face being declared as "Infidels" which the government has favourably considered. All pleadings of Indian Government under the international law for deporting Dr. Naik for facing trial for his heinous crimes committed in India before fleeing to Malaysia are being rubbished by that government. Presently a change.org. petition started by one Colin Nathan addressed to Tun Dr. Mahathir, titled: "Deport Zakir Naik" is doing the round in social media.

Identical to Malaysia, England has already been Islamized to the extent of 90%. The entire posts of Mayors of all the cities of England are presently occupied by Muslims and there are no chances that the said posts are ever reverting to non-Muslim citizens of England. Similar is the gradual process of other democratic countries such as France, Sweden, Germany, Australia, etc.

CONCLUSION:

The greatest threats presently faced by India to its very survival as a civilized nation are from the very Indian citizens living within the country as parasites. They are on the pay-rolls of various world-wide NGOs hostile to majority citizens of India and India as a whole. The "weapon" in attacking India in their hands was the indiscriminate granting of licenses under the FCRA.

There are mainly two categories of these antinational citizens thriving in India. The first category includes highly educated citizens, calling themselves "Left-Liberal-Intellectuals" and those who are professing imported Saudi-Arabia originated ideologies. The second category includes mostly uneducated Muslim citizens of India, professing imported Wahabi fundamentalism whose aims and objectives are transforming India into a Dar-Ul-Islam, like Pakistan, which is the fundamental doctrine of Islam to be compulsorily followed by every adherents of Islam.

The Islamic fundamentalism was originated in the frightening desert land where it is not easy to get even a glass of natural potable water to drink. While this class of threat had remained dormant since the advent of Islam 1400 years ago, it gained enormous fighting strength for the imposition of their doctrine for world-wide expansion only in the 1930s when certain infidels from the US discovered vast oil deposits in the soil beneath the desert land. This discovery led to revolutionize economy in Saudi Arabia, where Islam was born. Along with this sudden economic prosperity, the fundamentalism also grew side by side to impose the Islamic doctrines of expansion across the world.

The well-known YouTuber and public orator, Australian Imam Tawhidi speaks about Islam in the following words:

Islam is a religion like Christianity, Judaism or any other religion, came with one man's thoughts to guide human beings and not to rule over the human beings. Political Islam comes from the problem that some scholars believe that Islam can be used as a tool to govern human beings. This is the problem. Islam is not a constitution one can use for governing a country. This is why all the Islamic governments are total failures. They have the worst economy, worst standard of life, people are all upset, which is the reasons that they flee to Western countries for better lives. Can you show me just one Islamic country which is successful in term of human welfare, economy, better standars of lives, etc. All of them have failed. [Please watch video on YouTube by the link words: "Aussie Imam makes shocking confessions about Islam" as well as the other links of the Imam's YouTube speeches].

It is a universal fact that when political Islam and communism works together in any country, the destruction of that country is imminent and faster. A classical illustration in this regard is the countries like Afghanistan, Syria, etc. The political Islam and communism turn by turn destroyed the countries beyond redemption. [Readers are urged to watch a video-clip on YouTube by the link words: "Afghanistan: Land of Endless War – DW Documentary"].

It was Mark Twain who once said: "Truth is stranger than fiction". It is the case with all the Islamic countries. Although Islam is said to be representing "peace", there are no peace in any of the Islamic countries, but only "pieces", viz. destructions.

A "peaceful" uprising against the then President of the Islamic country, Syria, more than a decade ago turned into a full-scale civil war and the conflagration that followed left over 4,00,000 Muslim citizens dead. It devastated its cities and towns.

The war ruthlessly demolished ancient monuments, which were once symbol of peace.

Similar is the case of Afghanistan. Afghanistan regained independence from British influence in 1919. However, as on today it couldn't stand as a civilized nation or as a developing or developed country. It has witnessed only civil wars from time to time. At present the dreaded terrorist organization Taliban captured the political power there.

Coming back to the allegations of human rights violations against Muslim citizens in India by the UNHCHR, it is the height of hypocrisy on the part of the present Commissioner who is a woman hailing from a country, called Chile. The human right violations in Chile are of blood curdling magnitude. The Wikipedia lists in its website the human right violations of Chile, inter alia, in the following words:

QUOTE:

"Human rights violations in Chile were the crimes against humanity, persecution of opponents, political repression, and state terrorism committed by the Chilean Armed forces, members of Carabineros de Chile and civil repressive agents members of a secret police, during the Military dictatorship of Chile under General Augusto Pinochet. The number of direct victims of human rights violations in Chile accounts for around 30,000 people: 27,255 tortured and 2,279 executed. In addition, some 200,000 people suffered exile and an unknown numbers were sent to illegal detention centers.

UNQUOTE:

The million dollar question that would arise in the mind of any sober-minded citizens in this regard is why doesn't this woman concentrate upon her own nation in solving the human rights violations rather than poking her nose into the affairs of India which have democratic and secular credentials since time immemorial? Does this woman or the UN Body ever raised even an eyebrow when lakhs of Kashmiri Hindus were forced to flee their hearth and home in Kashmir in the wake of the spread of Islamic terror in the recent past? In fact as recently as May 2018, an organization called "Global Kashmiri Hindus Diaspora" has appealed to the UNHCHR regarding the genocide and ethnic cleansing of the Hindus by the majority Muslims of the Kashmir State. However, the UNHCHR refused to show any respect or response to their appeal. Does this woman, called Michelle Bachelet or her immediate predecessor, Zeid Raad Al Hussein, regard the native Hindus of Kashmir as "ethno-religious groups" not deserving any human right concern? It is utterly shameful, immoral and highhanded attitude on the part of the UNHCHR in characterizing the CAA as "limited to specific ethno-religious groups, may not be sufficiently objective and reasonable in light of the broad prohibition of refoulement under international human rights law" without understanding even an iota of the truth and realities of India.

About 40% of membership of UNO is Jihadi Muslim countries. Can India be allied with the UNO which has largest number of member countries professing Islamic fundamentalism? It would be amazing for any citizens of ordinary prudence that Islamic terrorism is taking place around the world at increasing frequency. And yet these so-called protector of human rights, the UNHCHR maintains disturbing silence over such incidents and focus their guns at Hindus and India as their soft targets. The Islamic terrorism has killed and maimed millions of innocent lives across the world since the advent of Islam 1400 years ago.

In this context it is noteworthy to mention here that when the Taliban carried out large scale terror strikes in many parts of the world, the UNO could only remain as a silent spectator. On demand by various member countries to ban Taliban, the General Committee of the UNO illogically and foolishly stated that "there are good Talibans and Bad Talibans" and therefore a proper definition regarding "Terrorism" could not be adopted as on today. It is elementary common sense that whether good or bad, the fundamental doctrine of Islam is superiority over the rest of the religions which itself is sufficient to define the term "Islamic Terrorism". And yet, the UNO drags on the matter without taking any remedial steps and the member countries continue to suffer as victims of these atrocious elements.

When a sober-minded citizen of India takes a close analysis of the track records of the UNHCHR since its establishment, it had taken up cases only on behalf of the Muslim fundamentalists anywhere in the world. It can also be established that over the years UNO and the other UN Bodies have become tools in the hands of the Jihadi Muslim countries to spread their ideologies around the world. They are least bothered to tackle any human right violations committed by Muslims against any non-Muslims.

If at all India agrees to let millions of illegal Bangladeshi and Rohingya Muslims into the country, as constantly demanded and worked for by anti-nationals and anti-Hindus like Harsh Mander and his international cohorts it would lead to (i) gradual weakening of Indian democracy and ultimately wiping out the democracy as it happened in Lebanon and many other countries as democracy and secularism are ruthlessly opposed by Islam. (ii) It will lead to civil war which would per force be imposed upon the peace-loving Hindus by these "Holy War Mongers" for fulfilling the fundamental Islamic doctrine of making the politically captured country a Dar-ul-Islam.

Thus, if India starts dancing in tune with the false and illogical accusations made by the UN Bodies, which are totally blind to the realities of India and is carried away by the false propaganda by the anti nationals living in the country like parasites, it would have the effect of collapsing its democratic principles and secular ideals and values, thereby creating chaotic situations in India sooner than anybody can expect.

India can therefore lead the multi-racial world to a peaceful coexistence with its ten-millennia-old time tested policy of "Samasta Lokah Sukhina Bhavantu" [May all the beings of all the worlds be happy]. In short, India is capable of dictating terms to the UN bodies and to the other countries and it can never be the other way round.

It might be mentioned here in this connection that a survey conducted in America reveals that 90% of the crimes committed in that country are out of the schizophrenic nature of Americans' views. It is therefore primarily the duty of American government to tackle this lunatic, called "George Soros", who is seeking to impose his lunatic ideas upon other sovereign nations by exercising extra territorial jurisdiction. If America keeps a blind eye towards these lunatic citizens of their country, the relationship between America and India is bound to get jeopardized.

Similarly, if UN Bodies like the UNHCHR are whole-heartedly supporting George Soros and try to thrust his megalomaniac ideas upon the Member-countries it would create chaotic circumstances in all such countries, rather than uniting the countries for which alone the UNO was established. Incidentally, Myanmar Military Junta has recently seized the entire Bank Accounts of the lunatic, George Soros, and his Open Society Foundation. Hence, if Indian authorities do not open their eyes to the internal gravest threats faced by the country and unless India confiscate the foreign illegitimate fund received by Harshad Mander and other anti-nationals, India would witness in the near future total chaotic situations which would be beyond the capacities of the government to tackle.

In this short write-up I have mentioned only five such elements who regularly pose greatest threats to the internal safety and security of India only in very sketchy details concerning them. However, there are several books detailing the crimes committed against India by these anti-nationals living in India as parasites. Two of these books are: (1) "Crimes Against India" By Stephen Knapp (2) "Breaking India: Western Interventions in Dravidian and Dalit Fault-lines" by Rajiv Malhotra. Yet another informative essay is available on the internet, which is titled: "Fifty People & Entities Dead or Alive Who Have Affected Hindus and Hinduism in a Negative Way", by Francois Gautier, a renowned French Indologist, which throws light on several leftist ideologues of India who are enemies of Hinduism and have dedicated their lives in destroying the country by putting up road-blocks in its march towards progress and prosperity.

It is therefore high time that India withdraws urgently its membership from the UNO and simultaneously take steps to form a coalition of world body tentatively called, "Coalition of Democratic Countries" before it is too late. [I am ready and willing to work in this direction in the capacity of a patriotic citizen of India and also to prosecute all those who poked their noses into the internal affairs of India before the International Court of Justice in my capacity as a Lawyer fully conversant with international laws and practices].

[SEPTEMBER 2014]

[An unedited version of this essay was published in NRI INTERNET.
COM - GLOBEL TECH., USA, issue dated 25/09/2014].

THE ROLE OF INDIAN AMERICAN INTELLECTUALS FORUM IN MAKING NARENDRA MODI AS PRIME MINISTER OF INDIA IN 2014

In a couple of days, Hon. Prime Minister of India, Narendra Modi, will be arriving in America at the invitation of President Barack Obama. In all probability, the first-ever official visit of Modi is likely to be an epoch-making event for the people of Indian origin. It is particularly noteworthy that the visit is in the month of September. The month of September has great historic significance in the relationship between India and America. It was in the month of September that Swami Vivekananda arrived at the American shore a century ago to address the Parliament of Religions, which paved the way for the people in the West to love

India and its civilization; It was in September that the *"The City of Sparta"* carrying Sri Sri Paramahansa Yogananda, the Yogi-Christ of modern India, arrived at the shore of Boston at the invitation of American Unitarian Association; it was in the month of September that the world-renowned newspaper "The New York Times", which had extensively covered both the events of Swami Vivekananda as well as Sri Sri Paramansa Yogananda, was born; it was in the month of September that the concerted efforts of both the people of Indian origin and the American disciples of Martin Luther King, Jr. culminated in unveiling a statue of India's Mahatma Gandhi at the capital city of Washington; it is again the 15th of September that was declared as international day of democracy, and the list goes on and on.

Narendra Modi is representing the largest and the sub-continental sized democratic country in the world with over 834 million eligible voters. The last parliamentary election in India was a mind-boggling democratic exercise which is unique for India because of the huge population – almost one fifth of human race inhabiting the earth compared with the oldest democratic America wherein only about 4% of the world population inhabits. It is on account of this uniqueness that David Cameron, the then British Prime Minister, who called up Modi on his winning the election and congratulated him by saying: *"It's great to be talking to someone who just got more votes than any other politician anywhere in the universe"*.

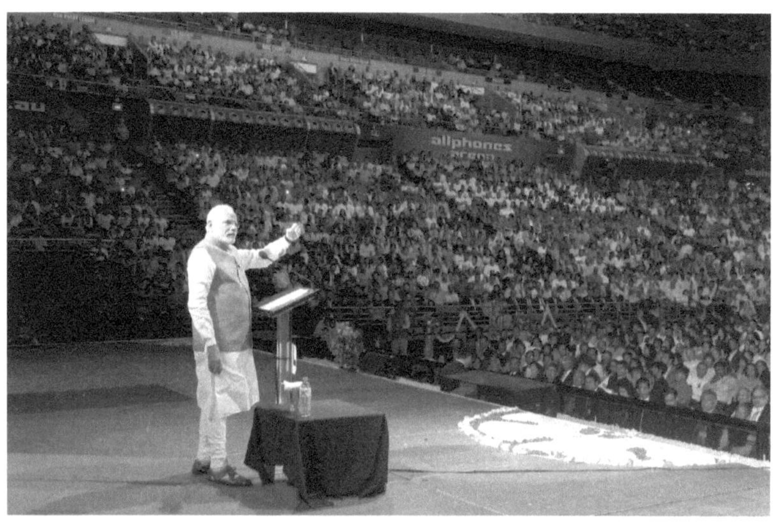

Prime Minister Narendra Modi addressing the gathering at Madison Square Garden in the USA which has been billed as the largest congregation ever witnessed in the soil of USA for welcoming and hearing a political head of a foreign nation.
[Photo Courtesy: Google Images]

The dominant citizens of India are those professing *Sanatana-Dharma* (the eternal path of duty, wisdom and spiritual growth), which came to be known as "Hinduism", which is not a religion in the real sense of the term but a way of life. The Hindus are a peace-loving, God fearing people and the fundamental tenets of Hinduism is *Samastha Lokah Sukhinobhavantu* (May all the people of the world be Happy) and *Vasudevaka Kutumbakam* (the entire world is a single unified family). However, at some point in time in the evolution of the civilization, these traits were degenerated into weakness and lack of self-respect on the part of those professing Hinduism as a consequence of which India was invaded by various evil forces from beyond its borders. It was the Nobel Laureate, V.S. Naipaul, who observed about this phenomena as: *"No civilization was so little equipped to cope with the outside aggression; no country was so easily raided and plundered and learned so little from its disasters. Five hundred years after the Arab conquest of Sind, foreign Muslim rule was established in Delhi which lasted for over five hundred years and then the British rule, which lasted for the next 150 years, ending only in 1947".*

It was at this juncture when India was ruled by the British, Swami Vivekananda, whose family name was also "Narendra", arrived at Chicago in the month of September 1893 to address the Parliament of Religions. Swami's address at the Parliament and his subsequent speeches across America were instrumental in kindling the spirit of freedom and sowed the seed of awakenings amongst the Indians against the foreign domination of their motherland. It is generally believed that Mahatma Gandhi was highly inspired by the speeches and writings of the Swami. Gandhi while living in South Africa came face to face with the magnitude of slavery and racial discrimination. As a Practicing Lawyer in that country, he took an overnight train ride from Durban to Pretoria and halfway to Pretoria a man stalked into his first-class compartment and ordered him into the baggage car. Gandhi held a first-class ticket, refused to move out and at the next halt the ticket examiner called policemen, who, unceremoniously, threw Gandhi off the train along with his luggage in the middle of the night. The incident was the turning point in Gandhi's life and his iron determination to kick out the British from the Indian soil took a decisive shape in his mind which grew day by day and eventually culminating into the freedom movement in India and the country attaining independence from Britain in 1947.

Why the Indian electorates defeated the Congress-led coalition government of United Progressive Alliance (UPA) headed by Sonia Gandhi could not have been fully grasped by the natives of any Western countries. The decade-long government of UPA was not in fact a true government representing the dominant citizens of India, viz. Hindus.

It was at the instance of the former Prime Minister of India, Indira Gandhi, that after having imposed the widely-unpopular Emergency in India to cling on to power that The Constitution (Forty-second Amendment) Act, 1976 was passed, whereby the term "Secular" was deliberately inserted to the Preamble of the Constitution, as though India were "communal" till then. Ironically, however, the Congress headed by Indira Gandhi and her son, Rajiv Gandhi, practiced just the opposite, viz. "appeasement of the Muslim minority at the cost of majority Hindus".

When the son of Indira Gandhi, Rajiv Gandhi, was assassinated, the Congress party elected his widow Sonia Gandhi, a Christian woman hailing from the fundamentalist Italy, as the President of the party. During the next general parliamentary election in India in the year 2004, the Congress party did not get an absolute majority to form the government and it took the support of several regional, communal, Leftist political parties, splintered national parties, break away groups having formed under certain insignificant political parties, etc. and thus formed a coalition government named and styled as "United Progressive Alliance" (UPA). Sonia Gandhi, who has had no proper education or any experience in heading the government of such a vast continental-sized country as India inhabited by over one billion people, was made Chairperson of UPA. She and her family followed

Christian religion of the type practiced and preached world-over by the Vatican and harbored inborn contempt towards Hinduism and Sanathan Dharma. Although pressure was mounted by the Congress workers upon Sonia for becoming the Prime Minister of India, scared of a probable assassination, coupled with the advice of her children against such an eventuality, she declined and instead made Dr. Manmohan Singh as her puppet to act as PM on the unequivocal understandings that she would remain behind the "thrown" to control the PM and would be taking all the decisions on behalf of the government.

Thus, it was for the first time in the post-independent history of India that a non-Hindu (Dr. Singh), who had stood for election but was defeated by the electorates, was made the PM of India, remotely controlled by the Italian woman. The major constituents of the coalition UPA government were Islamic parties such as Indian Union Muslim League, All India Majlis-E-Ittehadul Muslimeen (AIMIM), Jammu & Kashmir National Congress, etc. It is again for the first time in the history of free-India that dedicated communal parties have captured power at the Central level, India ironically remaining "Secular" as per the aforesaid amendment to the Constitution.

It is everybody's general knowledge that the fundamental tenets of Islam are the concept of its "Superiority" over the rest of the religions and the Islam treats their adherents as "Infidels". Accordingly, Sonia Gandhi soon established a National Advisory Council headed by Ahmed Patel, a fundamentalist Muslim, who wielded enormous power within the government of India in the matter of appointment of ministers, evolving policies, conducting government business, charting out programs for the Union Government, etc.

It has already gone on record as vindicated by numerous authoritative books authored by those who were intimately connected with the UPA government that Prime Minister Dr. Manmohan Singh was literally a puppet of Sonia, who remotely controlled each and every action of him as well as each and every word uttered by him. Thus, at the commencement of the first term of UPA in 2004 Dr. Singh categorically declared that the "Muslim citizens of India shall get first priority upon the national resources of the country", indirectly meaning that the majority citizens of India, viz. Hindus, are second class citizens. [Watch a video on YouTube by the wordslink: "Muslims have the 1st right over the resources of India said PM Manmohan Singh"]

With a view to keep the communal Muslim parties in the UPA coalition happy and dancing in tune with the demands of the Muslim Advisors and Ministers, Sonia ensured that all the important positions in the government, both political and non-political, including the internal security portfolio, were given to Muslims. Thus, the External Affairs Ministry was headed by two Muslim Ministers of Cabinet Rank, viz. Salman Khurshid and A. Ahmed who was representing Muslim League of Kerala (The said Islamic Party whole-heartedly supported the Islamic preacher and fundamentalist of Mumbai, viz. Dr. Zakir Naik); the Attorney General of India was a Muslim (Mr. Goolam Hussain), the Chief Justice of India was a Muslim (Hon'ble Justice Altamas Kabir), the Chief Election Commissioner of India was a Muslim (Qureshi).

Similarly, Sonia also ensured that the Heads of non-political government organizations, Statutory and Autonomous Bodies, Administrators of Hindu Temples controlled by the Union Government, Commissioners of Devosworm Boards managing the Hindu Temples, etc. were held by Muslims or non-Hindus. In short, the UPA government was of the Muslims, by the Muslims and for the Muslims while India remaining "secular" as per the aforesaid Amendment to the Constitution of India carried out by Indira Gandhi.

The records would reveal that the then Home Minister, Sushil Kumar Shinde, who repeatedly referred to the members of the majority citizens, the Hindus, as "saffron terrorists", worked solely for the welfare of Muslims in the country in an ugly "appeasement policies" adopted by the UPA government so as to ensure en bloc votes from the Muslims while at the same time knowing thoroughly well that the slave-minded Hindus would in any case vote for the Congress, the political party represented by Sonia and Shinde.

During the UPA regime the Islamic terrorism and Jehadi violence and bloodsheds in India were the highest. And yet, the UPA Home Minister, Shinde, wrote individual letters to all the State and Union Territories in India and the Police Commissioners across the country instructing them: "not to harass innocent Muslims", by which Shinde indirectly restrained the Investigating Agencies and Law Enforcing Authorities of India from carrying on their official duties and responsibilities without fear or favour as it is the fundamental principle of jurisprudence that the "innocence" of an accused person can never be established by his/ her outer look. Shinde also spearheaded for the promulgation of a legislation known as "Communal Violence Bill" aimed at stifling the collective voice and power of the majority citizens of India, viz. the Hindus, and make them slaves of Muslims at the behest of several Islamic fundamentalist NGOs flourishing in the Western countries through their foot soldiers in India like Harsh Mandar who was reportedly paid a huge sum of over Indian Rupees 12 Crores by an American NGOs comprised of Muslims of Indian origin for drafting the Bill. The UPA government was, therefore, like any other despotic Mogul ruler under whom the majority Hindus had no voice and has had to live like slaves.

In addition to being totally communal, the UPA government indulged in corruption of unprecedented magnitude and enormity. Various skeletons of frightening proportion involving large scale scams and financial bungling were started falling down from the cupboard of UPA day after day one of which being the payment of Rs.2 crores to the Lawyer-wife of former UPA Finance Minister, P. Chidambaram, towards her "professional fee" for the alleged professional services rendered by her, from the crimes-and-fraudsters-ridden Sharada Chit-fund Company of Kolkata, whose promoters and directors are presently languishing in jails. The said fee as per the Indian standard is at least one hundred times larger than the fee paid to any Lawyer for similar professional services. The fee payment was over and above the lavish spending of money like water towards her Executive Deluxe Class flight journeys from her far-off Chennai home-town to numerous cities across India, stay at Five-Star Deluxe Hotels, etc. as though there was not even a single competent Lawyer available locally within the city of Kolkata where the fraudulent company, Sharada Chitfunds Co., was head-quartered. During the decade-long rule of UPA Government, Sonia Gandhi became the Fourth Richest Politician in the world as per the survey conducted and reported by Forbes magazine of USA. Aravind Kejriwal, the activist-turned-politician and founder President of Aam Aadmi Party openly asserted that Sonia Gandhi and her family members looted the resources of India which was much larger in magnitude and ramification than what was looted by the British colonial masters during their colonial rule of the country.

It was in the aforesaid unprecedented circumstances that a large number of nationalist Hindus considered it as their duty to overthrow the UPA government and regain independence for the Hindus. The Parliamentary election campaigns held in 2014 were therefore regarded as the second freedom struggle for the Hindu majority citizens of India.

The tremors of these yearnings for freedom were high amongst the patriotic and nationalist people of Indian origin settled in America. Various Non-Resident Indians (NRI) of America formed themselves into Associations so as to carry on the campaign of emancipation of the dominant Hindus by throwing out the communal UPA government for which they untiringly worked for the success of the Prime Ministerial candidate of Bharatiya Janata Party (BJP), Narendra Damodardas Modi. Out of all these NRI organizations, the Indian American Intellectuals Forum (IAIF), under the dynamic leadership of New York based Narain Kataria emerged as a major force to reckon with, which relentlessly worked for defeating the UPA government and ensuring the victory of Narendra Modi and his BJP.

Kataria and his dedicated team have had excellent track records of carrying on the campaign against UPA Government headed by Sonia Gandhi right from the year 2005 – a year after UPA government came to power. Thus, in the year 2008, the Indian National Overseas Congress of Sonia Gandhi (INOCSG), consisting mostly of the People of Indian Origin who had earlier professed Hinduism but converted themselves into Christianity, having had filed three defamation cases in the amount of US$220 million against Kataria and his team members, viz. Arish Sahani and Satya Dosapati, in the New York and New Jersey Courts for publishing a full page advertisement regarding Sonia Gandhi in The New York Times, which was allegedly "defamatory". However almost 90% of the Indian community in the USA supported Kataria and he won two cases as the courts found them as false and frivolous lawsuits and the remaining one suit was unconditionally and shamelessly withdrawn by the INOCSG.

A year prior to the general election date in India, held in 2014, Kataria started working round the clock to organize and sensitize the Indians of America as well as in India by his talk, T.V. interviews, essays, seminars, etc. by way of effectively utilizing the electronic/social media. As a first step, Kataria sent out the essence of the Indian epic-story Mahabharata of defeating evil forces and establishing righteousness (Dharma) by E-mails to like-minded Indian citizens across the world, containing the following message: ***"Voice of India – Namo Namo! The bugle for Mahabharata war has been blown. Entire India is waking up very fast. There is an utter confusion in the ranks and files of Kauravas. Kauravas are on the run. Demoralization has already set in their ranks. Will be completely wiped out***

during the fight in the next general election". *[In this "Kauravas" represents the evil forces of UPA government, headed by Sonia Gandhi and NaMo stands for Narendra Modi].* I had received this message by E-mail from Kataria during the early part of the electioneering in India in the year 2013, which I had forwarded to my clients, including NRIs, students I taught in the past and their friends and relatives across the country. It is indeed heartening that in the ultimate analysis, what Kataria wished for; what he untiringly worked for; what the ideology he stood for like a rock, have all indeed come to a reality with redounding success in India – BJP emerging victorious with absolute majority and Narendra Modi becoming Prime Minister of India.

Living in Mumbai, I have had the thrill of watching on the YouTube various programs organized under the leadership of Kataria and his dedicated team across the USA. Of all the programs arranged by him, the program which would linger on in my mind is the one sponsored by IAIF involving the speeches of Yoga Guru Baba Ramdev at New York along with Dr. Subramanian Swami in the month of September 2013. The program held at a prominent Hotel in the heart of New York has had a telling effect upon all the Indians settled in the USA and the Western world. Baba Ramdev's *"Vande Mataram"* (Salute to Motherland) call reverberated the huge hall of the Hotel which was attended to its full capacity. The enthusiasm generated amongst the participants was palpable even by watching the program on the YouTube which was reminiscent of Swami Vivekananda's wakening call exactly at the same city of New York and in the same month of September in the year 1893.

Yet another memorable event organized by IAIF was based on an idea stemming from the insulting remarks spat against Narendra Modi by Mani Shankar Aiyar, the senior-most Member of Parliament in the UPA government and one of the boot-lickers of Sonia to the effect: ***"A place will be identified for the Gujarat Chief Minister to distribute tea wherever Congress meetings take place. ...... I throw up a challenge that in 21st century Narendra Modi will never become the Prime Minister of the country....But if at all he wishes to distribute tea to Congress leaders here, we shall find a place for him"***.

The aforesaid remarks was not only a personal attack against Modi and an affront at the unorganized working class people like the tea sellers but an unprecedented event in the history of civilized dealings amongst the political aspirants the world over and a mass-insults to the electorates of such a large State as Gujarat and its then Chief Minister, Modi. No sooner the news of the insults appeared in the media, than Kataria woke up the members of his team and hurriedly adopted strategies to give a befitting reply to the insults. Thus, the program called *"Chai-pe-Churcha"* (Talks at Tea) was born. The program was organized in groups in the entire length and breadth of such a vast country as the USA, which snowballed into a mass movement, akin to "Quit India" movement started by India's Mahatma Gandhi. The idea was to discuss and sensitize the members of IAIF of the dangers that India would be facing in the event Congress under the leadership of this former Christian waitress of Italian origin, who had espoused total contempt towards Hindus and *Sanatan Dharma*, along with her slave-minded coteries like Mani

Shankar Aiyar, P. Chidambaram, Sushil Kumar Shinde, etc. come to power.

It was during the first year of the NDA government assuming power that Sonia sent out Manishankar Aiyer as her Emissary to Pakistan to seek their help in toppling the NDA government headed by Prime Minister Modi. [There are several videos available in this regard on YouTube, out of which watch a video by the linkwords: "Is Manishankar Aiyar seeking help from Pakistan to defeat Modi?"].

Kataria and his dedicated team organized "*Hawans*" all over the USA to propitiate Gods and Goddesses and to invoke the blessings of Lord Ganesha to remove all the obstacles on the path of BJP's Prime Ministerial candidate Narendra Modi coming to power. In this regard the Laser Show put up by the IAIF of Swami Vivekananda's birth day celebrations in New York was indeed a spectacular event. [Incidentally while the entire UPA Parliamentarians treated Vivekananda as a "Hindu fundamentalist mendicant", the birth day of Prophet Mohammed, PBUP, was celebrated across the country with pomp and show during the whole UPA government period of a decade).

Again at no point of time in the history of electioneering anywhere in the world, India had witnessed such a massive flow of people of Indian origin into India during the electioneering period prior to 2014 – over 10,000 from many parts of USA – for cheering up the electorates by personal contacts in India. It has now been transpired that the idea of setting up a tea stall at the city of Vadodara in Gujarat during the vote counting period serving cups of hot free "NaMo" tea at a tea-stall, named and styled as "Mani Shankar Aiyar Tea Addah" along with a life-size cut-out of Aiyar with a garland of slippers on it was originated from a group of visiting American NRIs.

The members of the IAIF carried on what is now termed as "phone campaign". Each one of them took upon himself/herself as a duty to call up his/her relatives, friends and friends' friends in India and implored them to vote only for BJP.

Ironically, however, while the India's intellectuals living overseas worked for the unity and integrity of India by way of ensuring the success of Narendra Modi, the so-called intellectuals living in India worked round the clock for defeating Modi without rhyme or reasons and constantly worked against the welfare and progress of the country. Thus, India's first-rated "intellectual", Amartya Sen, the Nobel Laureate, was living in India during the electioneering period. He regularly attacked Modi and worked for promoting what he called "Third Front" – an amalgam of small regional political parties, communal parties, and splintered national parties. He refused to recognize the mammoth mandate successively given to Modi on three consecutive terms as Chief Minister of the State of Gujarat by the electorates of that state, his track records of developments and total absence of riots, Jihadi bombings, corruptions, etc. from his State, etc. Sen also behaved like a stooge of Western power and often seemed to carry with him a hidden agenda to propitiate his Western Christian Masters who conferred upon him all the personal credentials and acclaims, including the Nobel prize, totally blind to the realities of the dire need of working for the unity and integrity of his country of birth as a whole.

Yet another so-called intellect of India is Late U.R. Ananthamurthy, the *"Jnanpitha"* and *"Padma Bhusan"* Awardee. Ananthamurthy posed an open challenge to Modi ever coming to power and declared that the moment Modi comes to power he would leave the country for good. It is quite amusing that while the Nobel Laureate Amartya Sen left the country quietly under the cover of darkness along with his Western fundamentalist Christian wife (Georgina Rothschild) at the vote-counting period itself when he realized about the spectacular victory of Modi, the poor Ananthamurthy could not instantly leave the country as declared by him as the old age had caught up with him, although various patriotic organizations in India had sent him and his wife (Esther, the *Desi* converted Christian) two one-way tickets to Pakistan. He cited advancing age (85 years) and poor health and remained in India, having left for his "heavenly abode" before the swearing in ceremony of Modi.

Yet another "intellectual" of India is Arundhati Roy, the Man Booker Prize winner. This Christian woman worked for the disintegration of India by overtly and covertly espousing the cause of Kashmiri separatists, Naxalite terrorists and Islamic fundamentalists and regularly whipped up their passion to attack India. Although married, she threw to the winds all that family/ social values and decency by periodically visiting the Kashmiri separatist leaders like Geelani at their bungalows for cheering them up for what she termed "Freedom Struggle against India". Roy was found often supporting the Islamic terrorists in India. She regularly framed Modi as a "mass murderer of Muslims", "sponsored Genocide of Muslims in Gujarat", etc. etc. She characterized BJP as "a Hindu fascist organization who has been conducting an elaborate pogram of Muslims in Gujarat", etc. She compared Narendra Modi as "Hitler", totally blind to the realities, although since birth she has been living in India. At a T.V. interview which she gave in an Islamic country, Roy categorically stated that Mohd. Afzal, a confirmed terrorist and Parliament Building attacker, was "totally innocent" even after his conviction by all the lower courts of law which was finally confirmed by the Hon'ble Supreme Court of India and awarded capital punishment finding the grave offences committed by the terrorist against India as "the rarest of rare case". Roy sympathized with his family and periodically visited his house in Kashmir.

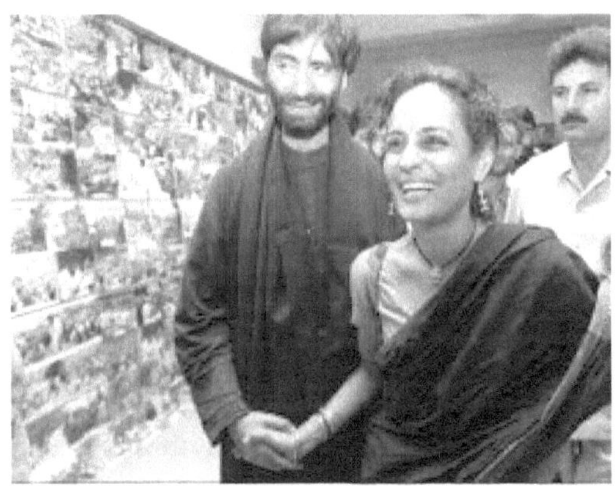

Arundhati Roy during one of her periodic visits to the bungalow of Yasim Malik, who was convicted for various terrorist strikes and terror funding for separating Kashmir from India. (Malik had also confessed to the killings of numerous Kashmiri Pandis, including Kashmiri Hindu Justice Neelkanth Ganjoo
[Photo courtesy: Google Images].

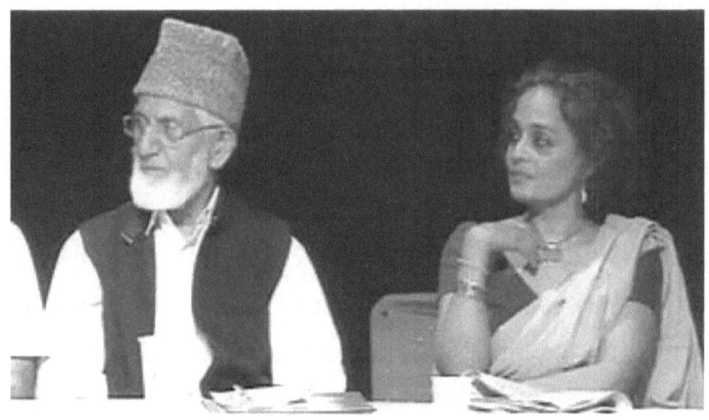

Arundhati Roy during one of her periodic stays at the bungalow of Pro-Pakistani-Kashmiri-Separatist leader, Sayed Ali Shah Geelani, who is regarded as the "Father of Kashmiri Jihads".

Roy described Afzal before his hanging by the Indian law enforcing authorities as "Prisoner of War", and after his hanging as "Martyr", etc. and whipped up the passion of Kashmiri separatists. Incidentally, when Kashmir is being treated for all intents and purposes as an integral part of India for over six decades and when lakhs and lakhs of innocent original and permanent inhabitant Hindus were assaulted and thrown out of their hearth and home from the State by these so-called separatists, such a conduct with impunity by a citizen would happen only in India under the much abused term: "freedom of expression". Had this woman been a citizen of Saudi Arabia or any other Islamic country such a conduct would have instantly attracted the punishment of beheading.

It is quite strange that when the highly researched book "Narendra Modi: A Political Biography" by Andy Marino, a Western scholar, containing incontrovertible documentary evidences, in which it was established that *"Narendra Modi wanted to quit as C.M., saying: It was unfair on the people of the State"*, and that *"No court has come even close to establishing his complicity in the violence"* was published, Arundhati Roy maintained a discreet silence when confronted by Reporters of both Western and Indian media. However, on the contrary, when a book titled: "Hinduism- An Alternative History" by a Western Christian fundamentalist woman, containing false and fabricated material stemming from the figment of imagination of the author was recalled by its publisher, Penguin, Roy made a hue and cry and carried on scathing attacks at the publisher and characterized their decision to recall the book as *"succumbing to the threats of Hindu fascist forces of India"*. It is probably on account of this double standards of promoting Christianity in India that Roy was featured in the Christian-dominated "2014 List of Time 100" as "the 100 most influential people in the world".

It is in the aforesaid realities prevailing in India where the so-called "Intellectuals" turning against India and relentlessly working towards anarchy and disintegration of the country that the selfless, sincere and outstanding works for the unity and integrity of the country carried on abroad by the patriotic members of the Indian American Intellectuals Forum are indeed to be commended, encouraged and rewarded.

Thus, it can easily be concluded that the credit for the spectacular victory of Narendra Modi and his becoming the Prime Minister of India should largely go to these unsung heroes of USA who came together under the umbrella of Indian American Intellectuals Forum held by a dynamic Indian, called "Narain Kataria". He was able to awaken the sleeping slaves of India and was instrumental to give a befitting reply to the characters like Mani Shankar Aiyar, Arundhati Roy, etc. by converting adversaries into victory. Shankar lost his election deposit and had to bite the dust.

It is worthwhile to mention here that Kataria and his team worked exactly similar to that of Late Netaji Subhash Chandra Bose, who had founded the Indian National Army (INA) to fight against the British regime and contributed to the achievement of independence for India from the British regime during his self-exiled life in Japan, while Kataria and his dedicated team at IAIF living as People of Indian Origin in the US fought against the Italian regime in India and gained independence for the Hindus of India. The differences in both the fighting instances are that while Netaji focused his entire attention upon India's independence, Kataria and his team focused their attention to the equal progress and prosperity of both America and India as the contribution of Indians settled in America in this regard are indeed admirable. In short Kataria treated both his *Karmabhoomi* (country of work) and *Janmabhoomi* (country of birth) on equal footing and dedicated his life to the cause and prosperity of both the countries. My hats off to him!

[Note by the Author: Mr. Narain Kataria has since then left for his heavenly abode].

SEPTEMBER 2015

[An unedited version of this essay was published in "HINDU VOICE" in its September, 2015 issue]

DR. APJ ABDUL KALAM: THE QUINTESSENCE OF SANATHAN DHARMA

From a tiny home full of poverty, starvation, deprivation and illiteracy in which Dr. APJ Abdul Kalam was born, he grew up to become a towering personality and lived like a spreading Banyan tree under which many souls found shelter, succor and growth. Dr. Kalam had been endearingly described as "Missile Man", "Peoples President", "Bharat Ratna", etc.

For me, however, Dr. Kalam was the greatest phenomena I ever came across in my life. At many stages of my journey through life, Dr. Kalam had indirectly influenced my life. My late father, who would have been of the same age as Dr. Kalam had he alive today, spent his adolescent years at a temple in Remeshwaram and from the anecdotes that my father related to us children later in his life, I realized that Dr. Kalam and my father were contemporaries in their respective adolescent years at the temple town.

One of the anecdotes I heard from my late father, which had poignantly started coming up to the surface of my mind ever since Dr. Kalam became the President of India was that: *"There was a Muslim youth who sold newspapers to the pilgrims at the Rameshwaram temples and in the vicinity of railway station for a living while at the same time he pursued his academic studies. He would come to the temple precincts in the evening, engage in conversation on spiritual subjects with the head priest and then sit quietly in Dyana (meditation)".*

I hardly realized at that period when my father was alive and narrated about "a Muslim youth" he encountered in his early life, would become a mighty personality in his life and in his own right!

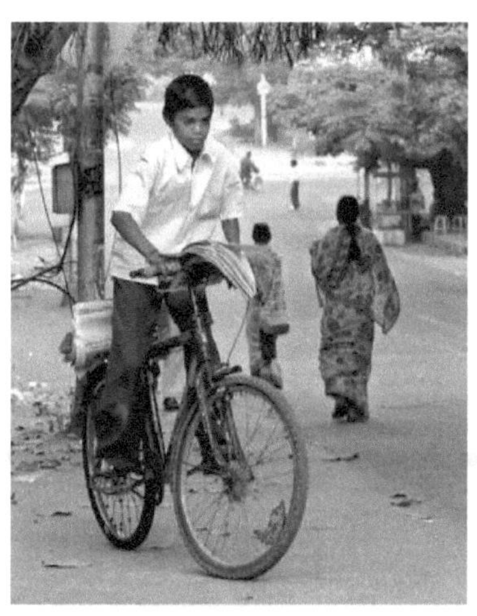

Dr. Abdul Kalam as a newspaper boy
[Photo courtesy: Google Images]
[The Author does not vouchsafe for the genuineness of this image]

What would be striking to one's mind upon intimately coming in contact with Dr. Kalam was his deeper absorption in the spirituality of India. In fact, he had been associated with several prominent spiritual centers of India from the South-most tip to the North-most tip of the country, viz. the Himalayas. To illustrate his spiritual journey, I would like to mention here an incident in the early part of his life.

As mentioned above, Dr. Kalam spent his adolescent life at a Hindu temple in the southern tip of India, viz. Rameshwaram, which paved the path for his spiritual journey in the materialistic world.

After leaving behind the adolescent period of his life at Rameshwaram and when he entered his career life, the first thing that Dr. Kalam did in the early part of his life was to meet Swami Sivananda who was hailing from Tamil Nadu and was a renowned Physician & Surgeon in the then Burma prior to independence. Swami Sivananda's Ashram was at the foothills of the Himalayas, which is the North-most tip of India and is diametrically in the opposite direction of Rameshwaram, the South-most tip of the country in the vast topography of India.

Dr. Kalam recollected his visit to the Ashram in one of his books: *"From a considerable distance away from the Ashram, I could easily sense the high spiritual vibration emanating from the Ashram. I walked into Swamiji's Ashram. My Muslim name aroused no reaction in him and as if he had read my agony and frustration in not being able to realize my childhood dream of flying an aircraft, he made me sit near him and then washed every single trace of despair out of my system through his gentle words. Even today, I can hear his words echoing in the deeper silence of my inner space. Swamiji said: 'Accept your destiny and go ahead with your life. You are not destined to become an Air Force pilot. What you are destined to become is not yet known, but it will manifest itself at the appropriate time. Forget this failure, as it was essential to lead you to your designated path. Search, instead, for the true purpose of your existence. Become one with your Self, my dear son! Surrender yourself to the will of God".*

The meeting with Swami Shivananda at the north-most tip of the country at the beginning of Dr. Kalam's career life was indeed the second phase of his journey through the path of Sanathan Dharma.

Dr. Kalam had been a regular visitor to the prominent Ashrams in the country such as the Ashram of Mata Amrutanandamayi in Kerala, Sri Satya Sai Baba at Puttaparthy, Ramana Maharashi's Ashram at Tiruvannamalai, Shri Ramakrishna Math at West Bengal and numerous other Ashrams across the country.

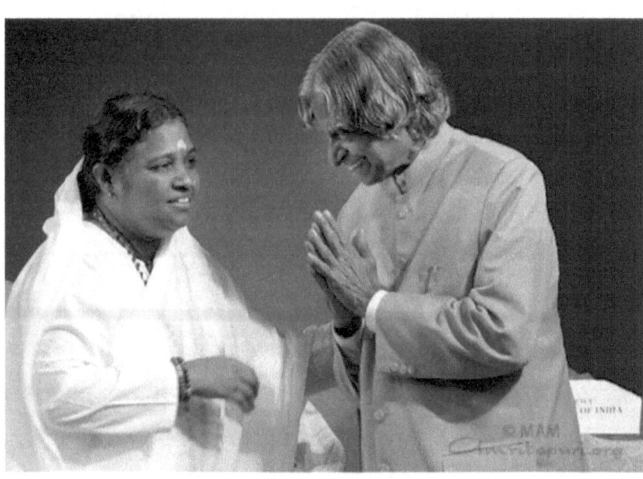

Dr. APJ Abdul Kalam with Mata Amritanandamayi of Kerala
[Photo Courtesy: Google Images]

I was fortunate to visit all these Ashrams that Dr. Kalam visited. There is an interesting connection with my visit to the Ashrams that Dr. Kalam visited during his life time which I would like to narrate here in brief.

During the early part of 1980s while I was employed with the Tata Iron & Steel Co. Ltd. [TISCO – presently known as "Tata Steel"] in their Headquarters at the then Bombay, I regularly attended the discourses on Bhagavad Gita by Swami Chinmayananda at the nearby Cross Maidan. As I am hailing from Kerala from where Swamy Chinmayananda hailed, I knew from the villagers that the Swamy was a born-again communist during his college life and after acquiring several Post-graduate degrees in various disciplines, he took up a job as an Investigative Reporter with the National Herald newspaper at Delhi. His first attempt in the capacity of a Newspaper Reporter was to produce an "all revealing Report" so as to "enlighten the gullible Hindus of India" by exposing the Sadhus and Swamis, as is the case with all the comrades of the Communist Kerala. However, to cut the long story short, instead of "exposing the Sadhus and Swamis", the so-called Investigative Reporter himself got merged into the "Institution of Swamis" after his first visit to Swami Sivananda's Ashram at Rishikesh, where Dr. Kalam visited. Thus, my initial intention to hear the discourses on Bhagavad Gita from the mouth of a "Godless communist man", of my native-state, Kerala, was out of fun and as a pastime activity. [For pastime I have never been a movie-theatre goer as we children were restrained by our parents from seeing commercial movies, but to watch only those movies which are based only on Hindu mythology, epics and philosophy]. However, the discourses on Gita by Chinmayananda became an important turning point in my life from which I had acquired a deeper meaning and understanding of the self and learned lessons in avoiding pitfalls in life.

During the later part of 1980s, after leaving my job at TISCO and then working in foreign countries thereafter, I came back to India and set up my legal practice in Mumbai. It was during my first professional year as a Lawyer in the 1990s that I ventured out on a pilgrimage into the Himalayas during the summer vacation for the courts. My first itinerary was Swamy Chinmayananda's Guru's Ashram "Tapovan" at Hardwar. On my trip from Delhi to Hardwar, I had purchased a book titled: "Living with the Himalayan Masters" by Swami Rama from the New Delhi Railway Station, which I read during my journey to Hardwar. Thus, after a day's sojourn at Tapovan Ashram, I visited the Ashram of Swami Rama from where I went to the Ashram of Swami Shivananda. I was there at the Ashram of Sivananda for a couple of days when I heard from all the senior monks regarding the visit and sojourn of Dr. Abdul Kalam, whom they spoke with great respect and reverence as someone with deeper understanding of India's spiritual ethos. They prophesied that Dr. Kalam would one day become a "great man" with the blessings of Swami Sivananda.

I have been associated with the Ashram of Sri Sathya Sai Baba of Puttaparthy, which is my second home-town, for over three decades. On my two pilgrimages during the period when Sri Sathya Sai Baba was in his body at his Ashram, Prasanti Nilayam, I could see Dr. Abdul Kalam and hear his speech that he delivered at the convocation of Sri Sathya Sai University, in close proximity. Incidentally, this University is the only University in India which

is rated by NAAC with the highest standard of rating, viz. "A++".
Dr. Kalam was, in short, an ardent devotee of Sri Sathya Sai Baba.

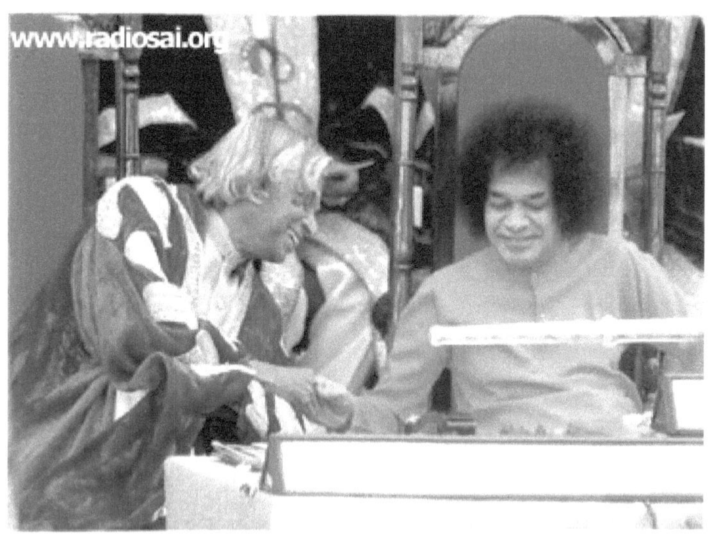

Dr. APJ Abdul Kalam with Sri Sathya Sai Baba at a Convocation
ceremony of Sri Sathya Sai University
[Photo Courtesy: www.radiosai.org]

It is pertinent to mention here that Sri Sathya Sai Baba
discouraged his devotees from watching Television. Sai Baba
often called Television as "Tele-Visham" (Poison). The devotees
of Sri Sathya Sai Baba in India are aware that Dr. Kalam never
watched TV and instead he often kept with him a small transistor
radio to hear AIR news from time to time. He was also a born-
again vegetarian.

Apart from being a great scientist, Dr. Kalam was also a
Great Management Guru and a motivator. In this regard I would
like to quote below an anecdote from his life, which happened

about four or five decades ago. The anecdot may not be in the public domain which was made as a lesson in the text book of Bal Vikas Schools run by Sri Sathya Sai Baba Trust.

QUOTE:

HUMILITY IS THE HALLMARK OF THE GREAT

Scientists at the rocket launching station at Thumba were in the habit of working for nearly 12 to 18 hours a day. There were about seventy such scientists working on a project. All the scientists were really frustrated due to the pressure of work and the demands of their boss, but everyone was loyal to him and they did never think of quitting the job.

One day, a scientist came to his boss, and told him: "Sir, I have promised my children that I will take them to the exhibition which is going on in our township. So I would like to leave office at 5.30 p.m.".

His boss replied: "OK. You are permitted to leave the office early today".

As usual, this scientist got fully absorbed into his duties without realizing the passage of time and when he felt that he was close to completion of his job in hand for the day, he looked at his watch. The time was 8.30 p.m.! Suddenly, he remembered of the promise he had given to his children in the morning before leaving his home. He looked for his boss. He was not there. Having told him in the morning itself, he hurriedly closed everything and ran to his home.

On the way to his home deep within himself, he was feeling guilty for having disappointed his children. He reached home, heavily panting for breath. The children were not around. His wife alone was sitting in the hall, reading some magazines. The situation was explosive as any talk to his wife would boomerang on him. He tiptoed to her.

*His wife asked him: "Would you like to have coffee or shall I straight away serve dinner if you are hungry?" The man replied with little hesitation: "If you would like to have coffee, I too would have, **BUT WHAT ABOUT THE CHILDREN?".** The wife let out a roaring laughter and asked him: "You don't know? Your Director himself came here at 5.30 p.m. and had taken the children to the exhibition. They are very happy and are fast asleep now; don't disturb them".*

What had really happened was:

The boss who granted permission to this scientist was observing him working seriously at 5.30 p.m – the time at which he was permitted to leave for home. The boss thought to himself, "this person will not leave his work, but if he has promised his children, they should enjoy the visit to the exhibition". So the boss took the lead in taking the children to the exhibition himself.

> *The boss does not have to do it every time. But once it is done, mutual trust and loyalty is established. That is why all the scientists at Thumba Space Centre continued to work under the boss with great dedication and devotion even though the stress was tremendous.*
>
> *By the way, can you hazard a guess as to who the Boss was??*
>
> *It was none other than Dr. APJ Abdul Kalam.*

UNQUOTE

I have realized over the years that speaking about any anecdote from the life of Dr. Kalam is of great mass inspiration. I have a personal experience in this regard which I would briefly touch upon here:

During the first year of his Presidency, in the year 2002, I was invited by one of the prominent colleges of Mumbai, viz. "Sree Nayaraya Guru College of Commerce" at Chembur, Mumbai, to deliver a public talk at its sprawling auditorium on the eve of an annual function.

Incidentally, the college was established in the pious memory of a great social reformer and Saint of Kerala, Sri Narayana Guru, who dedicated his whole life to bring mankind as a unified cohesive divine sparkle of God Almighty and worked tirelessly to achieve his goal on the theme of "One Caste, One Religion, One God For Man". The College, which is one of the largest, oldest and permanently affiliated to the University of Mumbai, is a classic living example of the Guru's philosophy and object.

The majority of the students of the college are Muslims hailing from the socio-economically weaker segments of Chembur and the neighboring Govandi. I have personally seen those Muslim students shun the religious obscurantism and fully merge themselves within the mainstream life, considering themselves as part and parcel of great cultural ethos and tradition of ancient civilization of India. For instance, during the period when various Muslim fundmamentalist organizations across India objected to the recital of "Vande Mataram" (Salute to the Motherland) by Muslim students, these students echoed these words in chorus in reverence to the Mother India at all College functions.

Thus, during the year 2002, I delivered a public talk, addressing students their parents and friends. The huge hall was packed to its capacity. The topic of my speech was "The Spiritual Law of Success". The major part of my speech was centered on the life of Dr. Abdul Kalam and similar other personalities who came up in life in spite of grinding poverty and adversities in life. During the course of my speech I had also mentioned that Dr. Kalam had donated his entire salary which he drew in the capacity of the President of India of one year to the Charitable Trust being run by Mata Amritananandamayi of Kerala for social services like the establishment of hospitals, schools, reliefs for natural calamities around the world, etc. etc. [It is pertinent to mention here that Dr. Kalam had never spoken about this to anybody and I came to know about it only because of my association with the Ashram at that time]. What stuck in my mind was regarding the response of the students to my speech. For most part of the hour-long speech, they stood up and gave a standing ovation. In fact, I had mistakenly thought it as a sort of heckling behaviors of the students. However, the then Principle of the college, Dr. Ravindran, and the entire college faculty unanimously opined that the speech, centered on the life of Dr. Abdul Kalam, was very much inspiring and the students very much appreciated it.

In life, as in death, Dr. Kalam epitomized India's secular and spiritual values. He was a role model of India's age old philosophy of simple living and high thinking, hard-work and devotion to duties, morality, wisdom and benevolence. Millions of youth were motivated by his inspiring speeches around the country and many parts of the world, apart from numerous motivational books authored by him.

One of the significant aspects of his inimitable personality was that, Dr. Kalam has never ever entertained any negative thoughts. His thoughts were invariably positive and optimistic which gave great inspiration to those who were facing adversities in life. An oft-quoted saying of Dr. Kalam is reproduced here:

QUOTE:

If you Fail, Never give up because F.A.I.L. means "First Attempt In Learning".

End is not the end. In fact E.N.D. means "Effort Never Dies".

If you get NO as an answer, Remember N.O. means "Next Opportunity".

| *So let's be positive* |

UNQUOTE:

Indeed Dr. APJ Abdul Kalam was an outstanding world citizen and a glittering star of India, to be emulated by every Indian irrespective of religion, region, caste or creed. The perpetuation of the legacy left behind him is a duty of every citizen of India.

MAY 2014

[An unedited version of this essay was published in "Hindu Voice" in its May 2014 issue]

THE IDEA OF ACADEMICS BECOMING IGNORAMUS: THE CASE OF 75 ACADEMICS WRITING TO "THE INDEPENDENT", U.K., ASSASINATING THE CHARACER OF NARENDRA MODY

---

*T*he Independent, U.K., in its edition dated 23rd April 2014 carried a letter jointly written by 75 academics of Indian Origin, serving at various Universities in the U.K. titled: *"The Idea of Modi in power fills us with dread"*.

It is amazing, to say the least, that there is not even an iota of truth or even a single cogent argument in the whole letter, which can be termed even by a child as an utter stupidity. This nonsense is not worth even for taking a cursory glance at it. However, in order to drive home the gravity of the stupidity, a few of the contentions raised in the letter, published in The Independent, are taken at random and are analyzed below:

Ignorence No.1: "There is widespread agreement about the authoritarian nature of Modi's rule in Gujarat".

The letter did not spell out as to the group of people or citizens amongst whom the purported "widespread agreement" arrived at. Is it confined to these 75 self-styled "intellectuals" of Indian origin? Elementary commonsense is that if at all there is even an iota of authoritarianism, how could Mody win numerous elections in the State of Gujarat for over twelve years, each time with larger margins of votes than the earlier election? Are these these rogue elements insinuate that all those inhabitants in the State of Gujarat are fools to vote to power Narendera Modi in spite of his allegedly being "Authoritarian"? These stupids, calling themselves "academics" seems to have not even an elementary idea of the term "authoritarianism". The common dictionary definition of the word "authoritarianism" is: "Strictly <u>forcing</u> people to obey a set of <u>rules or laws that are often wrong or unfair</u>". Do these 75 simpletons know that there are judiciary in India who are ever watchful to the conducts of the political masters and restrain them from their erring conducts not only at the State levels but also at the Central level; that there are well-informed public spirited citizens in India who would at the very moment when they detect any wrong or unfair rules or laws having been forced down the throats of any citizens by the political masters restrain them by way of Public Interest Litigation, etc.? Can these 75 morons point out even a single instance wherein either the judiciary or the public took up any action against Narendra Modi for over ten years of his government on the ground of adopting any rules or laws that are wrong or unfair? Do these imbeciles know that there is something called "Constitution of India" and if any government in power deviate even slightly beyond the purview of the constitution, there would be *suo motu* action by the judiciary to contain such unconstitutional action, apart from the effective checks and balance system prevailing in the parliamentary form of democracy in India? It is strange, to say the least, that these so-called academics were/are totally silent on the authoritarian regime and the emergency unleashed by Congress Prime Minister, Indira Gandhi, in the recent past just for clinging to power. It would have been ideal had these 75 fools prior to sending their joint-letter to such a pulp fiction newspaper, controlled by Leftist ideologues, called: "The Independent", consulted at least a KG-going child in India to understand the exact connotation of the term "authoritarianism" vis-à-vis Narendra Modi.

<u>Ignorence No.2: "We recall the extreme violence by the Hindu Right in Gujarat in 2002 which resulted in the deaths of at least 1,000 people, mostly Muslims".</u>

Why can't these stupid "recall" the daylight murders of innocents Sikhs, numbering over 8000 by the elite members of Congress in the recent past, viz. in 1984, as reported by the international media? "The Time" of the U.K. reported about the genocide in Punjab as: *"Such wide-scale violence cannot take place without police help. Delhi Police, whose paramount duty was to upkeep law and order situation and protect innocent lives, gave full help to rioters who were in fact working under able guidance of sycophant congress leaders like Jagdish Tytler and HKL Bhagat".*

The Wikipedia reported as follows:

QUOTE

After the assassination of Indira Gandhi on 31 October 1984 by two of her bodyguards, anti-Sikh riots erupted the following day. They continued in some areas for several days, killing more than 3000 Sikhs in New Delhi alone and an estimated 8000 – 20,000 Sikhs in total were killed across 40 cities in India.

UNQUOTE

There are truckloads of incontrovertible documentary evidences against all these prominent Congress ministers, clearly establishing their direct complicity in the genocide of Sikhs. And yet they were allowed to roam freely by the successive Congress governments in power. The Human Rights Watch of the USA reported as recently as in 2011 that the "Government of India is yet to prosecute those responsible for the mass killings of the Sikhs". All the Congress leaders, particularly the United Progressive Alliance (UPA) government headed by an Italian fundamentalist Christian woman, whose independent work experience was that of a Waitress at a U.K. Restaurant prior to her success in hooking a man, called Rajiv Gandhi, as her husband, wanted to pass the buck upon someone else for the large scale 1984 Sikh genocide in Punjab and Haryana on the assassination of Indira Gandhi. Indira Gandhi's son, Rajiv Gandhi's response to the carnage was: "When a big tree falls, the earth shakes". Even a recent instance shows that Rajiv Gandhi's widow, presently heading the UPA government, during her sojourn in the USA, the United States District Court for the Southern District of New York sought to serve upon her a summons to appear before it so as to examine the complicity of her in-laws and Congress Ministers in the Punjab and Haryana anti-Sikh carnage upon a petition filed by the American-based NGO, Sikhs for Justice. However, she sneaked out of the USA and made an affidavit, falsely stating under oath that she was not in the USA during the time when the summons was sought to be served upon her, which would attract prosecution for perjury upon her. In fact, the magnitude of the premeditated planning, violence, cruelties, death and destruction of properties at the behest of the Congress party in power was much larger in Punjab compared to the Gujarat's spontaneous violence which stemmed from the cold-blooded killings of innocent Hindu train pilgrim passengers, mostly women and children. In contrast, Modi has openly challenged that if at all there is even a grain of truth in the allegations of his complicity either directly or indirectly in the alleged crime against minority he can be publically flogged to death, which he kept on demanding since the year 2002.

There are several prominent Muslim leaders in India who are active members of BJP. M.J. Akbar, a former bureaucrat and a renowned writer is the national spokesman of BJP. At an interview he gave to a foreign T.V. Channel he declared: *"In ten years, no other politician has gone through so much scrutiny as Narendera Modi. He was scrutinized by police, central government, CBI, court-appointed institution, etc. etc. All of them have jointly and severally given clean chits to Narendra Modi".*

The analysis made by Akbar through his investigative journalistic eyes has now vindicated. In the highly researched book "Narendra Modi: A Political Biography" by Andy Marino, a Western scholar, containing incontrovertible documentary evidences, it was established that **"Narendera Modi wanted to**

quit as C.M., saying: *It was unfair on the people of the State"*, and that *"No court has come even close to establishing his complicity in the violence".* Modi did whatever he could do in his capacity as the C.M. of the Gujarat State to avert the violence. In fact, immediately after the Godhra train carnage he wasted no time in appearing on *Doordarshan,* appealing to the people to maintain peace and calm and not to react, threatening that any act of violence would be sternly dealt with. In addition, no stone was left unturned by Modi in earnestly requesting the Congress Chief Ministers of neighboring States to send adequate contingents of their police forces to Gujarat to contain the violence. However, those Congress Chief Ministers, particularly the then Congress C.M. of Madhya Pradesh, Digvijay Singh, adamantly refused to accede to his requests.

Coming back to the genocide of Sikhs by the Congress party workers, it would seem that these 75 myopic academics consider Sikhs of India as "Sick", not worth for protection from the so-called human rights violations.

It is amazing, to say the least, that every year there has been an "Amritsar genocide Commomoration March" by the Sikh community of London under the very nose of these sick-minded "intellectuals" of Indian Origin living in London. It would also seem that these "academics" are unable to see such yearly march while sitting in the balconies of their respective houses in London and shedding crocodile tears on the alleged plight of Muslims in India.

<u>Ignorence No.3:</u> "Narendra Mody is embedded in the Hindu Nationalist movement, namely RSS, with its history of

inciting violence against Muslims. Some of this group stand accused in recent terrorist attacks against civilians".

A week prior to writing this joint letter by the 75 self-styled intellectuals, Blair, the former British Prime Minister of U.K. (wherein these idiots presently carry on their livelihood undeservedly), called upon the world community to contain "the growing jehadi threats from Radicalized Islam" in England. In fact, there are on an average 40 reported and unreported terrorists attacks per month in India, particularly during the period of UPA regime. In a 2014 US National Counter-Terrorism Centre publication, titled: "A Chronology of International Islamic Terrorism", it was stated: "India suffered more terrorist attacks than any other country". The million dollar questions that would arise are: Have these 75 simpletons ever raised even an eye-brow or even a single word in condemning the terrorist violence in India and why can't these idiots appreciate the fact that after the major Akshardham terrorist attacks in Gujarat about a decade ago there were no more such terrorist strikes in that State on account of the able administration given by Modi? Incidentally, the purblind view of these simpletons on "RSS" is totally against the real nature, characteristics and history of RSS. In this regard these stupid academics should have read some of the observations made by the true, secular intellectuals of India, notably the Supreme Court Judges regarding RSS, published in the mainstream print media like "The Times of India". One such observation made by a former Senior Supreme Court Judge, K.T. Thomas, taken from The Times of India is quoted here for the enhancement of capacities of the corrupted brain of these so-called "intellectuals":

At a function attended by RSS Chief Mohan Bhagat, Justice Thomas observed:

QUOTE:

I am a Christian. I was born as a Christian and practice that religion. I am a church going Christian. But I have also learnt many things about RSS. There is a smear campaign that RSS was responsible for Gandhi's assassination, just because the assassin was once upon a time an RSS worker and the organization was completely exonerated by the court. Can the entire Sikh community be held responsible for Indira Gandhi's assassination? I became an admirer of the RSS in 1979 when I was posted as a District Judge of Kozkhikode. Simple living and high thinking is the hallmark of RSS. During the emergency, RSS was the only non-political organization which fought against it. We owe very much to RSS for sacrificing many lives for regaining our fundamental rights..."

UNQUOTE

As recently as 2018 Justice Thomas observed at a public function as: "After Army, RSS keeps Indians safe" (The Times of India issue dated January 4, 2018).

Similarly, Late Dr. A.P.J. Abdul Kalam, the former President of India, who was the quintessence of Sanadhan Dharma, and an apostle of peace, paid number of visits to the Headquarters of RSS when he was alive.

A photo snap taken at one such occasion is reproduced below:

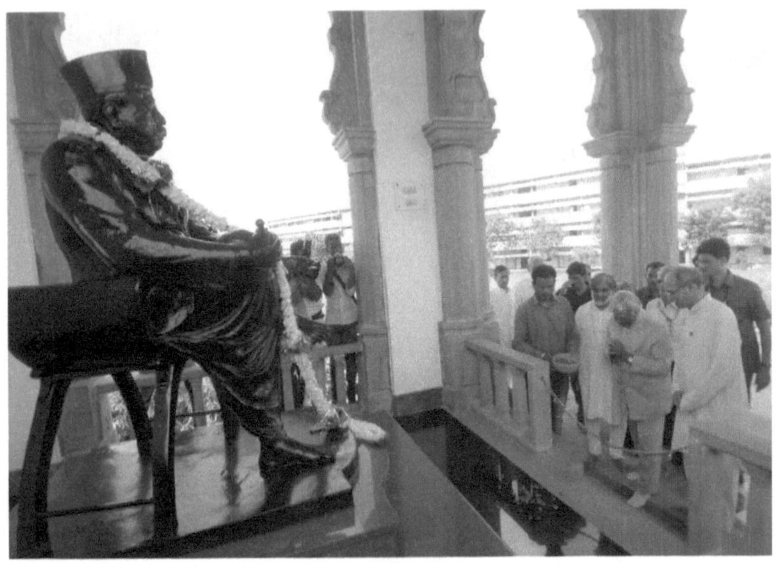

Dr. A.P.J. Abdul Kalam, visiting RSS headquarters and offering tributes to its Founder Dr. Keshav Baliram Hedgewar at "Smruti Mandir" in Nagpur.
[Photo courtesy: Google Images]

<u>Ignorence No.4: "The Modi-BJP model of economic growth involves close linking of government with big business, generous transfer of public resources to the wealthy and powerful, and measures harmful to the poor".</u>

One of the newspapers of India termed these 75 irresponsible U.K. academics as "Left-oriented academics, teaching at U.K. universities". Aravind Kejriwal has also been termed by the media as a "left-oriented activist". Kejriwal has openly declared at all public meetings that he addressed that "the UPA Government under an uneducated Western Christian woman has looted the resources of India in such a colossal scale that the total loot would be larger than the loot of India by the British colonial masters of nearly two century, which has greatly harmed the poor of India". In these realities, can anybody make out even a semblance of any cogency in the argument contained in the letter? On the contrary, there cannot be even a single instance of corruption or any financial bungling on the part of the decade-long government of Narendra Modi in Gujarat. The question, therefore, is: are these self-styled intellectuals of Indian origin not concerned with the large-scale corruption and looting of country's resources indulged in by the congress/UPA government and consequently harming the poor by the heavy burden of galloping inflation, never before witnessed by India?.

<u>Ignorence No.5</u>: "Some of Modi's close aides have been convicted for their involvement, and legal proceedings are ongoing in the Gujarat High Court which may result in Modi being indicted for his role. He has never apologized for hate speech or contemptuous comments about various groups – including Muslims, Christians, woman and Dalits. His closest aide has been censured recently by India's Election Commission for hate speech used in his election campaign.

These comments, made without furnishing any documentary evidences or even citing a single instance, in spite of the fact that Modi has been demanding to show him even a semblance of evidence regarding the truth of these allegations, are like the chattering of a psychopath.

Incidentally, "the closest academic aids" of these idiots are one Rajat Gupta who is presently serving life-long jail term in the USA for financial bungling. Does it mean that these idiots are involved in the crime committed by Rajat Gupta?.

<u>Ignorence No.6: "We are deeply concerned at the implications of a Narendra Modi-led BJP government for democracy, pluralism and human rights in India"</u>

By "Human Rights" these simpletons seems to be referring to only Muslims and not of the genocide of over 8000 innocent Sikhs on the streets of Punjab, Haryana and New Delhi by the high-profile congress ministers and the idiots seems to suggest that Sikhs are not entitled to protection from "Human rights violations".

Similarly in 1990s, the Hindus of Kashmir, who were the original inhabitants and sons of the soil of the State, were driven out of their hearth and home by the Jihadi Muslims of the State and they were made to live in sordid conditions in camps for refugees in various parts of India. Are these blind academics not concerned with the human rights of these innocent Hindus who were victims of Islamic terrorism?.

<u>Ignorence No.7: Modi victory would likely mean greater moral policing, especially of women, increased censorship and vigilantism".</u>

Apart from this remark being a figment of crude and wild imagination, these contentions are stemming from the fact that all these 75 so-called people of Indian origin are wallowing in the decadent Western cultures such as promiscuous life-styles, homosexuality, gay marriage, pub-cultures, dating cultures, blue-film watching, liquor consumption, etc. etc. Nobel Laureate Amartya Sen whole-heartedly supported gay marriage, homosexuality, etc. for Indians. Having thoroughly enjoyed these sense gratifying life-styles of the U.K. these idiots are now apprehensive of they and their offspring facing "moral policing" under Narendra Modi's rule whenever they visit India. In fact, during the whole UPA government rule, all these Western decadent cultures were freely flowing into India. It was Anand Grover, formerly a British citizen of Indian origin, who was instrumental for the repeal of Section 377 of the Indian Penal Code, 1860, which restricted homosexuality in India. In the internet this former British citizens was described as "The Lawyer who fought the 377 Law and won". Mr. Grover had declared himself as "the Honorary Gay" in the internet. One would wonder whether he is also a "Professional Gay". On winning his case for the repeal of Section 377 of the Indian Penal Code (IPC) at the Allahabad High Court, Grover gave interviews to U.K. T.V. channels, calling the judgment as "Historic Moment for India", as though making the Indian masses to indulge in homosexuality is the magic wand by which the Indian poverty could be removed. Presently the Hon'ble Supreme Court has again made the said Section 377 remain in the statute book of India. It is everybody's knowledge that the so-called Indian origin academics are working round the clock to get the said law again repealed through a curative petition before the Supreme Court, so as to spread the cultures of homosexuality, gay marriage, etc. into the ancient, traditional, spiritualized societies of India.

During the earstwhile UPA regime New Delhi was being nicknamed as "Rape Capital of India" and India as "The Rape Capital of the World". As a result of these realities the number of overseas female tourists coming into India is getting drastically reduced day by day on account of fear of female tourists getting raped at the Airport itself. The incident at New Delhi during the

UPA regime involving a young woman (Nirbhaya) is a classic case in this regard. This young woman was caught hold off by the male crew members of a transport bus at night and under the cover of darkness she was subjected to turn-by-turn gang-rape and after fully getting satisfied of their sexual cravings they threw her out. [It is pertinent to state here that the mothers of all those boys accused of the crime emphatically stated before the Trial Court that none of the boys have had any past history of any sexual misconducts]. This incident, to say the least, is just a casting of shadows of the coming events. In short, on account of the militant feminism being carried on by Indian feminists with the active financial support, encouragement and full cooperation of the Western feminists under the overall supervision of the Western Christian woman who had headed the Indian government, the women on the move in India would be treated as a "Use-and-throw product" in the days to come – like that of Nirbhaya at New Delhi, the 2012 rape and murder of a young Software Engineer with Tata Consultancy Services, Miss Esther Anuhya at Mumbai committed during the first UPA regime, etc.

In fact the aforesaid realities of India are solely on account of the unrestrained flow of Western cultures into India during the UPA government headed by an Italian Christian woman. Women getting boozed up at pub and then moving through out India with least regards of time and place, boys and girls living without marriage, single-motherhood, homosexuality, etc. etc. were the Western cultures which were freely flowing into India since the time the UPA government came to power. In fact, Dr. Subramanian Swamy, former Professor at Harward University, openly called Priyanka Gandhi, who was contesting election in 2014 and if elected she is likely to become a cabinet rank minister, as "pub cultured alcoholic". In other words the crime against women in India is mainly because of the total absence of "moral policing". In any case, it is elementary common sense that whatever be the circumstances, Narendra Modi will never be able to enforce the type of moral policing as existing in countries like Saudi Arabia because of the democratic principles of India. Hence the apprehensions of these 75 idiots of "moral policing of the type imagined by them" are based on the figment of their strange imagination.

It is a mystery to me as to how these stupid got into the noble profession of teaching at the elite Universities in the U.K. I am deeply concerned at the implications of these so-called "intellectuals" corrupting the minds of the youngsters pursuing education under the care of these misplaced academics. In fact, several commonwealth laws and regulations have banned the academics tinkering with the politics of the countries of their origin on the laudable objective that the youngsters should have the ability to cultivate independent thought process rather than being subject to the brain-washing by their teachers. It is high time that the concerned Universities wherein these characters are purportedly employed take stern actions against them. If not, it would be seriously detrimental to the fare name and fame of these institutions of academic excellence.

In the meantime the Indian patriots and People of Indian Origin, who are well-wishers of India living anywhere in the world, are sincerely called upon to keep a watch upon the affairs and conducts of these sense-gratifying Non Required Indian (NRI) "intellectuals". They are to be blacklisted with regard to any academic or other programs associated with the government under Narendra Modi in India, as and when he comes to power.

The list containing the names and the institutions represented by these 75 simpleton academics is given in the table below:

LIST OF INDIAN ORIGIN ACADEMICS WHOSE JOINT-LETTER WAS PUBLISHED BY "THE INDEPENDENT", U.K.

<u>NOTE</u>: I have deliberately avoided the titles "Prof" & "Dr." from the names of these 75 simpletons as it is likely that these titles might have been self-awarded ones and even if they have genuinely acquired these academic titles from any recognized Universities it will not have any significance with regard to the internal subject matter of India about which these people are abysmally ignorant.

Sr. No.	NAME	INSTITUTION PURPORTEDLY REPRESENTED
1	Chetan Bhatt	London School of Economics
2	Kalpana Wilson	London School of Economics
3	Sumi Madhok	London School of Economics
4	Gautam Appa	London School of Economics
5	Shakuntala Banaji	London School of Economics
6	Rashmi Varma	University of Warwick
7	Shirin Rai	University of Warwick
8	Dwijen Rangnekar	University of Warwick
9	Goldie Osuri	University of Warwick

10	Gurminder Bhambra	University of Warwick
11	Pablo Mukherjee	University of Warwick
12	Bishnupriya Gupta	University of Warwick
13	Murad Banaji	University of Portsmouth
14	Leena Kumarappan	London Metropolitan University
15	Subir Sinha	School of Oriental and African Studies
16	Amrita Shodhan	School of Oriental and African Studies
17	Brenna Bhandar	School of Oriental and African Studies
18	Jairus Banaji	School of Oriental and African Studies
19	Rachel Harrison	School of Oriental and African Studies
20	Alessandra Mezzadri	School of Oriental and African Studies
21	Gilberty Achcar	School of Oriental and African Studies
22	Rahul Rao	School of Oriental and African Studies
23	Phiroze Vasunia	University College London

Sr. No.	NAME	INSTITUTION PURPORTEDLY REPRESENTED
24	Srirupa Roy	University of Gottingen
25	Navtej Purewal	University of Manchester
26	Ravi Hensman	University of Manchester
27	Anandi Ramamurthy	University of Central Lancashire
28	Amit S. Rai	Queen Mary, University of London
29	Priyamvada Gopal	University of Cambridge
30	Joya Chatterji	University of Cambridge
31	Meena Dhanda	University of Wolverhampton
32	Hugo Gorringe	University of Edinburgh
33	Talat Ahmed	University of Edinburgh
34	Kerthikeyan Damodaran	University of Edinburgh
35	Nilina Deb Lal	University of Edinburgh
36	Nikki Dunne	University of Edinburgh
37	Patricia Jeffery	University of Edinburgh
38	Radhika Govinda	University of Edinburgh
39	Mary F. Hanlon	University of Edinburgh
40	Christopher Harding	University of Edinburgh
41	Gaia van Hatzfeldt	University of Edinburgh
42	Delwar Hussain	University of Edinburgh
43	Bethany Jennings	University of Edinburgh

44	Daniel O'Connor	University of Edinburgh
45	Kanchana N. Ruwanpaura	University of Edinburgh
46	Lauren Wilks	University of Edinburgh
47	Richard Whitecross	University of Edinburgh
48	Suprurna Banerjee	University of Edinburgh
49	Catriona Ellis	University of Edinburgh
50	Rowan Ellis	University of Edinburgh
51	Maggie Morrison	University of Edinburgh
52	Gargi Battacharyya	University of East London
53	Barbara Harriss-White	University of Oxford
54	Maan Barwa	University of Oxford
55	Nandini Gooptu	University of Oxford
56	Pritam Singh	Oxford Brookes University

57	Rohit K. Dasgupta	University of the Arts London
58	Shamira A. Meghani	University of Leeds
59	Amrita Dhillon	King's College London
60	Srila Roy	University of Witwatersrand
61	Sharad Chari	University of Witwatersrand
62	Vedita Cowaloosur	Stellenbosch University
63	Dibyesh Anand	University of Westminster
64	Nitasha Kaul	University of Westminster
65	Bhabani Shankar Nayak	Glasgow Caledonian University

66	Bashabi Fraser	Edinburgh Napier University
67	Shishir Nagaraja	University of Birmingham
68	Eurig Scandrett	Queen Margaret University
69	Steve Taylor	Northumbria University
70	Sukhwant Dhaliwal	University of Bedfordshire
71	Anderson Jeremiah	University of Lancaster
72	Anindya Raychaudhuri	University of St. Andrews
73	Sharika Thiranagama	Stanford University
74	Nayanika Mookherjee	Durham University
75	Uday Chandra	MPI-MMG, Gottingen

FEBRUARY 2016

[An unedited version of this Report was published in "Hindu Voice" in its February 2016 issue]

THE "MAKE IN INDIA WEEK" – FEBRUARY 13-18, 2016 HELD AT MUMBAI: THE MOTHER OF ALL ENTERPRENEURAL EVENTS IN THE WORLD

"This is the Best time ever to be in India and it is even better to Make in India. We have laid all round emphasis on Ease of Doing Business… On the issue of safety of properties and rights, we have already enacted a law for fast tracking of arbitration proceedings"

Narendra Modi, Hon'ble Prime Minister of India.

At no point of time in the history of the world, has there been such a mammoth entrepreneurial event, called "Make in India" Week, held at the MMRDA Grounds and at the sprawling

Girgaum Chowpatty, bordering the Arabian sea and kissed by the soft waves under the bright sun of the spring season of India.

On several counts the event was an unprecedented conglomeration of entrepreneurial think-tank from across the world. The Lion Mascot of the "Make in India" has literally come to life and kept roaring through-out the week-long event. Having lived and travelled through many parts of the world in the past, it was a sheer pleasure for me to move through the kaleidoscopic gatherings of divergent international personalities with animated faces. It is indeed heartening that the Lion's share of the foreign direct investments, pegged at Rs.7.95 lakhs crore, was bagged by the State of Maharashtra, which is presently under the young dynamic leadership of the BJP Chief Minister, Devendar Fadnavis.

I have had chances to interact with few of these delegates from across the spectrum of Western and European industrialized societies. Some of them said to me that their basic idea for attending the event was for "testing the water" by directly hearing from the charismatic leader of India, Modi, before taking decisions on investment in India. I could easily discern from the mood of the delegates that it was largely on account of the goodwill generated on "Brand Modi" ever since Modi came to power that these people from across the world converged at the venue.

There were sizeable numbers of corporate executives from South Korea. I could snatch a brief chat with one of them. On asking him as to what were the favorable points in making investment in India by his country, he mentioned to me: "Your present regime is headed by a dynamic Prime Minister, loved and respected world over. Your country has the highest pool of young and talented youth for whom work is devotion. The labor cost in India is comparatively very reasonable. Your government has initiated various pragmatic steps for ease of doing business in India".

It was amazing to me that Modi had touched upon every minute aspects of the whole Initiative, including the legal aspects when he said: "We have already enacted a law for fast tracking of arbitration proceedings".

Each day of the week witnessed intellectually stimulating presentations made by competent Indian government officials, highly advanced brain storming sessions held at artistically and ergonomically erected pavilions which were packed to the maximum capacities at both the venues of the event. One of the highly successful seminars was the one on "Renewable Energy". The idea initiated by Modi for the establishment of International Solar Alliance (ISA) with its Headquarters in Mumbai stole the show. The ISA is the conglomeration of 121 solar-rich nations who came on a common platform on a cooperative venture never ever heard before, which would bring out highly advanced solar technologies and power, generating millions of jobs for Indians in the years to come.

It is pertinent to state here that The Art of Living Silver Jubilee Celebrations 2006 hosted at Bangalore, which I had attended, was billed as the largest cultural event in the world attended by people from 155 countries. However, the "Make in India" event in Mumbai was on a different footing – an event centered on an Initiative for all round acceleration of economic progress and prosperity for India and the world. The Event has also given a shot in the arms of various other initiatives of the government such as Skill India, Digital India, Start Up India, etc. etc., leading to all-round progress of the country as a whole.

Incidentally the Global Leadership Forum of The Art of Living World Cultural Festival 2016 is also being hosted close on the heels of concluding the Make in India week [on 12th & 13th March 2016] at New Delhi. I had come across many of the international participants and visitors at the Make in India event having come to India to take part in the Cultural Festival as well and therefore the timing of the Make in India Week was also highly laudable.

One of the significant reasons for such an unprecedented enthusiasm and interest on investing in India from across the world is undoubtedly the confidence reposed by the international entrepreneurs in the present BJP governments both at the State of Maharashtra and at the Centre. Indeed there was an invisible synergy flowing between the State and the Centre which contributed to the massive success of the event. BJP is already billed as the largest political party in the world, known world over. Had there been regional political parties like Shiv Sena or the Maharashtra Navnirman Sena (MNS), and if at all they would have hosted such an event, there would have been only lukewarm response or even losing of their face. It is everybody's knowledge that the credit for the historical evolution of Bombay (renamed as "Mumbai" on regional sentiments) as a major financial centre of India goes to the British and to the entrepreneurs from outside the State of Maharashtra. However, both the Shiv Sena and the MNS thrived only on regional pro-Marathis sentiments. Shiv Sena founder Bal Thackeray, who started his life as a

Mumbai-based cartoonist, carried on the propaganda of South Indian migrants flowing into the city and taking away white-collar jobs, although the employment-generating industries were owned and established by entrepreneurs from outside the State of Maharashtra like Tatas, Dalmias, Birlas, Ambanis, etc. from Gujarat, Rajasthan, etc. as well as by multinational corporations in establishing industries and trade enterprises in Maharashtra, and the lions-share of jobs were gone to the so called sons of the soil. While the Shiv Sena unleashed violence in the past against the South Indians, the MNS which is a break-away group of the Shiv Sena, unleashed violence against North Indians.

With regard to the regional political parties in Maharashtra like Shiv Sena, MNS, etc. playing parochial politics and wrecking havoc in the matter of providing employment to the locals, a classical illustration is that of the fate of Indian School of Business (ISB), which was jointly promoted by senior executives of McKinsey & Co., USA, and by international conglomeration of Western and European Universities.

When the Shiv Sena was in power during 1995-1999 the ISB was allotted a parcel of land at the then newly created satellite city of New Bombay. Accordingly, as they were about to construct their buildings and campus, the Shiv Sena Government put up various conditions to ISB for the sole benefits of local people such as to fill upto 80% of their manpower requirements by recruiting only the sons of the soil from Maharashtra, showing respects to the locals (asmita), etc. Being an international consortium of academicians, intellectuals and think-tanks, who are concerned only with competitive results and proven merit of the candidates for employment, they were unable to abide by the said conditions.

It was at this juncture that the then Chief Minister of the undivided Andhra Pradesh, Chandra Babu Naidu, invited the ISB to set up its campus in his State without any preconditions, giving them a huge track of land admeasuring 260-acre at a throw away price in the suburb of the city of Hyderabad. I have had a chance to visit the sprawling campus of ISB at the suburb, called "Gachibowli" in 1999. The ISB was given free hand in recruiting their manpower requirements, as a result of which the sons of the soil of the then Hyderabad and Andhra Pradesh (part of which is presently in Telangana) indirectly benefitted and economically flourished like never before. Lakhs of small petty local shop keepers, Tourist Homes, eating houses, laundry services, agricultural producers, skilled and unskilled laborers, artisans, domestic servants etc. benefited beyond the imagination of any economic planners. In addition, prices of the land and property owned by the villagers around the city of Hyderabad shoot up from the dealings of which the local people made huge profits. The ISB had also started a unique initiative by establishing what they call "Student Villages" around its campus which was in a way adoption of the villages aimed at amelioration of the lives of poor people of the State and enriching the overall livelihood of the villagers, the sons of the soil.

Thus, the international investment communities would have never wanted to take risk in investing in Mumbai or Maharashtra in the face of such stiff parochial/regional sentiments and violence, had there been regional political parties in power. It is therefore the obligations on the part of the electorates to elect only the BJP at the Centre as well in the States in the years to come for the larger interest of the country as a whole. I am sure that World's

Largest Political Party (BJP) will make India the largest industrial hub in the world in the near future, generating millions of job to the countrymen, bettering the lives of every Indian, particularly the sons of the soil.

When one could look back in retrospect since the year 2016 when the "Make-in-India Week" event was held, one could realize that indeed the event was a giganatic step towards nation-building initiatives. Since then the country is being transformed into a global design and manufacturing hub, providing millions of employments to able-bodied, highly competitive, computer saavy and educated youths of the country. There has been an overwhelming increase in production and services of gadgets and vehicles of daily use, as for example research shows that between the year 2016 and 2022 the country assembled two billion smart phones and feature phones which are in high demands from across the world, benefitting not only the country in earning foreign exchange but also millions of youth of the country in getting employed directly and indirectly.

NOVEMBER 2015

[An unedited version of this essay was published in "Organiser" in its Nov. 2015 issue]

KERALA: GOD'S OWN COUNTRY OR GODLESS COUNTRY?

*I*n the wake of Delhi Police raiding Kerala Bhavan Canteen upon receiving clues that its canteen regularly served beefs to the bigwigs coming from Kerala, which is a direct defiance of the law and contempt towards the popular sentiments of the majority citizens of India; the Chief Minister of Kerala, Oommen Chandy, threatening to drag the police to the Court, etc. may be of great news values and amusements for the entire Hindus of India, except those living in that State. It is, therefore, essential to analyze the historical background of the evolution of food preference of Keralites.

If a person hailing from outside the State of Kerala happened to visit Kerala and ask any native Hindu of the State, professing leftist ideologies, regarding Hinduism, he/she would instantly respond by saying: "Oh! Religion is opium of the masses" while one would have heard or read in the media regarding reports concerning the former Kerala Marxist Chief Minister, V.S. Achuthanandan, openly declaring during the election campaign just prior to his assuming power in 2006: "It is the Government's obligation to bring all the Mullahs and Madrassa Teachers of Kerala on the pay-roles of the Government". True to the communist promises, he had ensured that he implemented the said election manifesto/promise after coming to power, thereby slowly and steadily Islamizing the State.

Achuthanandan, the Marxist-CPI Politburo member and one-time C.M. of Kerala publicly declared that the CPI-M would never pursue Gandhian non-violence and in fact the said declaration is regarded by the political Pandits in India as a call that legitimized the culture of violence and counter violence which devalued the rule of law and/or expunged every semblance of human values from the State.

Kerala is the only State in the country which has a gory tradition of political annihilation, popularly known as "the game of toppling of governments". Ever since the formation of the State and the first communist government came to power in 1957, there were numerous instances of "formation of governments" mostly by political parties represented by the CPI-M and intermittently by IUML, President's Rule, Indian National Congress, Praja Socialist Party, etc. till today, who upon coming to power on the political stage turn-by-turn on this toppling game remains seated for strange periods, ranging from few days to five years like in a musical chair game. Except one or two governments, none of them ever completed the prescribed term of office. Nowhere in the entire world can one find such radical political thinking and consciousness based on foreign-originated ideologies as that of the citizens of Kerala, although the State is a small narrow strip of land bordering the Arabian Sea.

Thus, Kerala is purportedly India's cent percent literate State while at the same time it has the history of the highest number of political murders ["Political killings remain unabated in Kerala amid blessings of State leadership" – Deccan Herald, issue dated 3/12/2021]; it has double the cases of national average of suicide cases [Onmanorama, dated 17/09/2022]; it has the highest number of people afflicted with mental ailments and various psycho-somatic disorders [About 6% of the population of Kerala suffers from mental illness compared with the national average of 2% as per Performance Audit Report by the CAG of India, reported in The Times of India, dated 29/06/2011]. All the mental hospitals in the State are burst at the seams; it has the highest number of divorce rates amongst its married people – five cases every hour [The Quint, dated 23/06/2016]; it has the highest number of youths of opposite sex living together without marriage ever since earstwhile United Progressive Alliance-Parliament enacted the legislation, viz. "The Protection of Women From Domestic Violence Act, 2004" which for the first time in India introduced the concept and practice of living without marriage known as "Live-In-Relationship". This concept was the brainchild of militant feminist and India's foremost communist ideologue, Indira Jaising, who is an iconic woman amongst the college-going girls of Kerala. The High Court of Kerala has observed that the "Live-in-relationships are increasing in Kerala. Use and throw culture affects marital lives in the State"

[Mathrubhumi, dated 01/09/2022]; it is the No.1 in alcohol consumption [Onmanorama, dated 02/12/2021]; it has the highest number of loss of man-hours due to industrial unrest; it has organized the highest number of strikes and hartals at the instance of the caders of the rival political parties at the drop of a hat ["Hartal's own State: Frequent strikes in Kerala combined with populace's laid back attitudes often bring public life to halt" – First Post, dated 11/01/2019]; it has the highest number of youth addicted to drugs and substances abuse ["Alarming spike in drug abuse in Kerala" – The Indian Express, dated 30/01/2023]; it has the highest number of Rationalist NGOs which were established exclusively for attacking everything dear to Hinduism and its faith system, branding them as "superstition".

These Rationalists NGOs regularly carry on street activism like the "Mangalsutra Burning", "Beef Festivals", etc. in connivance with the communist ministers of the State with whole-hearted supports and encouragements from the entire Muslims of the State. In contrast, these so-called NGO Activists, never even remotely dared to whisper even a single word regarding any customs and practices which are originated in the hostile desert land in the Middle Eastern countries followed in the State by the Muslim citizens, knowing fully well that any such move on the part of these Comrade Activists would instantly invite revengeful attacks by way of chopping off limbs and instant beheading of such "Activists" by the hawk-eyed Islamic adherents of the State as in the recent case of chopping off the right hand of Prof. T.J. Joseph on the allegations of his "insult to Islam".

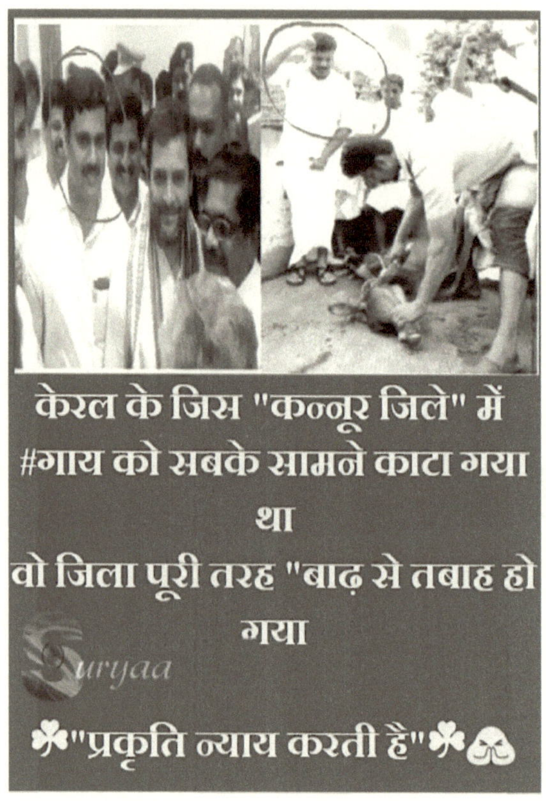

[A pregnant-cow is being slaughtered in the presence of Congress & Communist Stalwarts of the State in preparation for a beef festival]
[Image courtesy: Social media, WhatsApp post]

Political activism in Kerala starts at the High School level. In fact, the present C.M. of Kerala, Oommen Chandy, is credited to have the dubious distinction of carrying on the highest number of "Student Agitations" during his school and college days, qualifying him to become the C.M. of such a violent State. Chandy is a communist-sympathizer and a hard-core Christian, who opposed every move of sober-minded responsible Christian population of Kerala in discovering their original routes and coming back to Hinduism on their own accord ["Ghar Wapsi"] and fought tooth and nail at the Courts of Law against such, what he illogically termed "provoked conversion phenomena of the State", at the instance of the fundamentalist Christians of the State and Vatican. Chandy, who had undertaken numerous pilgrimages to Vatican during his tenure as the C.M. of the State, at the expenses of State Exchequer, is reported to have been funded by Vatican for stalling such "provoked conversion".

Sporadic political murders are a daily occurrence in the State, particularly in the northern District of Kannur from where all the communist stalwarts like A.K. Gopalan, Pinarayi Vijayan, etc. hails. Presently on account of the daily unabated murders, arsons and violence, such reports have lost its news-worthiness in the mainstream media, although the District is known amongst the Malayalees world over as "Killing Field". [Refer cover story titled: "Killing Fields of Kannur" published in "Organiser", issue dated 8th May 2016 and in numerous other Kerala-based non-communist newspapers and periodicals].

Kerala received a worldwide attention in 1956 when E.M. Shankaran Namboodiripad (popularly known as "EMS"), a top-class Brahmin, founded the "world's first democratically elected communist government". He lived and dedicated his entire life for the cause of popularizing communism in the State. It was in 1945 during his college life that EMS was enamored by the success of implanting communism in the Republic of San Marino (a tiny City State near Italy) that he focused every bit of his living moment, every breath that he took for espousing the cause of communism. His whole time, money, energy and efforts were directed to establish communist government in Kerala. For this purpose he adopted unprecedented down-to-earth strategies. Thus, with a view to wooing the Muslims of Kerala, he individually met each and every Muslim League leaders and sought their help for casting their votes in the democratic elections for the formation of Communist Government for which he promised them, in return, that upon his assuming power as Chief Minister of the State, the Muslims would be allowed to live in a separate District for themselves. Accordingly, the District of Malappuram for Muslims was carved out of the State during his tenure as the C.M.

Malappuram located in the central part of Kerala is a miniature of the Kingdom of Saudi Arabia where the Muslims are allowed to live undisturbed by carrying on the practice and propagation of Islam and to receive funding from wealthy Arabs of the Kingdom of Saudi Arabia and other Islamic countries around the world. In the District of Malappuram, one can find cow slaughter houses/shops at every nook and corner and a thriving leather industry. The unwritten law strictly enforced by threat and social ostracism in the District is that if at all any Muslim of the District wanted to sell his/her land it should be offered to only Muslims. Similarly if at all any of the remaining Hindus of the District wanted to sell his/her land it should be bought only by the Muslim.

Similarly, with a view to wooing the Dalits of Kerala, EMS adopted various drastic steps for the appeasement of the Dalits for garnering their votes in the democratic elections. Thus, he described Mahatma Gandhi as a "Hindu Fundamentalist". He fully agreed with the view of Kancha Illaiah, a prominent fire-brand Southern Dalit leader, that "Gandhi and his 'Brahmin' principles such as vegetarianism, swadeshi, cow protection, Brahmacharya and non-violence, etc. should be out-rightly shunned and discarded forever". EMS also regularly visited the houses of Dalits and took part in their social functions at which dishes of beef were served which he partook, affirming to them with his purported logic that "there is nothing wrong in eating beef when one can eat mutton". Thus, the hotels and restaurants across the length and breadth of Kerala started serving beef as a staple diet since the time Communists captured power in the State in the 1950s.

EMS during his life time often described RSS as "militant organization" without any shred of evidence and encouraged the CPI-M workers to attack RSS cadres, which is unabatedly being carried on almost every day. It is a curious case of the CPI-M workers belonging to Hinduism with its murderous violence-ridden foreign-originated ideologies of Karl Marx, Lenin, Mao, Cheguveera, etc. attacking RSS professing ancient Sanathan Dharma and nationalist ideologies which one can never find in any human settlement at any point of time in the history anywhere in the world. It is precisely this reason that Kerala had become a fertile ground for the Islamic fundamentalism to entrench deeply in the social milieu of the State, the intensity and enormity of which has since then alarmingly grew in the state. Presently the State is regarded as the nursery of Islamic fundamentalism, financially and logistically supported by Saudi Arabia, Pakistan and various other Islamic countries.

Thus, Abdul Nazer Mahdani is regarded as the Bin Laden of Kerala. He and his wife are reported to have carried out large scale bombings, killings and destruction of properties in

CPM-headed Kerala and in the neighboring States who are presently languishing in a Tamil Nadu Jail. Mahdani's political party, Peoples Democratic Party, is a coalition member of the Kerala government. He is highly respected by all the Communist and Congress stalwarts, including the present Communist-sympathizer Chief Minister, Oommen Chandy.

It is these realities that the food preference of the Comrade Hindus writ large in the State, which totally engulfed the vegetarianism of Kerala propagated by the State's Hindu Saints of the yore.

It is pertinent to state here that similar to the grabbing of world-wide attention on the formation of the first communist government in Kerala in the democratic India, it was in Kerala in post-independence of the country, which brought the first Islamic rule by Indian Union Muslim League (IUML) under C.H. Mohammed Koya, a hard-core Muslim fundamentalist. Strangely IUML was also a coalition partner in the defeated UPA government at the Centre under the leadership of Congress party, although it was the former Congress Parliament who carried out the amendment to the preamble to Indian constitution, thereby introducing the term "Secular", in spite of the fact that the Indian constitution has always been inherently secular on account of the ancient civilization, which equally embrace and celebrate all the religions on the concept of Vasudeva Kutumbakam (world is but ones own family), Samastha Lokha Sukhino Bhavantu (Let all humans and animals be happy) etc.

During the rule of IUML and by all the subsequent governments coming to power with the support of IUML, there were periodic overhauling of the books and other educational material prescribed for the educational institutions of the State funded by the government of Kerala. Thus, upon being discovered in any prescribed book or any reference carrying any negative portrayal of Islamic Intellectuals was out-rightly removed from the syllabus.

[There are numerous instances of "book burning" campaigns by Muslim students of the State in this regard]. Conversely any study concerning Hindu warriors and saints were strictly prohibited in the name of "secularism".

In fact it is only in Kerala that the text book concerning the life and time of Chatrapati Shivaji Maharaj the benevolent Founder of Maratha Empire of the 18th Century was banned throughout the State by a government Notification. It is pertinent to state here that during my childhood pursuing my educational life at a Government High School, prior to the consolidation of communist power in the State, I had to study the life of Hindu saints, warriors and Kings like Raja Harish Chandra, Shivaji, etc. whose lives were centered around human nature of compassion, love, spirituality, patriotism, moral philosophy, vegetarianism, etc. However, those studies were removed from the syllabus of educational institutions funded by the government in the name of "secularism" and in their places books pertaining to the life and time of public prostitutes [like "The Autobiography of a Sex Worker" By Nalini Jameela); the life and time of notorious thief (like "The Autobiography of Maniyan Pillai, The Thief") etc. were introduced. Likewise, a compilation of poems, viz. "Ode to the Sea" authored by a Saudi Arabian fundamentalist who was active in the high ranks of Al-Qaida, viz. Ibrahim Al-Rubaish alias Ibrahim Sulayman Muhammed Arbaysh, was an optional non-detailed book prescribed for the undergraduate students at Calicut University located at the heart of the Islamic District, Malappuram, where 90% of the regular students, staff, officers, V.C., etc. are per force Muslims.

The Nobel laureate Gabriel Garcia Marquez had opined that "Every country should have national heroes as otherwise it would be something like a house without doors". Kerala, however, has no real State or Indian national heroes. Its heroes were/are Marxist leaders of China, Russia, Cuba, etc. and heroes of Islamic countries like Saudi Arabia. Presently none of the youths who were born after the communist government consolidated power in the State knows anything about the ancient spirituality, human values-based scriptures, folklores of the renowned Hindu epics, etc. as they were consistently deprived of these studies of virtues by all the successive governments of the State in the name of "secularism".

For over fifty years of communist activism in Kerala, its ideologies of violence, atheism, purported rationalism, etc. have reached every nook and corner of the State. There is nothing called "collective consciousness of Godliness" amongst the Kerala Hindus as they are deprived of the understanding of the ancient spirituality of India through the educational system on account of false propaganda and pseudo secularist policies dictated by the communist stalwarts and Islamic fundamentalists. In this regard there is a curious case of the famous Guruvayoor Sri Krishna temple, which was brought under the athiest government from the time the communist government came to power and managed by a government appointed body called "Deveswom

Board". The majority of members of the Board are hard-core CPI-M politicians. The income generated by the temple by way of gold offerings and cash donations to the temple made by pilgrims mainly from outside Kerala, are being directed to fund various Islamic projects and payment of salary to the Mullahs and Madrassa teachers of Kerala under the threats from IUML of withdrawing their coalition support to the government. Incidentally, I have personally observed that Kerala Hindu Marxists after eating stomach-full of beef dishes from the restaurants located outside the temple complex entering the temple for "Darshan of the Krishna deity" just as a show business while at the same time the temple strictly prohibits the entry of any "Non-Hindus". It is pertinent to state here in this regard that I have pathetically witnessed several instances of even the Western ISKCON members being prohibited entry into the temple, although they and their family members are strict adherents of Sanathan Dharma and practising pure vegetarianism as per the teachings of Lord Krishna in Bhagavad Gita, disseminated by ISKCON.

The question, therefore, of beef being regularly served at the Kerala Bhavan canteen at the far-off New Delhi, in direct contempt of the popular sentiments of the Hindus of India as a whole, the threat held out by the Communist-minded, Christian fundamentalist, C.M. of the State of dragging the Delhi Police to the court, etc. are to be taken in the light of the factors which evolved the beef-based non-vegetarian food preference of Kerala Hindus.

Incidentally, it is interesting to state here that a few years ago a group of students from a College in Rajasthan established by Brahmakumari Sansthan visited Kerala on a study tour. They toured the entire length and breadth of the State for about a month. Thereafter, back in their college at a public function they observed that 90% of the non-vegetarian Hotels and Eateries run by the Hindus of the State display a board fixed at a conspicuous part of their establishments, carrying the words: "Fresh beef fried in ghee is available". These students opined that from this piece of external evidence one can easily gauge the internal mental aspects of Kerala Hindus. They further observed that many of these Hindus regularly visit Lord Krishna temples in the State which is purely a mechanical bodily function without even an iota of devotion and dedication, resulting into mockery of "Godliness".

APRIL 2016

[An unedited version of this essay was published in "HINDU VOICE" in its April 2016 issue].

FLUSH OUT THE ANTI-NATIONALS BY STRENGTHENING SEDITION LAWS IN THE LIGHT OF THE JNU EPISODE

---

*I*n no sovereign nation can one find that while her political head is paying homage to Martyr Jawans who sacrificed their lives in protecting the national monument, the iconic Parliament building, when attacked by the Islamic terrorists who had also slaughtered innocent citizens, the students at the nation's top Government University eulogizing and paying tributes/homage to the said terrorists!

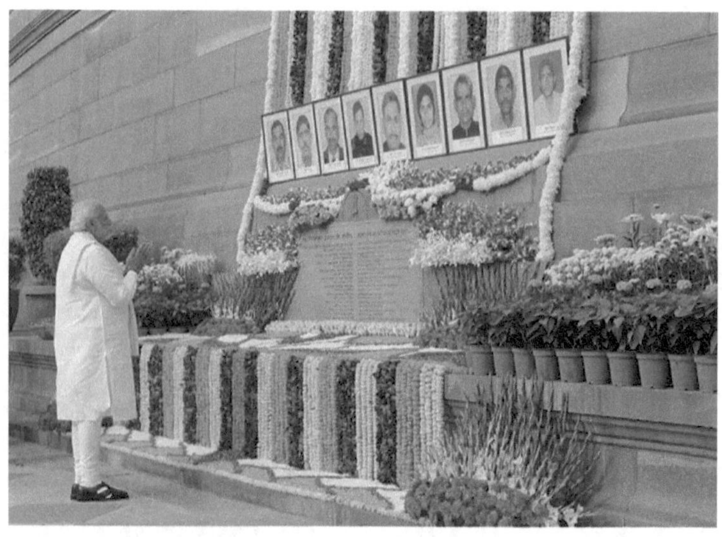

Prime Minister Narendra Modi pays homage in 2014 to those who lost their lives in the terrorist attack of Indian Parliament building.

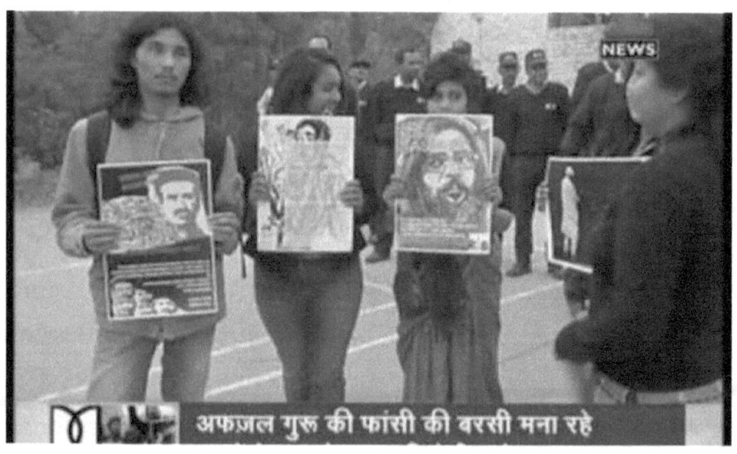

JNU students pay homage in 2016 to the terrorist, Afzal Guru, who attacked Indian Parliament building, killing several innocent Security Guards and civilians.

The youths in question in this bizarre incident are students having come under the banner of All India Students Federation (AISF), the student-wing of Communist Party of India (CPI) belonging to the Jawaharlal Nehru University (JNU) under its President, Kanhaiya Kumar.

The incident in question was a purported "Cultural Evening" for celebrating the first death anniversary of the convicted terrorist, Afzal Guru. The posters put up at various parts of the venue for organizing this event shows the picture of Kashmiri terrorists and it proclaimed that the event was organized for achieving the objectives of (i) rejecting "Brahmanical collective conscience", (ii) protesting against "judicial killings" of Afzal Guru and Maqbool Bhat, (iii) protesting against "the occupation of Kashmir by India", (iv) For expressing solidarity "with the struggle of the Kashmiri people" (read Muslims) (v) for espousing the cause of exercising "their democratic rights to self-determination".

A copy of one of the posters put up at the venue is reproduced below:

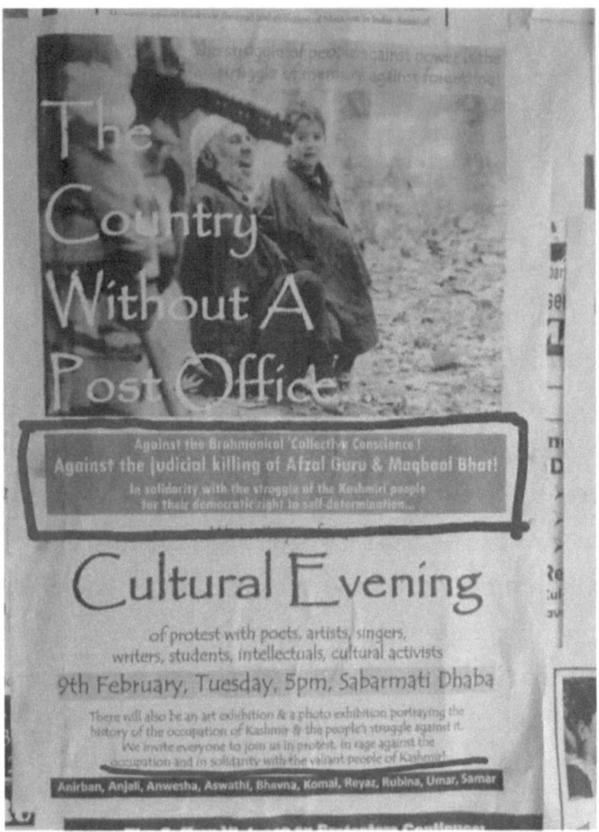

Let me at the outset analyze, in brief, the aforesaid objectives of the event, the purported Cultural Evening, in seriatim:

(i) **Rejecting "Brahmanical Collective Consciences":**
What does it mean? Are these idiots terming the "collective patriotic conscience amongst the citizens of India" as "Brahmanical Collective Conscience"? This new phrase coined by these rascals is fraught with catastrophic consequences, leading the country to a splintered entity as these anti-national elements themselves have expressed

through their slogans vociferously raised against India at the Cultural Evening.

(ii) **Protesting against "Judicial Killing":**

Are these so-called students of the Government University seeking to rise against the authority and decisions of the Apex Court in India by rubbishing its decisions? Has anybody ever thought that when the citizens of the country loss trust and confidence in the highest judiciary, particularly in a case involving life and death of its citizen, what would be the serious repercussions to be faced by the country as a whole?

(iii) **Protesting against the "Occupation of Kashmir by India":**

Kashmir has been an inalienable and integral part of India ever since the country attained independence for over six decades and there has never been any dissenting voice against this reality from any legitimate quarters.

(iv) **To give solidarity with the "Struggle of Kashmiri people":**

How daring these idiots are to omit the word "Muslims" from the terminology used by them, viz. "Struggle of the Kashmiri people". It is incredible, to say the least, that there is not even a whisper with regard to the lakhs and lakhs of Hindu Kashmiri Pandits, the original inhabitants of Kashmir, who were brutally attacked and ruthlessly evicted from their hearth and home in Kashmir by these so-called "Kashmiri People". It has been reported in a section of the print media that the person who held out Rs.11 lakhs reward to anybody for the head of Kanhaiya Kumar, the President of AISF, is a Kashmiri Pandit who had to run away for his life along with his family leaving aside his family's life-time savings of money, material and property, when they were brutally kicked out by the so-called Kashmiri people.

(v) **Espouse the cause of "Democratic Right to Self-determination":**

It is elementary common sense that Islam is totally against the very concept of democracy and the Indian Parliament building, the iconic monument of Indian democracy, was attacked on this ground alone. When Islam does not even remotely believe in "democracy", what does this bunch of idiots mean to say: "exercising the democratic rights" by the Kashmiri Muslims?.

It is generally said that "public memory is short" and therefore it is essential to recall, in brief, those dastardly days of terrorists attacking the Indian Parliament building and mercilessly slaughtering the security guards and the civilians for understanding the gravity of the anti-national activities carried on by these bunch of hooligans calling themselves as "students" at a premier University of the Central Government.

In December 2009 Pakistani backed terrorists entered the Parliament building, disguising themselves as the Indian government officials, carrying AK47, grenade launchers, pistols, etc. and opened fire, killing several Security Guards and civilians, including a young female constable, Kamlesh Kumari who was shot in the head when she bravely raised the alarm during the attack. The police arrested four of these terrorists including Mohammad Afzal Gura - the one who was at the centre of the so-called "Cultural Evening" on the eve of his first death anniversary.

After conducting an extensive and impartial trial through the democratic process (instead of the Sharia law as existing in Pakistan being applied to the case which would have meted out instant punishment by way of publicly beheading the terrorists) establishing the complicity of Afzal Guru beyond any shadow of doubt and by incriminating and incontrovertible documentary evidences, including the seizer of Indian currency of Rs.1 million from his possession, he was convicted by the Hon'ble Supreme Court of India.

It should specifically be noted here that the terrorist strikes, the trial of the terrorists, the punishment meted out to them, etc. were during the period of the unconstitutional coalition government of United Progressive Alliance (UPA) whose main coalition partner was Indian Union Muslim League (IUML). And yet, none of these IUML Parliamentarians raised even any eyebrow to the whole process of trial and execution of the terrorist, as they were fully satisfied with the truckloads of incriminating evidences against them as well as the impartial trials. It is pertinent to state here that the foreign-originated ideologies of IUML are diametrically opposed to the "secular" idea which was introduced earlier by the Nehru Dynasty government in the Preamble to the Constitution by an Amendment Act when an Emergency was clamped down by Indira Gandhi and her opponents were put behind the bars.

It is all the more strange that the Home Minister during the period was a Lawyer, viz. P. Chidambaram. He had all the while acquiesced to the whole trial, findings and the conviction of Afzal Guru. And yet, Chidambaram most strangely has now come up with a "doubt" regarding Afzal Guru's role in the dastardly attack, the reason of which even a child could discern is that he has an axe to grind by way of finding everything in the negative during the current legitimate regime under Modiji for the purpose of remaining consistently in the good book of the Italian woman under whom he had been serving like a slave until the UPA government was defeated by the patriotic citizens of India.

It is diabolical and beyond the comprehension of any sober-minded human being that these terrorists killed several Jawans of India and innocent citizens. And yet there has never been even a single word of compassion from the agitating JNU students towards these victims and on the contrary they were paying homage to the terrorists! In no civilized nation at no point of time can one could witness a similar parallel event wherein the perpetrators of heinous crimes are eulogized and the victims are condemned!

It is therefore essential to analyze the aforesaid bizarre circumstances and find ways and means to avert such recrudescence in the country by taking remedial measures without any delay.

It is pertinent to recall here that in the later part of 1990s, the authorities at the JNU had woken up at the rampant anti national activities being carried on by the Leftist students and guests at the JNU campus in support of Pakistan and meetings were convened to discuss the issue. However, as no concrete remedial action was forthcoming from the concerned authorities, one Adal Ghana Chakravorty, who was a faculty member at the University at that period, wrote a letter dated 7th February 1996, addressed to the Registrar of JNU, stating, inter alia, as follows:

QUOTE:

> *The agents of Pakistan have become vigorously assertive on the issue of Kashmir in recent times. The valley of Kashmir, following total physical liquidation of all the non-Muslims, has practically become an all-Muslim territory. This has emboldened the agents of Pakistan on the JNU campus to intensify their vicious campaign for a full-scale secession of Kashmir from India. A seminar was held on 15 November where a full throated declaration was made for another partition of India. According to my information, armed terrorists, staying as guests in Aravali and Gomti, were present with arms hidden on their person. Some terrorists are staying as unauthorized occupants in different hostels even today. Kindly press I.B. into immediate action. Once again the campus is awash with poster campaign by PDSU (financed by Islamic terrorists from Pakistan) asking for withdrawal of the army from Kashmir so that Kashmir can fully become an Islamic State outside the territorial jurisdiction of India. Pakistani agents are brazenly endorsing the infamous 2-nation Theory of Mohammed Ali Jinnah*

UNQUOTE.

However, the successive Nehru Dynasty governments ignored the aforesaid warning letter and kept a blind eye towards the sordid anti-national affairs going on unabated in the JN University on the basis of the much abused term: "freedom of expression". Herein below is a copy of the aforesaid letter.

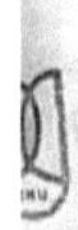

JAWAHARLAL NEHRU UNIVERSITY
NEW DELHI- 110067

ADAL GHANA CHAKRAVORTY
M.A. (Indiana, Bloomington, U.S.A.)
Ph. D. (J. N. U., New Delhi)
ASSOCIATE PROFESSOR
DEPARTMENT OF GERMAN

Res : 6965096
1314, NEW CAMPUS,
JAWAHARLAL NEHRU UNIVERSITY
NEW DELHI-110067.

7.2.96

To
The Registrar,
Jawaharlal Nehru University
New Delhi – 110 0067.

(Through Proper Channel)

Subject: <u>Rampant anti-national activities of the agents of Pakistan on J.N.U. campus.</u>

Madam Registrar,

This has reference to the Academic Council Meeting held on 21 December 95, chaired by the Vice-Chancellor. I had raised the above issue and was asked by the Vice-Chancellor to write to you for follow-up action at your end.

The agents of Pakistan have become vigorously assertive on the issue of Kashmir in recent times. The valley of Kashmir, following total physical liquidation of all the non-Muslims, has practically become an all-Muslim territory. This has emboldened the agents of Pakistan on the J.N.U. campus to intensify their vicious campaign for a full-scale secession of Kashmir from India. A seminar was held on 15 November (Zerox copy attached) where a full-throated declaration was made for another partition of India. According to my information, armed terrorists, staying as guests in Aravali and Gomti, were present with arms hidden on their person. Some terrorists are staying as unauthorised occupants in different hostels even today. Kindly press I.B. into immediate action.

Once again the campus is awash with poster campaign by PDSU (financed by Islamic terrorists from Pakistan) asking for withdrawal of the army from Kashmir (copy enclosed) so that Kashmir can fully become an Islamic State outside the territorial jurisdiction of India. Pakistani agents are brazenly endorsing the infamous 2-Nation Theory of Mohammad Ali Jinnah.

GRAM : JAYENU TEL.: 667676, 667557/557.   TELEX :031-73167 JNU IN FAX 91-11-686 5886

Viewed from an independent stand point, without giving effect to the provisions of even any trace of Constitution, laws, judiciary, etc. undoubtedly in no country except in India this unprecedented, unimaginable and bizarre incident of the students at a Government University paying homage to the terrorists could take place. This incident will, therefore, remain etched forever in the "Collective Conscience of the Patriotic Citizens of India".

It is indeed extremely disgusting and diabolical to see the pictures of young teenage University girls, wearing skin-tight pants, hugging the pictures of convicted terrorist, Afzal Guru, against their projecting bosoms flashed in the morning newspapers across the country. This would give a clear message to the world at large that these teenage girls are of loose moral character who are even ready to fight for the cause of ISIS terrorist organization and give them moral and physical comfort. A retired Professor of JNU University once mentioned to me that 90% of the girls at the University are totally immoral and are serving on the Panel of Call Girls clandestinely maintained by most of the Star Hotels located around the University at Delhi.

As usual, the English language newspapers published from India, particularly The Times of India, Indian Express, etc. whole-heartedly supported the students under the much abused term of "Freedom of Expression". English being the international language, these news papers are serving the taste and opinions of English speaking citizens of Western and European countries - least bothered about the slave-minded majority citizens of India or the safety, security and integrity of the country. This is the main reason that the mainstream media in the country stridently carried on illogical propaganda for repealing of the sedition law as contained under Section 124A of the Indian Penal Code.

It was Bertrand Russell who gave his theoretical opinion in his celebrated book "Education and the Social Order" that: "Communism, as it has developed in Russia, is a political religion analogous to Islam". This theory of Russell will become clear by looking at the photo-snaps of JNU students congregated for raising slogans against India, holding placards of AISF, enlarged pictures of terrorist Afzal Guru, etc. On a closer observation it would also be clear that the members of the congregation were a collective representation of fundamentalists with Islamic outfits and purdah along with Hindu youths professing Leftist ideologies. [Refer: Photos published in Organiser, issue dated February 28, 2016 as well as photos published in the mainstream print and electronic media].

Marx advocated that "During the period of transition, propaganda must play a large part. The aim is the indoctrination of the youth in the proletarian philosophy". In regard to the JNU background, indoctrination of students, propaganda, brain-washing, fabrication of lies, etc. are in great measure used in an unprecedented manner in the 7th decade of the free India.

In this regard Sitaram Yetchury, a top-class Brahmin from A.P., is the main brain behind the provocation and brainwashing of the students. JNU is the alma matter of Sitaram and during his student days in the 1990s he stepped up combined Jihadi and Leftist activism within the campus. He seems to have dedicated his life to ensure total wipe out of Hinduism and its Sanathan Dharma from this ancient land. His wife, Seema Chisti, is the Resident Editor of Indian Express Group of Newspapers. Indeed a fire-brand Leftist-brain as the Resident Editor of a mainstream media coupled with a hard-core Leftist activist as husband is a dangerous proposition which can be used to put down even the faintest voice of the slave Hindus and do greatest damages to the sovereignty, integrity and unity of India as a whole.

When Kanhaiya Kumar was arrested, Sitaram was the first to raise hue and cry under the bogey of "Intolerance", "Freedom of Expression", etc. while at the same time his Naxalite-minded wife carried on the strident media propaganda through the Indian Express edited by her. The article of a straw man, viz. Rajesh Misra, who is reportedly her beck and call, titled "Umar Khalid, My Dear Son" was published in the Indian Express issue dated 23rd Feb. 2016, which is an insult to the law enforcing authorities of India and the judiciary when they carry truck load of incriminating and incontrovertible evidences against Khalid. [Refer: http://indianexpress.com/article/ opinion/editorials/ afzal-guru-film-jnu-student-protest-do-not-disagree/].

It is worthwhile to mention here that when PM Modiji was taking all-out efforts to internationally popularize Yoga, Sitaram, could not digest the world-wide response received to the same and accordingly he specifically flew down to communist Kerala and camped there for a fortnight. His daily activism in addressing the students belonging to SFI and DYFI affiliated to CPI and CPM, respectively, was "incredible" as one of my contacts mentioned to me recently. At all functions which Sitaram addressed, he referred to Modiji as "Indian Hitler", "the hater of Muslims who committed Gujarat Genocide", etc. Sitaram repeatedly referred to "Yoga Aasanas" as "Nothing but the body movement of street dogs".

With regard to the large number of Faculty Members of JNU having come forward in support of Kanahaiya Kumar, it would be amazing, to say the least, that the entire top faculty and administrative members of the JNU are Leftist-oriented "intellectuals" who consistently devised a "filtering mechanism" to admit students to various courses conducted by JNU. By this mechanism the potential Proletarian Activists were selected and any students who have any background of having even any remote connection with Sanathan Dharma are filtered out. On a closer scrutiny of the question papers devised for the entrance examinations for admission to various academic disciplines of the Central University will speak for themselves.

The aforesaid "filtering procedure" for admission of students into the various courses of the University was reportedly done by a woman called Nivedita Menon, one of the so-called faculty members of the University. During her lectures at the Government University she regularly provoked her students to fight for "Kashmir's freedom". A video clip from one of her lectures was shown on a news channel in which she, inter alia, alleged: "Hindu society is the most violent, to the root violent society in the world". On 18th October 2016 one of her essays was published by a newspaper in which she tooth and nail attacked the Uniform Civil Code. She, inter alia, wrote: "The talk of Uniform Civil Code has nothing to do with gender justice. It has entirely to do with a Hindu Nationalist Agenda to *discipline Muslims*". A piece of news report appeared in "Dainik Bharat", a popular Hindi Newspaper, in this regard is reproduced below, which is self-explanatory.

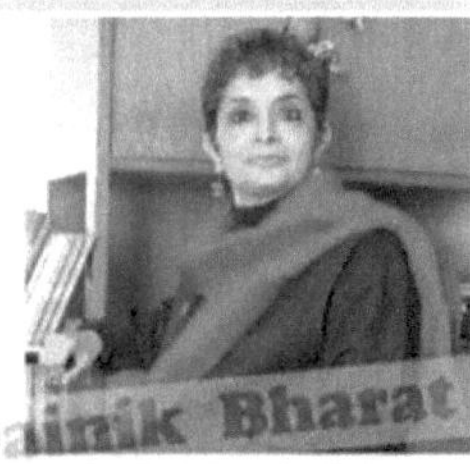

The British governments, who are the ultimate authority in giving the status of territorial jurisdiction of both India and Pakistan, have time and again affirmed that the Jammu and Kashmir as well as the Pak occupied Kashmir are integral parts of India. In such circumstances, how dare these idiots of an Indian Government University carrying on false propaganda and agitation in favour of an enemy country in contradiction to the prevailing realities? What makes this woman holding the position of Professor who has the capacity to indoctrinate the minds of the wards under her tutelage, to be allowed to speak for the fundamentalist Pakistan who is perennially at unprovoked proxy war against India? Does this woman deserve any salary being paid out to her month after month apart from lavish perks from the tax-paying money of the Indian citizens? Why doesn't she migrate to Pakistan? Serious questions pertaining to the internal and external security of India such as how a Chief Minister like Arvind Kejriwal, who has had a track record of supporting Pakistan with regard to the question of Kashmir, and who had the temerity to address the anti-national JNU students could be allowed to continue to be the C.M.; how an opposition member like Rahul Gandhi who had also addressed the said JNU students can be allowed to contest the next elections under the provisions of Representation of Peoples Act, etc. are to be addressed by the Law Enforcing Agencies and National Security Officials in the country before it is too late. At present the only "tool" in the hands of these National Safety and Security Authorities are a piece of legislation called "sedition law" as provided under Section 124A of the Indian Penal Code. If at all such a law is repealed, undoubtedly the anti-society, anti-Hindu and anti-national forces flourishing in the country would prey on Indian societies like a pack of jackals!

FEBRUARY, 2018

[An unedited version of this essay was published in "ORGANISER", in its issue dated 04/02/2018]

THE POLITICS PLAYED BY THE S.C. JUDGES

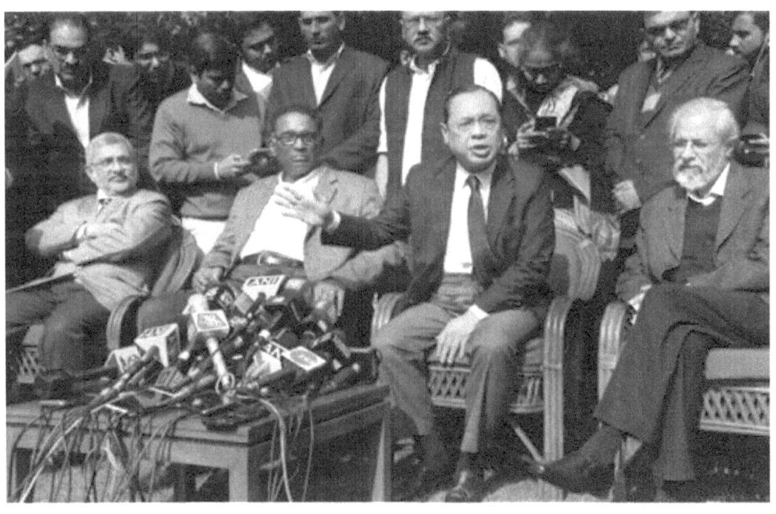

Four Senior Supreme Court Judges, appointed by erstwhile Nehru Dynasty governments, sitting in "Revolt" in a busy part of the Delhi street [Image Courtesy: Getty Images]

*I*t is for the first time in the judicial history of free India that four senior most Supreme Court (SC) judges redressing their purported grievances at the feet of pulp fiction writers and media personnel by coming out of their plush government allotted Lutyens bungalows and sitting in "Dharna" at a chaotic part of the public street of New Delhi in the presence of mendicants, hawkers, drunkards, street hooligans, pedestrians, etc.! [Refer: The Times of India, issue dated 13/01/2018]. This single most episode is enough for the total erosion of respect, faith and trust towards judiciary in the minds of the ordinary Indian citizens.

By Resorting to this unprecedented move by the so-called conscience keepers of the law, they have violated all the cannons of justice delivery system and transgressed all the Constitutional provisions pertaining to upholding of the dignity and integrity of judiciary.

Under Article 124 of the Indian Constitution, the Judges of the Supreme Court are required to subscribe, in the presence of the President, to an oath which, inter alia, states as follows: "He/she will bear true faith and allegiance to the Constitution of India as by law established; that he/she will uphold the sovereignty and integrity of India; that he/she will duly and faithfully and to the best of his/her ability, knowledge and judgment perform the duties of his/her office without fear or favor, affection or ill-will and that he/she will uphold the constitution and the laws; that he/she shall conduct himself/herself in a dignified manner upholding the majesty of judiciary".

Apart from the aforesaid unequivocal constitutional provisions which are aimed at ensuring the dignity and the venerable status enjoyed by the judiciary in the country, there are well laid out judicial ethics followed in all the civilized and democratic nations of the world. These judicial ethics are particularly adhered to by the International Court of Justice. A couple of these ethics are quoted here: "(1) A Judge shall not enter into public debate or express his view in public on political matters or on matters that are pending or are likely to arise for judicial determination, (2) A Judge is expected to let his judgments speak for themselves. He shall not give interviews to the media".

It is quite unfortunate that the aforesaid unprecedented episode occurred close on the heels of the CBI Special Judge, O.P. Saini, acquitting all the accused in the 2G spectrum scam cases which occurred during the erstwhile unconstitutional regime of UPA government headed by the Italian Christian woman.

It is, therefore, essential to analyze these unprecedented episodes so as to find out ways and means to avert recrudescence of similar revolting scenes by those holding judicial positions.

It is already well-known that these four Judges revolted against the then Chief Justice of India (Dipak Mishra, a corruption free and impartial Judge, whose appointment was not blessed by the Italian Head of the UPA Government) by going to the public were included in the list of SC Judges who were indulging in corrupt practices as per the reported statements made by yet another Senior Judge of the Hon'ble High Court of Calcutta, who has now retired. Thus, in 2013 and 2014 Justice (Retd.) Karnan of the Madras High Court wrote to the then Chief Justice of India and to the PM regarding the corrupt practices indulged in by 20 Judges of the SC, which included the four revolting Judges. However, for the larger interest of judicial propriety, the SC did not pay much heed to the said reported statements made by Justice Karnan in his letter. Justice Karnan himself had stated, inter alia, at a seminar organized by a Southern Law University: "The SC did not apply its mind (in investigating about the misdeeds of these Judges)...." and he added: "That's why public confidence in the judiciary is decreasing day by day".

It has now turned out to be a paramount duty cast upon the Appointing Authority of these Judges to set up appropriate Commission of Enquiry to unravel the mental aspects, character and a thorough background check of these Judges (whose appointments as Judges were all blessed by the Italian Head of the UPA government) as well as to find out the veracity of the pronouncements made by the then sitting Judge, Justice Karnan, so as to bring transparency in the functioning of judiciary.

It is pertinent to mention here that there are several leads which would conclusively clinch the fact that these four judges were influenced by the Left-wing political forces stemming from certain quarters of the country which are akin to the episode of "Break India Gang Agitation" resorted to by the students of the Central Governed owned JN University, as well as by the Lobby representing the Congress Stalwarts at the Hon'ble Supreme Court.

TRIGGERING FACTOR:

What triggered for the unprecedented conduct of the Judges is a Public Interest Litiation (PIL) regarding the death of the Special CBI Judge BH Loya [who was earlier presiding over the Sohrabuddin Sheikh encounter case in the CBI Court] filed before the SC. It was alleged in the said PIL that Amit Shah, the then BJP President, was involved in the said case as one of the accused and therefore the Petitioners surmised that he had a hand in the death of Justice Loya.

It is all the more significant to state here that the said PIL was filed by an activist, who is a close associate of Teesta Setalvad, viz. Tahseen Poonawala. It is everybody's knowledge that Teesta was the foot soldier of certain foreign fundamentalist NGOs and money was pouring into her account from them for utilizing it for "trapping" the then CM of Gujarat, Narendra Mody, by hook or by crook as one of the accused in the Gujarat riots so as to debar him once for all from coming into power either in Gujarat or at the Centre.

It is pertinent to state here that as Teesta and her husband Javed Anand maintained their account through which they received money from the foreign NGOs, they were bound and liable to file returns regarding the remittances of foreign money in to their account with the FCRA authorities, which they adamantly rejected and on the contrary they splurged up the money towards various anti social, anti-Hindu and anti national activities at the instance of their foreign Masters.

It is significant to mention here that it is well-known across the country that Teesta had been fighting a long battle against the then CM Modi over the 2002 Gujarat riots during which period she had left no stone unturned in "trapping" him by way of hoisting upon him numerous false, frivolous and fabricated criminal cases, all of which came to be dismissed one after the other, the Courts finding them as bogus and frivolous.

Teesta is, therefore, like a wounded and defeated war horse brimming with unfounded revenge and getting ready for committing further damages to Modi and his political party at the behest of her foreign masters. It is in these circumstances that she simply passed on the baton to her trusted friend and co-activist, Tehseen Poonavala, for going in full steam against Modi's trusted friend Amit Shah by way of filing a false PIL, containing fabricated allegations and made-up stories!

It is pertinent to state here that the elder son of late Judge, Anuj Loya, aged about 22 years, has categorically ruled out the possibilities of any foul play in the death of his father. He further added that none of the immediate family members of his father has any suspicions regarding the death of his father and that he died of certain coronary artery ailments which he said his father had suffered in the past too.

It is, therefore, elementary logic that when the immediate kiths and kins of the deceased has no suspicion regarding any foul play in the death of the Judge, the *locus standi* of the petitioners, if any, in filing the said PIL should have automatically nullified and the PIL should have been dismissed with exemplary costs.

In any case even if the PIL is to be tried, the cooperation from the immediate family members of the deceased Judge is to be enlisted, which is fundamental to an impartial trial.

The million dollar question, therefore, was how and why the four Judges, particularly Chemaleswar, were so anxious to get allotted the said PIL, seeking Court's directions to probe into the said death, to any one of them for "trial".

1984 RIOTS CASES:

It could be discerned that the paramount reasons for the revolt are that the CJI (Dipak Mishra) has reopened the 1984 riots cases pertaining to the genocide of Sikhs from Punjab, Haryana and Delhi involving high-profile Congress and left-wing political leaders. In addition, the Ram Mandir Vs. Babri Masjid verdict will be coming up soon. The purported grievances of these revolting judges are that all these cases were not being assigned to any one of them so that they could have dealt with the same according to their whims and fancies and for serving the causes of their political masters who blessed their appointments, viz. the Italian Head of the erstwhile UPA government and her cohorts.

2G Spectrum Scam Case:

Coming back to the question of 2G Spectrum scam case judgment by CBI Special Judge, acquitting all the accused, any Indian citizens of ordinary prudence can easily realize that it has turned out to be one of the greatest blows to the edifice of the Indian judiciary, compromising truthfulness and transparency.

The trial of 2G Spectrum case was highly vitiated by way of nullifying the entire trial on account of the conflict of interest of the persons who handled the cases.

Thus, the Special Public Prosecutor, who was assigned the prosecution duties against all those found guilty in the 2G Spectrum scam cases was a lawyer named: "Anand Grover". His mistress, Indira Jaising, was appointed as the First Female Additional Solicitor General of India, who is a hard-core leftist ideologue, harboring utter contempt towards Sanathan Dharma.

It must be born in mind that the whole period of the erstwhile unconstitutional UPA government had witnessed unprecedented scams and corruption cases which happened with the connivance of Indira Jaisingh who was the Additional Solicitor General of India appointed at the instance of the Italian Head of the Indian government. It is therefore elementary common sense that her so-called "husband" Anand Grover who was entrusted with the trial of the scam cases would be interested only to defeat the entire cases with a view to save his Mistress, Indira Jaising, her Italian God Mother and all the tainted UPA Ministers from the entanglements of the cases. Grover's appointment as Lawyer to handle the trial of the cases, therefore, was something like the idiom fox guarding the hen house.

It is therefore common sense that both Indira Jaising and Anand Grover were overwhelmingly interested in defeating the whole trial for their selfish and personal interests to save themselves from the predicament of prosecuting the accused. I have gone through the entire judgment passed by CBI Special Judge, O.P. Saini and I would like to analyze here just one observation out of numerous observations made in the 1500-page judgment.

Under para 1817 he observes as follows: "There is no evidence on the record produced before the court indicating any criminality in the acts allegedly committed by the accused". When the 2G Spectrum scam episode exploded like a powerful bomb during the UPA regime headed by the Italian woman, which led the Hon'ble Supreme Court to cancel the whole allocation made by the then Telecom Minister, there used to be daily reports in the mainstream media wherein truck load of documentary evidences regarding the illegality in the whole conduct of those ministers involved as well as illegal gratification, etc. were accurately reported. Moreover, for cancelling the allotment, the Hon'ble SC has considered the evidentiary values of all the documents pertaining to the scam submitted before it and found that those evidences would conclusively clinch the complicity of the accused. And yet it is unbelievable, to say the least, that the prosecution could not adduce even a shred of evidence before the CBI Court!

It can therefore be easily concluded that Anand Grover who has had overwhelming interest in defeating the entire cases so as to save his Mistress, Indira Jaising, her Italian God Mother and all the tainted Ministers of the UPA government from all the predicaments as the 2G spectrum scam and other corruption cases arose with the connivance or negligence of Jaising as she was simultaneously working for numerous foreign NGOs while holding the constitutional post of the Additional Solicitor General of India, he has willfully concealed and/or destroyed the whole evidences pertaining to the cases.

It is now for the citizens of the country to consider and try the aforesaid historic episodes in the People's Court in the larger interest of safety, security and integrity of the country through the Ballot Box.

LIST OF ANCIENT UNIVERSITIES DESTROYED BY THE MUSLIM INVADERS

Sr. No.	Name of the destroyed Universities & Libraries and their location.	Brief description of Universities/ Libraries and the names of the destroyers
1	Bikrampur University, which was located in the undivided India (Akhanda Bharat) and presently located in Bangladesh.	This ancient University was established in 7th century and it steadily expanded through the 11th century. This centre of education attracted students from various countries, including China, Thailand, Tibet, Nepal, etc. Archaeological evidences excavated in 2013 reveals that it was one of famous Buddhist education centres in ancient India. It was destroyed by the invading Mughal armies.

2	Jagaddala University. It was located in the undivided India (Akhanda Bharat) of North Bengal and in the present day it is in Bangladesh.	This University is regarded among five great ancient Indian Universities, the other being Nalanda, Vikramshila, Sompura and Odantapuri. It was established by King Rampala in the early 11th Century CE. It taught wide ranging subjects and specialized in Vajrayana Buddhism. Buddhist scholar, Vidyakara, was a faculty member. He compiled anthologies of Sanskrit verses known as "Subhasitarantnakose". There were large volumes of Tibetan scriptures. The University was destroyed by the armies of Mughal invaders.
3	Nalanda University, located in the state of Bihar.	This University was one of the ancient Universities. It was established by Emperor Gupta which boasted magnificiant temples, spacious classrooms, meditation halls, monasteries, etc. Its sprauling campus was over 2000 years old. This University was destroyed by Bakhtiyar Khilji of the Mughal army.

4	Odantapuri University. It was located in the Magadha region of Bihar	This University was founded by King Gopala of Pala Dynasty during the 7th century CE. Students from all over the country sought admission in the University for pursuing various academic studies. Bhaktiyar Khilji and his army destroyed this University.
5	Pushpagiri University. It was located in ancient Kalinga which covered Districts such as Cuttck and Jajpur of present day Odisha.	Emperor Ashoka established this University in the last years of BCE and it was as old as Nalanda University. It was said that its campuses spread across three adjoining hills known as Lalitgiri, Ratnagiri and Udayagiri. This University attracted students from all over the world. A famous Buddhist monk Prajna from Gandhara came to study at this ancient University. Unfotunatley, however, this ancient University perished due to neglect by the Mughal rulers.

6	Somapura University located in the present-day Azad Kashmir.	The University was established by Pala King Dharampala in 7th century. It was one of the largest centres of education – larger than Nalanda University. It taught various subjects, including scriptures of Hinduism, Buddhism, Jainism, etc. and it stood for over four centuries. The University was destroyed by Sikander Butshikhan for establishing Islam in Kashmir.
7	Sharada Peeth Temple University. It was located in the undivided India (Akhanda Bharat) in the region of Kashmir which is now in Pak-occupied-Kashmir.	Sharada Peeth is one of the 51 Shakti Peethas in ancient India. Many ancient Hindu scholars studied at this University. It is said that Adi Shankara graduated from this University which was said to be at least 2500 years old. Muslim invaders headed by Sikander Butshikan destroyed this University and established Islam in Kashmir.

APPENDIX-2

THE HINDU •LETTERS TO THE EDITOR•

Being a Hindu In Bharat

Sir, — I am a Hindu and have been a Hindu since my birth. As I call myself a Hindu, the Indian Government will look on me as a communalist. A Hindu in India is expected to be ashamed of his religion and not talk about it in public. He must proclaim that he is secular. He must be tolerant when Hindus are attacked and Hinduism is ridiculed. Hindus believe that all religions lead to the same truth. Some other religions proclaim their uniqueness and feel that there can be salvation only through their religion. They want us to embrace their religion out of concern for the pagan Hindus. Hindus accept the right to convert others. Some ridicule Hindu gods and goddesses at street-corner meetings and Hindus do not protest. Hindus accept others' right to propagate their faith by fair or foul means.

Governments manage Hindu temples. They do not interfere in the administration of the religious places of other religions as they belong to minority religious groups. Governments enact laws governing the life of Hindus but minority groups are given freedom to do what they want to.

Sri Rama's birthday and Sri Krishna's birthday are not national holidays. The Prophet's birthday is a national holiday. The Hindus do not mind as they are a tolerant people. They recite "Iswar Allah tere nam" and no one else does.

Ambedkar ridiculed and abused Hindus and Hinduism. As tolerant Hindus, we love him, adore him. Alladi Krishnaswami Iyer, B. N. Rao, and others also contributed a great deal towards the drafting of the Indian Constitution. We have forgotten them as they were foolish enough not t criticise Hindus and Hinduism.

Hindus adore Max Mueller for his translation of Hindu religious works into English. Some call him a Rishi. We forgive him for his views on Hindus and Hinduism. He translated Hindu religious works to prove that Christianity is superior to Hinduism. In 1886, Max Mueller wrote to his wife: "I hope I shall finish the work, and I feel convinced though I shall not live to see it, yet this edition of mine and the translation of the Veda will hereafter tell to a great extent on the fate of India and on the growth of millions of souls in that country. It is the root of their religion and to show them what the root is, I feel sure, is the only way of uprooting all that has sprung from it during the last three thousand years." He wrote to the Secretary of State for India that "the ancient religion of India is doomed and if Christianity does not step in, whose fault will it be?" As true Hindus, we forget his motives and value him for his work.

I am distressed at the way Hindus aretreated by every government. Our governments are more interested in the minorities than in the majority community. Hindus are taken for granted. Their tolerance is mistaken forweakness.

n the name of secularism, governments trample on the feelings of Hindus. The present tensions in the country are due to the one-sided policy of the governments. Governments are united in dividing people on the basis of their religion. The British divided and ruled. The British have left us; their legacy remains.

K. Subramanian, Secunderabad

APPENDIX-3

CENTRAL GOVERNMENT SCHEMES/PROJECTS/ ROADS/RIVERS/BUILDINGS NAMED AFTER NEHRU DYNASTY MEMBERS

[Permission for reprinting has been obtained from Dr. Surya Prakash, who compiled these names]

1. Rajiv Gandhi Grameen Vidyutikaran Yojana, Ministry of Power – A scheme "Rajiv Gandhi Grameen Vidyutikaran Yojana" for Rural Electricity Infrastructure and Household Electrification was launched for the attainment of the National Common Minimum Programme of providing access to electricity to all Rural Household by 2009. Rural Electrification Corporation (REC) is the nodal agency for the scheme. Rajiv Gandhi Grameen Vidyutikaran Yojana to

be continued during the Eleventh Plan period with a capital subsidy of Rs. 28000 Crore;

2. Rajiv Gandhi National Drinking Water Mission (RGNDWM), Ministry of Rural Development, Annual allocation plan – from Rs.6,000 crore to Rs 10,000 crore per annum. Total spent until now – around Rs 70,000

3. Jawaharlal Nehru Urban Renewal Mission, Ministry of Urban Development, – Total spent until now – Rs 62,000 crore.

4. Indira Awas Yojana, Ministry of Rural Areas and Environment – IAY is a CSS funded on cost-sharing basis between the Centre and the States in the ratio of 75:25. In the case of UTs, the entire funds are provided by Centre. The target groups for housing under IAY are households below poverty line living in rural areas, particularly those belonging to SC/ST and freed bonded labourers. Annual Allocation – Rs 8000 – 11,000 crore

5. Indira Gandhi National Old Age Pension Scheme

6. Rajiv Gandhi National Crèche Scheme for the Children of Working Mothers, Department of Women & Child Development, Ministry of HRD, New Delhi – Budgetary allocation of around Rs 100 crore per year

7. Rajiv Gandhi Udyami Mitra Yojana for benefit of NE entrepreneurs, Ministry of Micro, Small & Medium Enterprises, Government of India

8. Jawaharlal Nehru Rojgar Yojna – Ministry of Labour and Employment – A Self- employment programme for urban poor

9. Rajiv Gandhi Shramik Kalyan Yojna, Employees' State Insurance Corporation

10. Indira Gandhi Canal Project, Funded by World Bank
11. Rajiv Gandhi Shilpi Swasthya Bima Yojana, Union Ministry of Textiles, in association with ICICI Lombard General Insurance Company Limited
12. Indira Vikas Patra
13. Rajiv Gandhi Equity Savings Scheme
14. Rajiv Gandhi Panchayat Sashaktikaran Abhiyan
15. Rajiv Gandhi Scheme for Empowerment of SAdolescent Girls
16. Indira Gandhi National Widow Pension Scheme
17. Indira Gandhi National Disability Pension Scheme for BPL beneficiaries 18. Rajiv Gandhi Geamin LPG Vitrak Yojana

State Government Schemes

1. INDIRAMMA, an acronym for Integrated Novel Development In Rural Areas and Model Municipal Areas – a programme for integrated development of villages and municipalities –Andhra Pradesh
2. Indiramma Pachcha Thoranam – An Action Plan for Village Organisations –Andhra Pradesh
3. Indiramma Amrutha Hastham Scheme – To provide nutritious food to pregnant and lactating women –Andhra Pradesh
4. Amma Hastham – A kit containing nine essential commodities for Rs 185 –Andhra Pradesh
5. Indiramma Kalalu – To identify individual and community needs among Scheduled Castes and Scheduled Tribes – Andhra Pradesh
6. Indira Kranti Pratham, Andhra Pradesh

7. Rajiv Gandhi Abyodhaya Yojana, Andhra Pradesh
8. Rajiv Gandhi Rehabilitation Package for Tsunami Affected Areas, Tamil Nadu Rajiv Gandhi Social Security Scheme for Poor People, Pomndicherry
9. Rajiv Ratna Awas Yojna, Delhi to provide housing facilities to the poorer sections in Delhi.
10. Rajiv Gandhi Prathamik Shiksha Mission, Madhya Pradesh
11. Rajiv Gandhi Shiksha Mission, Chhattisgarh
12. Rajiv Gandhi Mission on Food Security, Madhya Pradesh
13. Rajiv Gandhi Mission on Community Health, Madhya Pradesh
14. Rajiv Gandhi Rural Housing Corporation Limited, Karnataka
15. Rajiv Gandhi Tourism Development Mission, Rajasthan
16. Rajiv Gandhi Computer Literacy Programme, Assam
17. Rajiv Gandhi Swavlamban Rojgar Yojana, Govt. of NCT of Delhi
18. Rajiv Gandhi Vidyarthi Suraksha Yojana, Maharashtra
19. Rajiv Gandhi Mission for Watershed Management, M.P.
20. Rajiv Gandhi Food Security Mission for Tribal Areas, MP
21. Rajiv Gandhi Home for Handicapped, Pondicherry
22. Rajiv Gandhi Breakfast Scheme, Pondicherry
23. Rajiv Gandhi Artisans Health and Life Insurance Scheme, Tamil Nadu
24. Rajiv Gandhi Zopadpatti Nivara Prakalpa, Mumbai
25. Rajiv Arogyasri programme, Gujarat
26. Rajiv Gandhi Computer Saksharta Mission, Jabalpur
27. Rajiv Gandhi Bridges and Roads Infrastructure Development Programme, Haryana
28. Rajiv Gandhi Gramin Niwara Prakalp, Maharashtra Govt.

29. Indira Gandhi Utkrishtha Chhattervritti Yojna for post-plus II students, Himachal Pradesh
30. Indira Gandhi Women Protection Scheme, Maharashtra -158- -3-
31. Indira Gandhi Prathisthan, Housing and Urban Planning Department, UP
32. Indira Kranthi Patham Scheme, Andhra Pradesh
33. Indira Gandhi Vruddha Bhumiheen Shetmajoor Anudan Yojana, Maharashtra
34. Indira Gandhi Niradhar Yojna, Govt. of Maharashtra
35. Indira Gandhi Drinking Water Scheme-Haryana Govt.
36. Indira Gaon Ganga Yojana, Chattisgarh
37. Indira Sahara Yojana, Chattisgarh
38. Indira Soochna Shakti Yojana, Chattisgarh
39. Indira Gandhi Balika Suraksha Yojana, I IP
40. Indira Gandhi Garibi Hatao Yojana (DPIP), MP
41. Indira Gandhi Water Project, Haryana
42. Indira Gandhi Sagar Project, Bhandara District, Maharashtra
43. Indira Jeevitha Bima Pathakam, Andhra Pradesh
44. Indira Gandhi Priyadarshani Vivah Shagun Yojana, Haryana
45. Indira Mahila Yojana Scheme, Meghalaya
46. Indira Gandhi Calf Rearing Scheme, Chhattisgarh
47. Indira Gandhi Priyadarshini Vivah Shagun Yojana, Haryana
48. Indira Gandhi Calf Rearing Scheme, Andhra Pradesh
49. Indira Gandhi Landless Agriculture Labour scheme, Maharashtra

Sports/Tournaments/Trophies

1. Rajiv Gandhi Gold Cup Kabaddi Tournament

2. Rajiv Gandhi Sadbhavana Run
3. Rajiv Gandhi Federation Cup Boxing Championship
4. Rajiv Gandhi International Football Tournament
5. Rajiv Gandhi Road Race, New Delhi
6. Rajiv Gandhi Boat Race, Kerala
7. Rajiv Gandhi International Artistic Gymnastic Tournament
8. Rajiv Gandhi Memorial Roller Skating Championship
9. Rajiv Gandhi Memorial Marathon Race, New Delhi
10. Rajiv Gandhi International Judo Championship, Chandigarh
11. Rajeev Gandhi Memorial Trophy for the Best College, Calicut
12. Rajiv Gandhi Rural Cricket Tournament, initiated by Rahul Gandhi in Amethi
13. Rajiv Gandhi Football Gold Cup (U-21)
14. Rajiv Gandhi Gold Cup Football Trophy, Jammu & Kashmir
15. Rajiv Gandhi Instant Football Tournament, Mumbai
16. Rajiv Gandhi Award for Outstanding Sportspersons
17. All India Rajiv Gandhi Basketball (Girls) Tournament -159- -4-
18. All India Rajiv Gandhi Wrestling Gold Cup, organized by Delhi State
19. Rajiv Gandhi Memorial Jhopadpatti Football Tournament, Maharastra
20. Rajiv Gandhi Mini Olympics, Mumbai
21. Rajiv Gandhi Beachball Kabaddi Federation
22. Rajiv Gandhi Memorial Trophy Prerana Foundation
23. Indira Gandhi International Womens' Hockey Gold Cup Tournament

24. Indira Gandhi Boat Race
25. Nehru Cup – International Football Tournament.
26. Jawaharlal Nehru Hockey Tournament.

Stadia

1. Indira Gandhi Sports Complex, Delhi
2. Indira Gandhi Indoor Stadium, New Delhi
3. Jawaharlal Nehru Stadium, New Delhi
4. Rajiv Gandhi Sports Stadium, Bawana
5. Rajiv Gandhi National Football Academy, Haryana
6. Rajiv Gandhi AC Stadium, Vishakhapatnam
7. Rajiv Gandhi Indoor Stadium, Pondicherry
8. Rajiv Gandhi Stadium, Itanagar
9. Rajiv Gandhi Indoor Stadium, Ernakulam
10. Rajiv Gandhi Sports Complex, Kundli, Delhi
11. Rajib Gandhi Memorial Sports Complex, Guwahati
12. Rajiv Gandhi International Stadium, Hyderabad
13. Indira Gandhi Stadium, Vijayawada, Andhra Pradesh
14. Indira Gandhi Stadium, Una, Himachal Pradesh
15. Indira Priyadarshini Stadium, Vishakhapatnam
16. Indira Gandhi Stadium, Deogarh, Rajasthan
17. Indira Gandhi Sports Stadium, Shimla

Peaks and Geographical Landmarks

1. Indira Point (the southernmost point of India- formerly known as Pygmalion Point)
2. Indira Col (near trijunction of India-China-Pakistan)
3. Jawahar Dweep (formerly Butcher Island in Mumbai Harbour)
4. Mount Rajiv, a peak in the Himalayas

Airports/ Ports/Aviation Academies

1. Rajiv Gandhi International Airport, Hyderabad
2. Rajiv Gandhi Container Terminal, Cochin
3. Indira Gandhi International Airport, New Delhi
4. Indira Gandhi Dock, Mumbai
5. Indira Gandhi Rashtriya Uran Akademi, Fursatganj Airfield, Rae Bareli, Uttar Pradesh
6. Jawaharlal Nehru Nava Sheva Port Trust, Mumbai
7. Rajiv Gandhi National Aviation University, Rae Bareli, Uttar Pradesh
8. Rajiv Gandhi Aviation Academy, Secundrabad
9. Rajiv Gandhi Academy for Aviation Technology, Thiruvananthapuram, Kerala

Power Plants

1. Rajiv Gandhi Super Thermal Power Station (RGSTPS),Sipat, Chattisgarh
2. Rajiv Gandhi Combined Cycle Power Plant, Kayamkulam, Allappuzha, Kerala
3. Rajiv Gandhi Thermal Power Plant, Hissar, Haryana
4. Indira Gandhi Super Thermal Power Project, Haryana

Universities/Education Institutes

1. Rajiv Gandhi Indian Institute of Management, Shillong
2. Rajiv Gandhi Institute of Aeronautics, Ranchi, Jharkhand
3. Rajiv Gandhi Institute of Petroleum Technology, Rae Bareli

4. Rajiv Gandhi Technical University, Gandhi Nagar, Bhopal, M.P.
5. Rajiv Gandhi School of Intellectual Property Law, Kharagpur,
6. Rajiv Gandhi National University of Law, Patiala, Punjab
7. Rajiv Gandhi National Institute of Youth Development, Tamil Nadu
8. Rajiv Gandhi Institute of Technology, Kottayam, Kerala
9. Rajiv Gandhi College of Engineering Research & Technology, Chandrapur, Maharashtra
10. Rajiv Gandhi College of Engineering, Airoli, Navi Mumbai, Maharashtra
11. Rajiv Gandhi University, Itanagar, Arunachal Pradesh
12. Rajiv Gandhi Institute of Technology, Chola Nagar, Bangalore, Karnataka
13. Rajiv Gandhi Proudyogika Vishwavidyalaya, Gandhi Nagar, Bhopal, M.P.
14. Rajiv Gandhi D.Ed College, Latur, Maharashtra
15. Rajiv Gandhi College, Shahpura, Bhopal
16. Rajiv Gandhi Institute of Petroleum Technology, Raebareli, U.P.
17. Rajiv Gandhi Homeopathic Medical College, Bhopal, M.P.
18. Rajiv Gandhi Institute of Post Graduate Studies, East Godavari District, Andhra Pradesh
19. Rajiv Gandhi College of Education, Tumkur, Karnataka
20. Rajiv Gandhi College of Veterinary & Animal Sciences, Pondicherry, Tamil Nadu
21. Rajiv Gandhi Institute of IT and Biotechnology, Bhartiya Vidhyapeeth
22. Rajiv Gandhi High School, Mumbai, Maharashtra

23. Rajiv Gandhi Group of Institutions, Satna, M.P.
24. Rajiv Gandhi College of Engineering, Sriperumbudur, Tamil Nadu
25. Rajiv Gandhi Biotechnology Centre, R.T.M., Nagpur University
26. Rajiv Gandhi Centre for Biotechnology, Thiruvananthapuram, Kerala
27. Rajiv Gandhi Mahavidyalaya, Madhya Pradesh
28. Rajiv Gandhi Post Graduate College, Allahabad, U.P.
29. Rajiv Gandhi Institute of Technology, Bangalore, Karnataka
30. Rajiv Gandhi Govt. PG Ayurvedic College, Poprola, Himachal Pradesh
31. Rajiv Gandhi College, Satna, M.P.
32. Rajiv Gandhi Madhyamic Vidyalaya, Maharashtra
33. Rajiv Gandhi Institute of Contemporary Studies, Islamabad, Pakistan
34. Rajiv Gandhi Centre for Innovation and Entrepreneurship
35. Rajiv Gandhi Industrial Training Centre, Gandhinagar
36. Rajiv Gandhi University of Knowledge Technologies, Andhra Pradesh
37. Rajiv Gandhi Institute Of Distance Education, Coimbatore, Tamil Nadu
38. Rajiv Gandhi Centre for Aquaculture, Tamil Nadu
39. Rajiv Gandhi University, Arunachal Pradesh
40. Rajiv Gandhi Sports Medicine Centre (RGSMC), Kerala
41. Rajiv Gandhi Science Centre, Mauritus
42. Rajiv Gandhi Kala Mandir, Ponda, Goa
43. Rajiv Gandhi Vidyalaya, Mulund, Mumbai
44. Rajiv Gandhi Memorial Polytechnic, Bangalore, Karnataka

45. Rajiv Gandhi Memorial Circle Telecom Training Centre (India), Chennai
46. Rajiv Gandhi Institute of Pharmacy, Kasagod, Kerala
47. Rajiv Gandhi Memorial College Of Aeronautics, Jaipur
48. Rajiv Gandhi Memorial First Grade College, Shimoga, Karnataka
49. Rajiv Gandhi Memorial College of Education, Jammu & Kashmir
50. Rajiv Gandhi South Campus, Benaras Hindu University, Varanasi
51. Rajiv Gandhi Memorial Teacher's Training College, Jharkhand
52. Rajiv Gandhi Degree College, Rajahmundry, Andhra Pradesh
53. Rajiv Gandhi Centre for Biotechnology
54. Rajiv Gandhi Government Degree College, Shimla
55. Rajiv Gandhi Centre for Aquaculture
56. Rajiv Gandhi Ground Water Training and Research Institute
57. Rajiv Gandhi Computer Literacy Programme
58. Indira Gandhi National Open University (IGNOU), New Delhi
59. Indira Gandhi Institute of Development & Research, Mumbai, Maharashtra
60. Indira Gandhi National Forest Academy, Dehradun
61. Indira Gandhi Institute of Development Research, Mumbai
62. Indira Gandhi National Tribal University, Orissa
63. Indira Gandhi B.Ed. College, Mangalore
64. Smt. Indira Gandhi College of Education, Nanded, Maharashtra

65. Indira Gandhi Balika Niketan B.ED. College, Jhunjhunu, Rajasthan
66. Indira Gandhi Krishi Vishwavidyalaya, Raipur, Madhya Pradesh
67. Smt. Indira Gandhi College of Engineering, Navi Mumbai, Maharashtra
68. Smt. Indira Gandhi College, Tiruchirappalli
69. Indira Gandhi Engineering College, Sagar, Madhya Pradesh
70. Indira Gandhi Institute of Technology, Kashmere Gate, Delhi
71. Indira Gandhi Institute of Technology, Sarang, Dist. Dhenkanal, Orissa
72. Indira Gandhi Institute of Aeronautics, Pune, Maharashtra
73. Indira Gandhi Integral Education Centre, New Delhi
74. Indira Gandhi Institute of Physical Education & Sports Sciences, Delhi University, Delhi
75. Indira Gandhi High School, Himachal
76. Indira Kala Sangit Vishwavidyalaya, Chhattisgarh
77. Indira Gandhi Medical College, Shimla
78. Jawaharlal Nehru Technological University, Kukatpally, Andhra Pradesh
79. Nehru Institute of Mountaineering, Uttarakashi, Uttarakhand
80. Pandit Jawaharlal Nehru Institute of Business Management, Vikram University
81. Jawaharlal Nehru University, New Delhi
82. Jawaharlal Nehru Centre for Advanced Scientific Research, Bangalore
83. Jawaharlal Nehru Engineering College in Aurangabad, Maharashtra

84. Jawaharlal Nehru Centre for advanced Scientific Research, a deemed university, Jakkur, Bangalore
85. Jawaharlal Nehru Institute of Social Studies, affiliated to Tilak Maharashtra Vidyapith (Pune, Maharashtra)
86. Jawaharlal Nehru College of Aeronautics & Applied Sciences, Coimbatore, (ESTD 1968)
87. Jawaharlal Nehru Institute of Technology, Katraj, Dhankwdi, Pune, Maharashtra
88. Jawaharlal Nehru Engineering College in Aurangabad, Maharashtra
89. Jawaharlal Nehru Institute of Education & Technological Research, Nanded, Maharashra
90. Jawaharlal Nehru College, Aligarh
91. Jawaharlal Nehru Technological University, Hyderabad
92. Jawaharlal Nehru Krishi Vishwavidyalaya, Jabalpur
93. Jawaharlal Nehru B.Ed. College, Kota, Rajasthan
94. Jawaharlal Nehru P.G. College, Bhopal
95. Jawaharlal Nehru Government Engineering College, Mandi District, Himachal Pradesh
96. Jawaharlal Nehru Public School, Bhopal
97. Jawaharlal Nehru Technological University, Kakinada, Andhra Pradesh
98. Jawaharlal Nehru Technological University, Hyderabad, Andhra Pradesh
99. Jawaharlal Nehru Institute of Technology, Ibrahimpatti, Andhra Pradesh

Awards

1. Rajiv Gandhi Award for Outstanding Achievement

2. Rajiv Gandhi Shiromani Award
3. Rajiv Gandhi Shramik Awards, Delhi Labour Welfare Board
4. Rajiv Gandhi National Sadbhavana Award
5. Rajiv Gandhi Manav Seva Award
6. Rajiv Gandhi Wildlife Conservation Award
7. Rajiv Gandhi National Award Scheme for Original Book Writing on Gyan Vigyan
8. Rajiv Gandhi Khel Ratna Award
9. Rajiv Gandhi National Quality Award, Instituted by Bureau of Indian Standards
10. Rajiv Gandhi Environment Award for Clean Technology, Ministry of Environment & Forests, Government of India
11. Rajiv Gandhi Film Awards (Mumbai)
12. Rajiv Gandhi Khelratna Puraskar
13. Rajiv Gandhi Parisara Prashasti, Karnataka
14. Rajiv Gandhi Vocational Excellence Awards
15. Rajiv Gandhi Excellence award
16. Indira Gandhi Peace Prize
17. Indira Gandhi Prize for National Integration
18. Indira Gandhi Priyadarshini Award
19. Indira Priyadarshini Vrikshamitra Awards, Ministry of Environment and Forests
20. Indira Gandhi Paryavaran Purashkar
21. Indira Gandhi Award for National Integration
22. Indira Gandhi Official Language Award Scheme
23. Indira Gandhi Award for Best First Film
24. Indira Gandhi Rajbhasha Award
25. Indira Gandhi Prize for Peace, Disarmament and Development

26. Indira Gandhi Prize for Popularization of Science Implementation
27. Indira Gandhi Shiromani Award
28. Indira Gandhi NSS Award
29. Indira Gandhi award for social service, Madhya Pradesh
30. Indira Gandhi Postgraduate Scholarship for Single Girl Child, UGC
31. Indira Gandhi Rajbhasha Shield Scheme
32. Jawaharlal Nehru Award for International Peace
33. Soviet Land Nehru Award
34. Jawaharlal Nehru Balkalyan Award
35. Jawaharlal Nehru Memorial Fund, New Delhi
36. Jawaharlal Nehru Birth Centenary Research Award
37. Jawaharlal Nehru Award for International Understanding
38. Nehru Bal Samiti Bravery Awards
39. Jawaharlal Nehru Memorial Medal
40. Jawaharlal Nehru Prize for Popularization of Science
41. Jawaharlal Nehru National Science Competition Awards

Scholarship / Fellowship

1. Rajiv Gandhi Scholarship Scheme for Students with Disabilities
2. Rajiv Gandhi National Fellowship Scheme for SC/ST Candidates, Ministry of Social Justice and Empowerment
3. Rajiv Gandhi Fellowship, Indira Gandhi Open University
4. Rajiv Gandhi Science Talent Research Fellows
5. Rajiv Gandhi Fellowship, Ministry of Tribal Affairs

6. Rajiv Gandhi National Fellowship Scheme for Scheduled Castes and Scheduled Tribes candidates given by University Grants Commission

7. Rajiv Gandhi Fellowship sponsored by the Commonwealth of Learning in association with Indira Gandhi National Open University

8. Rajiv Gandhi Science Talent Research Fellowship given by Jawaharlal Nehru Centre for Advanced Scientific Research (to promote budding scientists) done in tandem with Department of Science and Technology and Rajiv Gandhi Foundation

9. Rajiv Gandhi HUDCO Fellowships in the Habitat Sector (to promote research in the field of sustainable Habitat development) for MPhil, PhD Students

10. Rajiv Gandhi Travelling Scholarship

11. Rajiv Gandhi(UK) Foundation Scholarship

12. Indira Gandhi Memorial Fellowships

13. Post-Graduate Indira Gandhi Scholarship for Single Girl Child

14. Fullbright scholarship now renamed Fullbright- Jawaharlal Nehru Scholarship

15. Cambridge Nehru Scholarships, 10 in number, for research at Cambridge University, London, leading to Ph. D. for 3 years, which include fee, maintenance allowance, air travel to UK and back

16. Scheme of Jawaharlal Nehru Fellowships for Post-graduate Studies, Government of India

17. Jawarharlal Nehru Science Fellowships for International Students in India

National Parks/ Sanctuaries/ Museums

1. Rajiv Gandhi (Nagarhole) Wildlife Sanctury, Karnataka
2. Rajiv Gandhi Wildlife Sanctury, Andhra Pradesh
3. Indira Gandhi National Park, Tamil Nadu
4. Indira Gandhi Zoological Park , New Delhi
5. Indira Gandhi National Park, Annamalai Hills, Western Ghats
6. Indira Gandhi Zoological Park, Vishakhapatnam
7. Indira Gandhi Rashtriya Manav Sangrahalaya (IGRMS)
8. Indira Gandhi Wildlife Sanctuary, Pollachi
9. Rajiv Gandhi Health Museum
10. The Rajiv Gandhi Museum of Natural History
11. Indira Gandhi Memorial Museum, New Delhi
12. Nehru Memorial Museum and Library, New Delhi
13. Nehru Planetarium, New Delhi
14. Jawaharlal Nehru Museum in Aurangabad, Maharashtra
15. Jawaharlal Nehru Memorial Gallery, London
16. Jawaharlal Nehru Planetarium, Worli, Mumbai.
17. Jawaharlal Nehru National Science Exhibition for Children

Hospitals/Medical Institutions

1. Rajiv Gandhi University of Health Science, Bangalore, Karnataka
2. Rajiv Gandhi Cancer Institute & Research Centre, Delhi
3. Rajiv Gandhi Home for Handicapped, Pondicherry
4. Shri Rajiv Gandhi College of Dental Science & Hospital, Bangalore, Karnataka
5. Rajiv Gandhi Centre for Bio Technology, Thiruvanthapuram, Kerala

6. Rajiv Gandhi College of Nursing, Bangalore, Karnataka
7. Rajiv Gandhi Super Specialty Hospital, Raichur
8. Rajiv Gandhi Institute of Chest Diseases, Bangalore, Karnataka
9. Rajiv Gandhi Paramedical College, Jodhpur
10. Rajiv Gandhi Medical College, Thane, Mumbai
11. Rajiv Gandhi Institute of Pharmacy, Karnataka
12. Rajiv Gandhi Hospital, Goa
13. Rajiv Gandhi Mission on Community Health, Madhya Pradesh
14. Rajiv Gandhi Super Specialty Hospital, Delhi
15. Rajiv Gandhi Homoeopathic Medical College, Bhopal, Madhya Pradesh
16. North Eastern Indira Gandhi Regional Institute of Health & Medical Sciences, Shilong, Meghalaya
17. Indira Gandhi Medical College, Shimla
18. Indira Gandhi Institute of Child Health, Bangalore
19. Indira Gandhi Institute of Medical Sciences, Sheikhpura, Patna
20. The Indira Gandhi Pediatric Hospital, Afghanistan
21. Indira Gandhi Institute of Child Health, Bangalore
22. Indira Gandhi Medical College, Shimla
23. Indira Gandhi Institute of Dental Science, Kerala
24. Indira Gandhi Memorial Ayurvedic Medical College & Hospital, Bhubaneshwar
25. Indira Gandhi Government Medical College and Hospital, Nagpur
26. Indira Gandhi Eye Hospital And Research Centre, Kolkata
27. Indira Gandhi Hospital, Shimla
28. Indira Gandhi Women and Children Hospital , Bhopal

29. Indira Gandhi Gas Relief Hospital, Bhopal
30. Kamla Nehru Hospital, Shimla
31. Chacha Nehru Bal Chikitsalaya
32. Jawaharlal Institute of Postgraduate Medical Education and Research, (JIPMER)
33. Jawaharlal Nehru Cancer Hospital and Research Centre, Bhopal
34. Jawaharlal Nehru Medical College in Raipur.
35. Nehru Homoeopathic Medical College & Hospital, New Delhi
36. Nehru, Science Centre, Worli, Mumbai
37. Pandit Jawaharlal Nehru Institute of Homoeopathic Medical Sciences, Maharashtra

Institutions / Chairs / Festivals

1. Rajiv Gandhi National Institute of Youth Development. (RGNIYD), Ministry of Youth and Sports
2. Rajiv Gandhi National Ground Water Training & Research Institute, Faridabad, Haryana
3. Rajiv Gandhi Food Security Mission in Tribal Areas
4. Rajiv Gandhi National Institute of Youth Development
5. Rajiv Gandhi Shiksha Mission, Chhattisgarh
6. Rajiv Gandhi Chair Endowment for South Asian Economics
7. Rajiv Gandhi Project – A pilot to provide education through massive satellite connectivity
8. Rajiv Gandhi Rural Housing Corporation Limited, Karnataka
9. Rajiv Gandhi Information and Technology Commission
10. Rajiv Gandhi Chair for Peace and Disarmament

11. Rajiv Gandhi Chair, Allahabad University
12. Rajiv Gandhi Music Festival
13. Rajiv Gandhi Memorial Lecture
14. Rajiv Gandhi Akshay Urja Diwas
15. Rajiv Gandhi Education Foundation, Kerala
16. Rajiv Gandhi Panchayati Raj Convention
17. The Rajiv Gandhi Memorial Educational and Charitable Society, Kasagod, Kerala
18. Rajiv Gandhi Memorial Trophy ekankika spardha, Prerana Foundation
19. Indira Gandhi National Centre for the Arts, Janpath, New Delhi
20. Indira Gandhi Panchayati Raj & Gramin Vikas Sansthan, Jaipur, Rajasthan
21. Indira Gandhi Centre for Atomic Research (IGCAR), Kalpakkam
22. Indira Gandhi Institute for Development and Research , Mumbai
23. Indira Gandhi Institute of Cardiology (IGIC), Patna
24. Indira Gandhi National Center for the Arts, New Delhi
25. Indira Gandhi National Foundation, Thiruvananthapuram, Kerala
26. Indira Gandhi Mahila Sahakari Soot Girni Ltd, Maharashtra
27. Indira Gandhi Conservation Monitoring Centre , Ministry of Environment & Forest
28. Jawahar Shetkari Sahakari Sakhar Karkhana Ltd.
29. Nehru Yuva Kendra Sangathan
30. Jawaharlal Nehru Custom House Nhava Sheva, Maharashtra
31. Jawaharlal Nehru Centre for Advanced Scientific Research, Bangalore

32. Jawaharlal Nehru Cultural Centre, Embassy of India, Moscow

33. Pandit Jawaharlal Nehru Udyog Kendra for Juveniles, Pune, Maharastra

34. Pandit Jawaharlal Nehru College of Agriculture and Research Institute, Pondicherry

35. Rajiv Gandhi Akshay Urja Diwas to commemorate his birthday on August 20

Roads/Buildings/places

1. Jawaharlal Nehru Bhawan, Headquarters of the Ministry of External Affairs, New Delhi

2. Indira Paryavaran Bhawan, Headquarters of the Ministry of Environment and Forests, New Delhi

3. Rajiv Gandhi Bhawan. Headquarters of the Ministry of Civil Aviation

4. Rajiv Chowk, Delhi

5. Rajiv Gandhi Bhawan, Safdarjung, New Delhi

6. Rajiv Gandhi Handicrafts Bhawan, New Delhi

7. Rajiv Gandhi Park, Kalkaji, Delhi

8. Indira Chowk, New Delhi

9. Nehru Yuvak Kendra, Chanakyapuri, New Delhi

10. Nehru Place, New Delhi

11. Nehru Park, New Delhi

12. Nehru House, BSZ Marg, New Delhi

13. Rajiv Gandhi Renewable Energy Park, Gurgaon, Haryana

14. Rajiv Gandhi Sea Link – Bandra-Worli, Mumbai

15. Rajiv Gandhi Chowk, Andheri, Mumbai

16. Indira Gandhi Road, Mumbai

17. Indira Gandhi Nagar, Wadala, Mumbai
18. Indira Gandhi Sports Complex, Mulund, Mumbai
19. Nehru Nagar, Kurla, Mumbai
20. Jawaharlal Nehru Ggarden, Thane, Mumbai
21. Rajiv Gandhi Memorial Hall, Chennai
22. Jawaharlal Nehru Road, Vadapalani, Chennai,
23. Rajiv Gandhi Salai (old Mahabalipuram road named after Rajiv Gandhi), Chennai
24. Rajiv Gandhi Education City, Haryana
25. Rajiv Gandhi IT Habitat, Goa
26. Rajiv Gandhi Nagar, Chennai
27. Rajiv Gandhi Park, Vijayawada
28. Rajiv Gandhi Nagar, Coimbatore, Tamil Nadu
29. Rajiv Gandhi Nagar, Trichy, Tamil Nadu
30. Rajiv Gandhi IT Park, Hinjewadi, Pune
31. Rajiv Gandhi Panchayat Bhavan, Palanpur Banaskantha
32. Rajiv Gandhi Technology Park, Chandigarh
33. Rajiv Gandhi Smriti Van, Jharkhand
34. Rajiv Gandhi Road, Chittoor
35. Rajiv Gandhi Memorial, Sriperumbudur, Tamil Nadu
36. Indira Gandhi Memorial Library, University of Hyderabad
37. Indira Gandhi Musical Fountains, Bangalore
38. Indira Gandhi Planetarium , Lucknow
39. Indira Gandhi Centre for Indian Culture (IGCIC), High Commission of India, Mauritus
40. Indira Gandhi Zoological Park , Eastern Ghats of India
41. Indira Gandhi Industrial Complex, Ranipet, Vellore District
42. Indira Gandhi Park, Itanagar
43. Indira Gandhi Square , Pondicherry
44. Indira Gandhi Road, Willingdon Island, Cochin

45. Indira Gandhi Memorial Tulip Garden, Kashmir
46. Indira Gandhi Sagar Dam, Nagpur
47. Indira Gandhi Bridge, Rameshvaram, Tamil Nadu
48. Indira Gandhi Hospital, Bhiwandi
49. Indira Gandhi Memorial Cultural Complex, Uttar Pradesh.
50. Indira Gandhi Panchayati Raj Sansthan , Bhopal
51. Indira Gandhi Nagar, Rajasthan
52. Indira Nagar, Lucknow
53. Nehru Nagar, Ghaziabad
54. Jawaharlal Nehru Gardens, Ambarnath
55. Jawarharlal Nehru Gardens, Panhala
56. Jawaharlal Nehru Market, Jammu.
57. Nehru Chowk, Ulhas Nagar, Maharashtra.
58. Nehru Bridge on the river Mandovi, Panaji, Goa
59. Nehru Nagar Ghaziabad
60. Jawaharlal Nehru Road, Dharmatala, Kolkata
61. Nehru Road, Guwahati
62. Jawahar Nagar, Jaipur
63. Nehru Vihar Colony, Kalyanpur, Lucknow
64. Nehru Nagar, Patna
65. Jawaharlal Nehru Street, Pondicherry
66. Nehru Bazaar, Madanapalli, Tirupathi
67. Nehru Chowk, Bilaspur. M.P
68. Nehru Street, Ponmalaipatti, Tiruchirapalli
69. Nehru Nagar, Ahmedabad
70. Nehru Nagar,. Nashik-Pune Road, Maharashtra

(This list reflects only 75% of the total naming schemes across the country made by the Dynasty Members]

APPENDIX-4

LIST OF PEOPLE WHO SIGNED AJMAL KASAB'S MERCY PETITION.

Source**: INDIAN DEFENCE NEWS** November 27, 2018 Ajmal Kasab

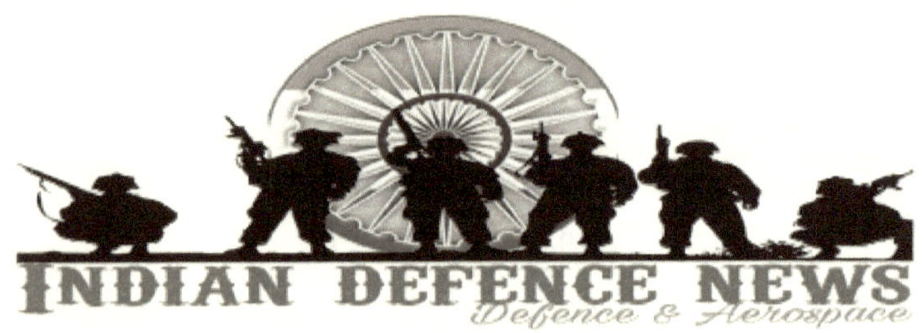

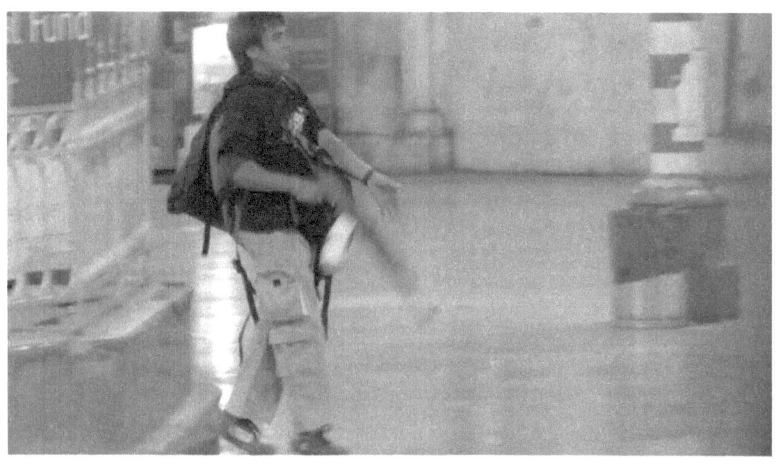

Total 203 people had filed mercy petition for 26/11 terrorist Ajmal Kasab but in this list some names are very shocking as for example <u>HARSH MANDER</u> also filed petition for Ajmal Kasab and he was considered as the right hand of Sonia Gandhi and he was also NAC (National Advisory council) member. Sonia Gandhi served as its Chairperson for much of the tenure of the UPA. <u>ARUNA ROY</u> who was also a NAC member, has also signed the petition. Here is the full list of people who signed the mercy petition :

List of people who signed Ajmal Kasab's mercy petition

NAME	PRFOFESSION	E-MAIL ID
Yug Mohit Chaudhry	Lawyer	<u>yugchaudhry@ hotmail.com</u>
Abdul Wahab Khan	Lawyer	<u>advocatekaw@yahoo. com</u>

Vrinda Grover	Lawyer	vrindagrover@gmail.com
Meenal Baghel	Editor, Mumbai Mirror	mbaghel@gmail.com
Anish Grewal	Entrepreneur	anish@winassetmanagement.com
Harsh Mander	Social Activist, NAC Member	manderharsh@gmail.com
Aakar Patel	Journalist	aakar.patel@gmail.com
Reena George	Ph.D. Student	reena.mary.george@univie.ac.at
Harish Dhawan	Associate Prof in Eco, Univ. of Delhi	locateharish@gmail.com
Swastayan Roy	Journalist	swastayan@yahoo.com
Mukul Mahant	Social Activist	mikemahant@hotmail.com
V. Venkatesan	Journalist	venkat.venkatesan@gmail.com
S. Thambisetty	Professor, LSE	S.Thambisety@lse.ac.uk
Anusha Rizvi	Independent Filmaker	anusharizvi@gmail.com
Bhaskar Hazarika		hazarika@gmail.com

K.P. Shankaran	Lecturer (Retd) in Philosophy	shankaran_kp@ yahoo.com
Byatha N. Jagadeesh	Lawyer	jagadeeshabn@gmail. com
Mayank Misra	Lawyer	adv.mayank.misra@ gmail.com
Babu Mathew	Professor of Law	
Surabhi Chopra	Law Professor.	surabhi.chopra@ gmail.com
Suroor Mander	Advocate	suroorm@gmail.com
Anuj Bhagwati	Entrepreneur	a_a_bhagwati@ ateindia.com
Kiran Bhatty	Independent Researcher	kiran.bhatty@gmail. com
Mahmood Farooqui	Historian, Artist, Filmmaker.	baankeraja@gmail. com
Jyoti Punwani	Journalist	jyoti.punwani@gmail. com
Colin Gonsalves	Senior Advocate, Supreme Court.	colin.gonsalves@hrln. org
Pritam Bhatty	Artist	pritambhatty@ rediffmail.com
Vijay Raghavan	Tata Institute of Social Sciences	vijay.r@tiss.edu
Abbas Kazmi	Lawyer	abbaskazmi@ rediffmail.com
Aditi Khanna		aditikhanna@hotmail. com

Andaleeb Alam	Social Worker	alam.andaleeb@gmail.com
Dr. Madhav Thambisetty	Professor of Medicine	madhavtr71@gmail.com
Prof Rupin Desai	Professor of English (retd)	desairupin@yahoo.in
Biraj Patnaik		biraj.patnaik@gmail.com
Sameer Sain	Entrepreneur	ssain@everstonecapital.com
Peoples Union for Democratic Rights		paramjeet.timmy@gmail.com
Shankar Raman	Cinematographer	shanker@chasingtales.net
Gautam Babbar	United Nations	gautam.babbar@unodc.org
Nandita Das	Actress	dasnandita@gmail.com
Gaurav Sinha	Lawyer	
Maharukh Adenwalla	Lawyer	mahrukhadenwalla@rediffmail.com
Gulnar Bandukwalla Pruisken	Entrepreneur	gulnarp@gmail.com
Kalyani Menon Sen	Feminist Learning Partnerships	kmenonsen@gmail.com

Vijay Hiremath	Lawyer	vijayhiremath@gmail.com
Kamla Bhasin	Social Scientist	kamla@sangatsouthasia.org
Devaki Jain	Development Economist & Writer	devakijain@gmail.com
Saumya Uma	Consultant on Gender, Law & Human Rights	saumyauma@gmail.com
Kamayani Bali Mahabal		kamayani@ymail.com
Urvija Priyadafrshini	Ph.D. Student	urvipriya@gmail.com
Kanamma Raman		kannamma24@gmail.com
Priyanka Vegad	Lawyer	priyankavegad@yahoo.com
Parul Gupta	Language Teacher	parulmudita@hotmail.com
Shruti Gupta	Telecom Professional	shrutig1@gmail.com
Kiran Shaheen		kiranshaheen@gmail.com
Harsh Bora	Lawyer	harshbora10@gmail.com
Kalpana Kannabiran		kalpana.kannabiran@gmail.com
Anju Talukdar		anju@ngo-marg.org

Rahul Roy	Lawyer	rebeccamammen@gmail.com
Rana Behal		rbehal@gmail.com
Navsharan Singh		nsingh@idrc.org.in
Binoo John		binoojohn@gmail.com
Shankar Sen	IPS, Retd. Director, NPA:DG (Investigations)	sankaran_ips@yahoo.com
Chetan Mali	Lawyer	chetanmalee@gmail.com
Dr. Walter Fernandes	North Eastern Social Research Centre	walter.nesrc@gmail.com
Manohar Elavarthi	Praja Rajakiya Vedike, Bangalore	manoharban@gmail.com
Geeta Thatra	Research Fellow, TISS	geeta.thatra@gmail.com
Jayashree Subramanian	Tata Institute of Social Sciences (TISS)	j_manian@yahoo.com
Susan Abraham	Lawyer	susangita50@gmail.com
Veena Gowda	Lawyer	gowdaveena@gmail.com

Flavia Agnes	Lawyer	flaviaagnes@gmail.com
Gautam Patel	Lawyer	gautampatel@gmail.com
Dale Luis Menezes		dale_menezes@rediffmail.com
Rariul Alom Rahman	Student	rafiul.delhi@gmail.com
N. Jayaram	Journalist	njabroad@gmail.com
Richa Minocha	Member Secretary, Jan Abhiyan Sanstha, HP	richa.minocha70@gmail.com
Paari Vendan	Lawyer	paarivendhan@gmail.com
Jeny Antony		jenydolly85@gmail.com
Namita Kohli	Student`	namitakohli83@gmailc.om
Rimple Mehta	JU-SYLFF Doctoral Fellow, Jadavpur University	rimple.mehta@gmail.com
Brinca Bose		brindab ose@gmail.com
Javed Iqbal	Journalist	imissyahoo@gmail.com

S. Anand	Publisher, Navayana	anand@navayana.org
Jinee Lokaneeta	Associate Professor, Political Science	jlokanee@drew.edu
Anu Salelkar		anu.salelkar@gmail.com
Sneha Krishnan		krishnan.sneha@gmail.com
Dr. Akhil Katyal	Assistant Professor, Delhi University	akhilkatyal@gmail.com
Shreelak Manohar	Researcher & Activist	sahreela_m_88@yahoo.co.in
Dr. Sandeep Bakshi	Postdoctoral Fellow, English	Sb583@leicester.ac.uk
Madhumita Dutta		madhudutta.new@gmail.com
Ashok Agarwaal		ashokagrwaal@gmail.com
Shalini Gera		shalinigera@yahoo.com
Jamal Kidwai		jamalkidwai@gmail.com
Anjali Dave	Tata Institute of Social Sciences	anjali@tiss.edu

Laxmi Murthy		murthy.laxmi@gmail.com
Harsh Kapoor		aiindex@gmail.com
Bondita Acharya		bondita12@gmail.com
Madhu Sarin	Psychoanalyst	msarin2011@gmail.com
Dilip Simeon		dilipsimeon@gmail.com
Rashmi Gera		g_rashmi@hotmail.com
Joe Ahialy		jJoe1@athyal.org
Lalitha Ramdas		lramdas@gmail.com
Abha Bhaiya		abhabhaiya@gmail.com
Malani S		malini_s@sify.com
Manisha Sethi	Jamiak Teachers Solidarity Association	manisha.sethy@gmail.com
Deepti	Saheli	deelited@gmailcom
Tarun Bhartiya		tarunbhartiya@gmail.com
Anuradha Chenoy		kamalchenoy@gmail.com
Kamal Mitra Chenoy		kamalchenoy@gmail.com

Aseem Shrivastava		maybeaseem@gmail.com
Sugari R. Ramdas		sagari.ramdas@gmail.com
Madhoo		sagari.ramdas@gmail.com
Kunjam Pandu Dora		sagari.ramdas@gmail.com
Akshay Pathak		pathak.akshay@gmail.com
Jagmohan Singh		bigideaszone@gmail.com
Dunu Roy		qadeeroy@gmail.com
Rituparna BorahManohar Elavarthi		rituparna.borah@gmail.com
Mansoor Nazeer		mansoor_nazeer
Bharti Ali		bharti@haqcrc.org
Sumi Krishna		sumikr@gmail.com
Dr. Ambrose Pinto SJ	Administrator, St. Joseph' Evening Colleges	23ambrose@gmail.com
Padmini Mirchandani	Publisher	padmini@pictorpublishing.com
Neha Majumdar		nehamujundar@gmail.com

Valmiki Naik		valmikinaik@gmail.com
Naresh Fernandes	Writer	naresh.fernandes@gmail.com
Sanchia de Souza		sanchiadesouza@gmail.com
Sonal Shah	Editor	sonal@paprikamedia.com
Ruthk Sequeira		ruthsequeira@gmail.com
Namisha Gupta		namishagupta1@gmail.com
Radha Thomas		radhathomas@explocity.com
Nikil Kumar		nikhil.sez@gmail.com
Shankar Singh		arunaroy@gmail.com
Achin Vanaik		achin.vanaik@gmail.com
Zubin Bharucha	Cricket Coach	zb100@aol.com
Siddharth Sharma	LL.M. Student, Berkeley	sid.ind@gmail.com
Mary Scaria	Lawyer	maryscaria@gmail.com
Sashwati Mishra		msashwati@gmail.com
Armin Solkar	Lawyer	aminsolkar@hotmail.com

Naima Shaikh	Lawyer	sheikh.naima@ymail.com
Samirak Sheikh		samira.sheikh@yahoo.co.uk
Neerajk Malik		nj_malik@hotmail.com
Nikita Agarwal		nikita.agarwal.delhi@gmail.com
Kritika Agarwal		nikita.agarwal.delhi@gmail.com
Kasim Sait		kasim@airtelmail.in
Sukla Sen		sukla.sen@gmail.com
Kareem Sait		sait.kareem@gmail.com
Amba Kak		ambakak@gmail.com
Nandini Dey		nandini.rv@gmail.com
Ajaya Kumar Singh		ajaysingho@gmail.com
Ashish Kothari		chikikothani@gmail.com
Vivek Sundara		viveksundara@gmail.com
Sabeena Gadihoke		sgadihok@gmail.com
HAQ: Centre for Child Rights		bharti@hazcrc.org

Amrita Nandy	Jawaharlal Nehru University	amrita.nandy1@gmail.com
Rakhee Joshi	Consultant, Social Research	rakheekj@gmail.com
Puneet Kohli		puneetkohli101@gmail.com
Gana Kurinji Shanmugasundaram	Vice-President, PUCL (TN & Puduchery)	newflower_kurinji@yahoo.co.in
Neha Choksi		nehabythesea@hotmail.com
Amita Chatterjee		amita_ju@yahoo.com
Jashodhara Dasgupta		jashodhara@sahayoginda.org
Gabriele Dietrich		reach.gabriele@gmail.com
Gayatri Menon		gayatri.menon@gmail.com
Bhairavi Sanghi	Designer	bhairavi77@hotmail.com
Siddharthk Narrain	Alternative Law Forum	sid@altlawforum.org
Murtaza Danish Husaini	Actor & Dramatist	dan.ayyaar@gmail.com
Aamir Bashir	Actor & Director	unattore1@gmail.com

Sonia Gandhi's NAC members tried to save Ajmal Kasab:

Congress-NCP government of Maharashtra, tasked the Lawyers, 'Amin Solkar' and 'Farhana Shah' to protect, Ajmal Kasab and Sonia Gandhi's NAC members tried to save 26/11 Mumbai Terror attack killer Ajmal Kasab. Aruna Roy , Harsh Mander , Vrinda Grover and 203 others sought mercy for 26/11 terrorist Ajmal Kasab.

NAC members tried to save Kasab

Aruna Roy, Harsh Mander among 203 sought mercy for 26/11 terrorist

KUMAR CHELLAPPAN/ANNAPURNA JHA ■ CHENNAI/NEW DELHI

A serving member and a former member in the Sonia Gandhi-headed National Advisory Council (NAC) were among the 203 petitioners to the President of India seeking mercy for Ajmal Kasab, the main accused in the 2008 Mumbai terror attacks, which claimed 164 lives.

An RTI reply in this regard has revealed that Aruna Roy, who is at present a member of the influential NAC, and Harsh Mander, a former member in the body, were among the scores of others, including several journalists and social activists who filed mercy pleas for Kasab.

"Mander, a former NAC member, wrote to the President of India seeking clemency for Ajmal Kasab, who had been sentenced to death by a trial court as well as the Supreme Court. But President Pranab Mukherjee was gracious enough to reject the clemency petition as well as the strong recommendation by the NAC member," Janata Party president Subramanian Swamy told reporters here on Friday. Kasab was hanged on November 21, last year.

Swamy distributed copies of the letter received under the Right to Information Act by one of his party members about details of persons who sent in mercy petitions to the President for Kasab. Both Roy and Mander figure in the 203-strong list.

Besides the two, another key social activist figuring in the list happens to be Nikhil Dey. "These are the kind of people sitting as members of the NAC to decide the fate of this country," Swamy alleged. Mander, who was a member of the NAC till last year, had also courted controversy for his pleas to save Afzal Guru, one of the main accused in the 2001 Parliament attack case, from the gallows.

When contacted, Harsh Mander sent an article, 'The Quality of Mercy', that he had written after Kasab's hanging in November last year saying it reflected his views on the issue. "I feel even more worried when the Supreme Court declares in a particular matter of a political crime of terror that the death sentence must be applied to 'satisfy the collective conscience' of the nation; or the clearly political motivations in the haste with which Kasab was executed," Mander said in the article.

He, however, admitted that Kasab's "trial was fair, his conviction just, his crime merciless and horrendous therefore many celebrated his hanging as fitting closure to a people traumatised by his offence."

Continued on Page 4

Also read: **List of people signed mercy petition for Afzal_guru**

Also Read: **List of people who signed mercy petition for Yakub Memon**

APPENDIX-5

CHIDAMBARA RAHASYA

Reprinted with prior permission from PGurus

CHIDAMBARA RAHASYA:
DETAILS OF HUGE SECRET ASSETS & FOREIGN BANK ACCOUNT OF CHIDAMBARAM FAMILY

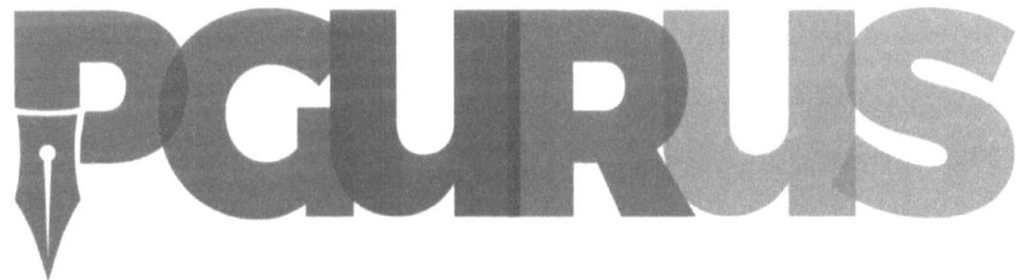

SUMMARY OF THE ASSETS & FOREIGN BANK ACCOUNTS OF THE CHIDAMBARAM FAMILY UNEARTHED BY THE ITD

BY

TEAM PGURUS

MARCH 15, 2017

The Income Tax's Chennai Investigation Unit's report having more than 200 pages about former Finance Minister P Chidambaram's family and especially son Karti and his company's huge assets in more than 14 countries are now out in the public domain. Recently some portion of this sensitive report was exposed in public by Bharatiya Janata Party (BJP) leader Subramaniam Swamy in a press conference. Many media houses whose owners are friendly and in collusion with Chidambaram tried to black out the news.

In the interest of public, we are producing the entire data or assets and bank accounts found in the join raid of Income Taxe and Enforcement Directorate.

21 foreign bank accounts by Karti and his companies in Metro Bank in UK, 4 accounts in OCBC in Singapore in the name of Advantage Strategic Consulting Pte Ltd., the controversial company caught in kickbacks in Aircel-Maxis scam, 2 banks in Spain namely Sabadell Atlantico, La Caxia Bank, HSBC UK, Barclays Bank in Monaco, Marseille BNP Paribas in France, UBS in Switzerland, etc. The detailed list of the 21 secret foreign bank accounts unearthed by investigators is published in the end of this post.

The Income Tax which seized hard disks from Karti's companies found that P Chidambaram, wife Nalini Chidambaram, son Karti and his wife Srinidhi jointly purchased a property and a big palatial house in Cambridge in UK. As per the Income tax seized documents, the property bought by Chidambaram and family is: 5, Holben Close, Cambridge, CB237AQ. This huge property and home was purchased from Edmund Suley Holt and Heather Holt and the money was transacted from Karti's personal account in London's Metro Bank account number: 16714313. Chidambaram never declared this property in any of his mandatory affidavits as Member of Parliament (MP) or Minister. Chidambaram in his affidavit to Rajya Sabha in May 2016 declared only 1/3rd portion of the property as wife Nalini's property. He also under-invoiced the value of this property of his wife's share at just Rs.1.55 crores, while UK's real estate websites estimate this property in Cambridge to be worth more than Rs.85 crores.

Karti's Advantage Strategic Consulting Private Limited's Singapore Company's bank accounts to buy properties in UK like purchase of 88 acres farm house known as Surridge Farm in Somerset, UK. The land value shown in the registry is one million pounds.

Another property in Cambridge is at Ceres, 29, Meade House at Cambridge.

Chidambaram's son Karti has built a massive empire in different parts of the world by making investments in real estate and engaging in other business activities in London, Dubai, South Africa, Philippines, Thailand, Singapore, Malaysia, Sri Lanka, British Virgin Island, France, USA, Switzerland, Greece and Spain. Most of the purchases happened during the period 2006 to 2014 when Chidambaram was Finance Minister and Home Minister. The probe agencies estimate these assets across the world are expected to be more than Three Billion Dollars. Why did the Chidambarams invest in real estate in first world countries? This post will give you a clue.

Karti's Singapore-based firm had acquired majority shares of a big resort in Sri Lanka, known as Lanka Fortune Residencies. This company owns the prestigious resorts 'The Waterfront', 'Weligama Bay Resort' and Emerald Bay Hotel.

Karti's Singapore firm routed money via Dubai to acquire three farms and vineyards in South Africa, identified as Rowey Farm in Grabouw, Cape Orchards and Vineyards Private Limited, and Zandvliet Enterprises, a wine and stud farm in Ashton.

The Dubai-based Desert Dunes Properties Ltd has also investment in Karti's Singapore-based company Advantage. The probes have unearthed a money trail of 1.7 million Singapore Dollars between these firms. Another Dubai-based company, Pearl Dubai FX LLCX, also had financial transaction with Advantage. This shows that Karti linked firms have offices and assets in UAE also.

The Advantage's Ceres, 29, Mede House had entered into joint ventures with the Philippines-based companies to obtain franchise team of International Premier Tennis League (Asia). The Philippine firms, which were engaged in joint ventures with the Karti-controlled company, are SM Arena Complex Corporation, Sports Entertainment Events Management Inc.

The Advantage had also had financial transactions with another real estate company in Singapore known as Real Beyond Pte. Ltd. having three subsidiaries in Malaysia. The investigation has unearthed that these transactions led to 16 land purchases in Thailand.

The Advantage's Singapore unit has set up a firm in British Virgin Island (VI), namely Somerset Surridge Ltd. Advantage also invested 400,000 Singapore dollars in another BVI firm known as Full Innovations Ltd. It also has financial dealing with Geben Trading Limited in BVI and offices in Switzerland. This firm's major transactions were through the famous Swiss Bank, namely UBS. The investigators got proofs of transactions in Dollars and Euro. The Advantage also has transaction of five million Singapore dollars with another firm in Singapore, namely Unison Global Investments Ltd.

The Karti-controlled company in Singapore entered into joint ventures with Gravitas Investments, Match Point International Tennis Events to buy a franchise Tennis Team called 'Manila Mavericks'. This deal was worth of 12 million US dollars and the money was paid in 10 installments.

Karti's Singapore company also acquired a residential flat in Malaysia worth 1.9 million Malaysian Ringgits from a firm called Peninsular Smart. The probe team also found some agreement papers which shows that the Advantage holds franchisees of Café' Coffee Day in some locations in Malaysia. The investigators have found several transactions to Karti's Singapore firm with Malaysian companies. Malaysia is the head quarters of telecom giant Maxis which acquired Aircel in 2006. The IT and ED officers seized payment details amounting to more than Rs.30 crore in foreign currencies.

The Advantage in Singapore also opened a subsidiary firm in Barcelona in Spain known as Advantage Estrategia Esportiva

SLU in August 2012. This is a sports academy having four acres with seven tennis courts in Spain.

Karti-linked Singapore firm has also one million US dollar investment in a company in France known as Pampelonn Organisation. The Advantage also has transactions with a Greek firm known as Pisani John Sakellarios in Athens.

Karti's firm Advantage Strategic Consulting Private Limited (ASCPL) had transactions with Aircel Televentures, DCB Client, Diageo Scotland Limited, Katra Group, Sri Lanka Export Development Board, Unifi Wealth Management Ltd., VST Tillers Tractors, Carlton Trading Company, Claris Life Sciences', ITC Centre, Best Land Realty Limited, Essar Steel Limited, Gokul Builders and Estates, S Kumar, INX Media, Reflections, Thiagarajar Mills Private Limited, Saksoft, EL Forge Limited.

The Income Tax which seized hard disks from Karti's companies also found that Karti used to get huge money as kickbacks in several Foreign Investment Promotion Board (FIPB) deals pending with father former Finance Minister P. Chidambaram.

On Sept 22, 2008, ASCPL received Rs.35 lakh from INX Media (now known as News XTV Channel), which applied for FIPB clearance of 220 million dollar during the period. Same day another Rs.60 Lakh was paid from INX Media to Northstar Software Solutions Pvt. Ltd. Major shares of this Northstar Software Solutions Pvt. Ltd. controlled by C B N Reddy, who is a Benami and Director of ASCPL and its Singapore subsidiary also. On Sept 24, 2008 another tranche of 20,000 Dollars were paid to ASCPL's Singapore subsidiary by INX Media.

On Sept 26, 2008, ASCPL had a money transaction of 50,000 dollars with Geben Trading Limited in Athens in Greece. This company's address is 4 Zaf. Mastsa Street, 14564 Athens, Greence and incorporated in British Virgin Island (BVI). The money transactions of ASCPL also show to Geben Trading's bank account in UBS, Geneva in Switzerland. The emails of banking transaction details were marked to Karti also and documents shows about a business takeover of healthcare and rehabilitation centers in Greece. All these transactions happened during the INX Media's Foreign Direct Investment (FDI) approvals for 220 million dollar were pending with Karti's father Finance Minister P Chidambaram. In short, the murder accused Peter and Indrani Mukherjee who sold their INX Media paid around 9 crores rupees to Karti linked firm for FIPB clearance.

In August 2008, Karti's Singapore company got 60 lakh shares in the media firm Network 18's London based company Artevea Digital UK. This deal happened when Network 18 applied for a series of FIPB clearances, when Chidambaram was the Finance Minister. This led to around 25 crores kickback for processing the FIPB clearance.

The documents unearthed by Income Tax shows that ASCPL received money from many companies when their FDI investments files were with FIPB and cabinet Committee on Economic Affairs (CCEA) during Chidambaram's tenure as Finance Minister. The companies which transferred money to Karti's ASCPL are Claris Life Sciences, Diageo Scotland Limited which acquired fugitive Vijay Mallya's UB Spirits, Katra Group, Arcelor Mittal linked Saksoft, Reflections belong to Spark Capital Advisory Private Limited. As per the Income Tax Analysis

Report, all these deals involve around Rs.500 crores kickback to Karti linked companies for necessary FIPB and CCEA clearances during Chidambaram's period in Finance Ministry.

The documents seized from the raid also show that ASCPL received money from Best Land Realty, when the company got a aRs.304crore loan from Public Secttor Undertaking (SU) Banks.

In a bizarre incident, the British company Diageo Scotland Limited which acquired fugitive Vijay Mallya's UB Spirits even paid 15,000 dollas as Service Charges to Karti's ASCPL for fixing appointments with then Prime Minister Manmohan Singh, Finance Minister Chidambaram. Diageo's emails thank Karti for fixing appointment of company owner Lord Blyth with Prime Minister Manmohan Singh, Finance Minister Chidambaram. The thanking email also attached the 15,000 dollar pay out receipt as Service Charges for fixing appointments with PM and FM. This is a clear case of abuse of power initiating case under Prevention of Corruption Act.

Another clear case of favoritism to son's company by abusing power by Chidambaram is – In September 2006, Russia's National Industrial Bank (Nazprom) appoints Karti's ASCPL as Business Consultant for their Joint Venture with Indian overseas Bank. The documents seized by Income Tax included ASCPL's agreement with Russian Bank Nazprom and Nazprom's series of communications with IOB including the meetings in Chennai. The emails show that in each transaction with the Russian bank and PSU IOB, Karti's ASCPL minted money in the form of consultancy. The Russian Bank's agreement says Karti's ASCPL's Singapore subsidiary will get 5% as commission with all transactions with Indian Overseas Bank, apart from the initial 25,000 collar processing fee. This is a clear case of abuse of power by Finance Minister Chidambaram to get a cut for son Karti's company for each money transfer between PSU Bank IOB and Russian Bank Nazaprom.

Karti's ASCPL also received huge money from a South African company Nicholas Stynes Associates Limited. This South African company was engaged in providing security to IPL Cricket and the money transactions with Karti's company happened when Chidambaram was Home Minister.

The documents also show that ASCPL got huge money as commission from Allianze Securities for sale of NABAD Bonds when Chidambaram was Finance Minister.

The money was paid to Finance Minister Chidambaram from Karti's Meltrack Ltd in relation to sale of shares and selling of huge tract of land in Mysore to VST Tillers & Tractors Limited. The land was mortgaged to Union Bank of India. P. Chidambaram was shown as unsecured creditor to Meltrack Limited.

A very interesting thing in all Karti companies including ASCPL- there are five common Directors like C B N Reddy, Bhaskar Raman, Mohanan Rajesh, Ravi Viswanathan and V Padma. The Income Tax found that all these five persons have entered into a curious WILL that they owe all properties and assets to Karti or his daughter Aditi in consideration of respect and love to P Chidambaram! This shows that these five persons are nothing but Benamis of Karti and P Chidambaram.

Hotel Mozart is a famous hotel in Croatia and the hotel building has historical importance. This building was the Headquarters of the Yugoslavian Army during Second Word War. Circumstantial evidence suggests that Karti may have invested $5 million into this hotel.

As per the Income Tax Report, Karti's company Advantage Strategic Consulting Private Limited (ACPL) even accepted 15000 dollars from UK's liquor giant Diageo for fixing appointments with the then Prime Minister Manmohan Singh and the then Finance Minister P Chidambaram.

Documents revealed that P Chidambaram pays a rent of Rs. 2 lakhs per month to his wife and only son for use of one floor of a four storey Jor Bagh house. Does the PC family own just only the one floor? Who owns the other three?

This is arguably one of the largest catch of black money in India from a politician's family.

The billion dollar question is when will the Government order CBI, ED and Income Tax to initiate proceedings under Prevention of Corruption Act, PMLA, Benami Transactions Act and seizure of Black Money against Chidambaram and his family members.

Here is a list of 21 forein Bank Accounts being held by Karti Chidambaram:

Institution	Account Number	Bank Name	Branch/ Country
Advantage Strategic Consulting Singapore Pte. Ltd.	629774019001 503107752701 601058811201 503260424301		Singapore
Advantage Estrstegia Esportiva SLU	00810052040 002247826	Sabadell Atlantico	Spain
	006500445000 01067492	La Caixa Bank	
Karti Chidambaram	16714313	Metro Bank	U.K.
Totus Tennis Limited	503280166301	OCBC	Singapore
	17397044	Metro Bank	UK
Scotch Club	73664449	HSBC	UK
Pampelone Organisation SAS France	00010674295	Marseille BNP Paribas	France
Sporting Advantage Monaco SARL	0065-0044-58-0001067492	Barclays Bank	Avenida Diagonal, Monaco

	0081-0058-04-0002247826	Bank Sabadell	Catalunya
Full Innovation Ltd.	0102175357	Standard Chartered Bank	Singapore
4Siam Tennis S.L.	0019 0066 51 401 0031003	Deustche Bank	France
Nano Holdings LLC	8227144170	Wells Fargo Bank	San Fransisco, California
Geben Trading Ltd.	240-405111.60K 240-405111.70Q	UBS S.A.	Geneva, Switzerland

APPENDIX-6

SUMMARY OF HARSH MANDER'S WORLD-WIDE DONORS:

[Source: Website of Ministry of Home Affairs]

Centre for Equity Studies, DL/231661130 (Summary of data from fcraonline.nic.in)

"Donor" Organization	Country	2010	2011	2012	2013	2014	2015	2016	2017	Total (INR)
American Federation of Muslims of Indian Origin	USA	724758								724758
Church in Action & ICCO	Netherlands	7064256								7064256
Partnership Foundation	Netherlands	36937568	57372333	82377391	1084010					177771302
Sangat	UK	86051								86051
IDRC (Govt. entity)	Canada	2583067	2646211	5489559	3487345	2248654	1626048	953599		19034483
Association for India's Development	USA		1000000	750000		1623500	2641367	3744059	636567	10395493
Dan Church Aid	Denmark		8622759	6344687	3224138	5082765	4832240	1087549	166624	29360762
Indian Muslim Relief & Charities	USA		499000							499000
Bodo Huetten Foundation	Germany		222900	264975	972479	509718	527972	870089	1038232	4406365
HSBC Limited	India		1611573	402893						2014466
American Muslim Physicians of Indian Origin	USA		491070	972261	580485	613641	327659	800214	765826	4551156
Bal Raksha Bharat	India		795000	1933140						2728140
Action Aid	UK/India		2241409	1119794						3361203
Oxfam	UK/India			2000000	4959250	1623500	3639905			12222655
Centre for Budget and Governance accountability	India					1140000	697562			1837562
Association for Rural and Urban Needy	Hyderabad, India					7210750	1635060			8845810
National Foundation India	Delhi					600000	290000	1097506	929968	2917474
Swiss Aid	Switzerland					914000				914000
International Food Policy Research Institute	USA					1988630	443550			2432180
Islamic Relief	India					3321388	803176			4124564
Christian Aid	UK							341876		341876
Asian Dev Res Institute	Patna							448885		448885
Fund for Global Human Rights	USA							1611184	2245819	3857003
Oxford Univ	UK							1027866	289868	1317734
Luxemberg Foundation	Germany							1617213		1617213
American Center	Delhi							332450		332450
Minority Rights Group	UK							212842		212842
Insaan Group	USA								3274494	3274494
Jal Seva Foundation	India								165531	165531
Bread for the World	Germany								2393354	2393354
Total		47395700	75502255	101654700	22658457	20858418	15131917	14145332	11906283	309253062

BIBILIOGRAPHY:

1. Jawaharlal Nehru: Rebel & Statesman By B.R. Nanda
2. The Naked Mughals: Forbidden Tales of Harem and Butchery By Vashi Sharma & Sanjeev Newar.
3. Crimes Against India: By Stephen Knapp.
4. Breaking India: Western Interventions in Dravidian and Dalit Faut-lines By Rajiv Malhotra.
5. Narendra Modi: A Political Biography By Andy Marino
6. The Autobiography of a Sex Worker By Nalini Jameela.
7. Living with the Himalayan Masters By Swamy Rama.
8. Reminiscences of the Nehru Age By M.O. Mathai
9. Public Money, Private Agenda By Dr. A. Surya Prakash.
10. The Coalition Years By Pranab Kumar Mukherjee.

YOUTUBE VIDEOGRAPHY:

1. Shocking testimony of Brigitee Gabriel on Islamisation of Lebanon.
2. How Lebanon was converted into Islamic country within few years? – Pankaj Saxena.
3. Dr. Subramanian Swamy calls for criminal action against Sonia Gandhi Amid RGF Row.
4. Former Assam CM Tarun Gogoi speaks to Arnab Goswami.
5. How Vatican used Sonia Gandhi – per Wikileaks
6. Angry Anupam Kher rips apart Rahul Gandhi, Kanahaiya Kumar at the ……
7. APJ Abdul Kalam inspiring speech on India at European Parliament.
8. Watch a special show on how illegal migrants cross over to India from Bangladesh.

9. Did Sonia Gandhi try to prevent deportation of illegal Bangladeshi immigrants?/ India First (India Today T.V.

10. India Responds to Imran Khan's speech and shames Pak at the UN – Vidhisha Maitra, First Secretary, MEA.

11. Pakistan is Hell for Hindus: Arif Ajakia, Ex-Mayor, Karachi.

12. Illegal immigrants from Bangladesh staying in Bangalore.

13. An angry Indian rips into Time Magazine for calling PM Modi Divider-in-Chief.

14. Story of Christian majority Lebanon, Brigette Gabriel and the deed…

15. Aussie Imam makes shocking confessions about Islam.

16. Afghanistan: Land of Endless War – DW Documentary

17. Muslims have the 1st right over the resources of India.

18. Is Manishankar Aiyer seeking help from Pakistan to defeat Modi?

www.ingramcontent.com/pod-product-compliance
Lightning Source LLC
LaVergne TN
LVHW040319200726
843493LV00014B/737